THE
BLACK MASK
BOYS

BOOKS BY WILLIAM F. NOLAN

William F. Nolan

THE BLACK MASK BOYS

Masters in the Hard-Boiled School of Detective Fiction

Featuring Classic *Black Mask* Fiction by:

Dashiell Hammett Raymond Chandler

Erle Stanley Gardner Horace McCoy

Carroll John Daly Frederick Nebel

Raoul Whitfield Paul Cain

•

WILLIAM MORROW AND COMPANY, INC.
NEW YORK

Library of Congress Cataloging in Publication Data

Nolan, William F., 1928–
  The Black mask boys.

  "Featuring classic Black mask fiction by: Dashiell Hammett, Raymond
Chandler, Erle Stanley Gardner, Horace McCoy, Carroll John Daly, Frederick
Nebel, Raoul Whitfield, Paul Cain."
  Bibliography: p.
  1. Black mask—Addresses, essays, lectures. 2. Detective and mystery stories,
American—History and criticism—Addresses, essays, lectures. 3. Authors,
American—20th century—Biography—Addresses, essays, lectures. 4. Detec-
tive and mystery stories, American. 5. American fiction—20th century. I. Black
mask.
II. Title.
PS374.D4N64   1985   813'.0872'09   84–14778
ISBN 0–688–03966–9

Printed in the United States of America

First Edition

1 2 3 4 5 6 7 8 9 10

BOOK DESIGN BY ROBERT FREESE.

To My Hard-Boiled Friend,
E. R. HAGEMANN
Pioneer of the Pulpwoods

Contents

●

Introduction

●

This book takes the reader on a journey into a dark and violent time in America, when a revolutionary new genre of crime fiction, the hard-boiled detective story, emerged from the pulp pages of a remarkable magazine.

Black Mask, and the fiction it printed, grew directly out of the era between the two world wars, when machine guns flashed fire from low-slung black limousines, when the corner speakeasy served rotgut gin, when swift rum-runners made night drops in dark coastal waters, when police and politicians were as corrupt as the gangsters they protected, when cons and crooks prowled New York alleys and lurked in trackside hobo jungles, when Dillinger and Pretty Boy Floyd and Al Capone made daily headlines and terrorized a nation.

The *Black Mask* boys wrote it as it happened. Their fiction captured the cynicism, bitterness, disillusionment and anger of a country fighting to survive the evils of Prohibition and the economic hardships of the Depression.

The stories in *Black Mask* were born of adversity, written to dramatize and delineate a nation in flux.

The fast-paced, action-packed mysteries of today are a direct by-product of what has become known around the world as "the *Black Mask* school."

The elegant, deductive sleuth, the calm, calculating sifter of clues, gave way to a new breed—the wary, wisecracking knight of the .45, an often violent, always unpredictable urban vigilante fashioned in the rugged frontier tradition of the western gunfighter.

In the pages of *Black Mask,* the private eye was born.

With this book, a mix of history, biography, and fiction, I celebrate the hard-boiled school and the men who made it famous.

Presented here is the fascinating, previously untold story of *Black Mask,* highlighting its editors, writers, and enduring series characters, tracing the magazine's

13

course from its first issue, in April of 1920, to its last, in July of 1951. Included in this history is the first full-scale portrait of Joseph Thompson Shaw, the legendary editor whose unwavering vision shaped the *Mask* and who guided it through its formative years.

Beyond my chronicle of the magazine itself, I have provided extensive life-and-career portraits of the leading "*Black Mask* boys"—the eight major innovators of the hard-boiled school: Dashiell Hammett, Raymond Chandler, Erle Stanley Gardner, Carroll John Daly, Horace McCoy, Paul Cain, Frederick Nebel, and Raoul Whitfield.

Each author-portrait is accompanied by a classic *Black Mask* story from the period. Included is the first hard-boiled detective tale ever printed, "Three Gun Terry," from Carroll John Daly. (Like most of the other selections, this story has never been reprinted anywhere since its original *Black Mask* appearance.)

I have also included chronological checklists of each author's work for the *Mask*, allowing the reader to trace individual contributions through the years.

Such major hard-boiled pioneers as Daly, McCoy, Nebel, Whitfield, and Paul Cain have been biographically and critically neglected. And *Black Mask* itself has never been fully chronicled.

Therefore, this book fills a special need, detailing the birth and development of a vigorous, new, truly *American* form of mystery fiction.

The *Black Mask* era awaits you.

Let the journey begin.

—WILLIAM F. NOLAN
Agoura, California
1984

"The greatest change in the detective story since Poe came in 1926 with the emergence of the *Black Mask* school of fiction."

—Russell B. Nye
The Unembarrassed Muse:
The Popular Arts in America

THE
BLACK MASK
BOYS

History of a Pulp: The Life and Times of Black Mask

●

No grand vision inspired the creators of *The Black Mask*. In fact, litterateur H. L. Mencken and drama critic George Jean Nathan despised their brainchild and refused to allow their names to be included on its masthead.

Black Mask was an economic necessity, created for the purpose of aiding another financially crippled publication edited by Mencken and Nathan.

By 1918, *The Smart Set* was in trouble. This highly regarded, innovative magazine, which had launched the professional career of F. Scott Fitzgerald and which was designed for the sophisticated reader, had never been a moneymaker. Subtitled "A Magazine of Cleverness," *The Smart Set* was a bit *too* smart and clever to reach a mass audience.

In order to keep it solvent, Mencken and Nathan (who also shared in its ownership) had entered the more lucrative field of the pulps with *Parisienne* and *Saucy Stories*. Both titles proved successful.

Pulp magazines were then of a standard size—seven by ten inches, with gaudy, bright-colored covers (a reflection of their Dime Novel origins). They could be produced at a relatively low cost due to the use of paper made from ground wood. This "pulp" paper was short-fibered, fragile, and difficult to preserve, and clearly separated these publications from the "slick" magazines printed on smooth, higher-quality paper stock.

Even though Mencken and Nathan did well with *Parisienne* and *Saucy Stories,* their financial battle had not yet been won. Another mass-market pulp publication seemed the only solution.

According to historian Ron Goulart, the editor-publishers "turned down the opportunity to do an all-Negro pulp . . . [and] finally decided they'd try a mystery magazine."

Their decision was no doubt inspired by the success that Street & Smith had achieved with *Detective Story*. As the only ongoing crime pulp, it had steadily increased its circulation since its first appearance in October of 1915.

Early in 1919, writing to his friend Ernest Boyd about the problems at *Smart Set*, Mencken declared: "I am thinking of venturing into a new cheap magazine scheme . . . The opportunity is good and [we] need the money."

A line drawing of Satan, in a black mask, was featured on each issue of *Smart Set* as part of its cover logo—which gave Mencken and Nathan the idea for their new title. The logo chosen for the new publication was a thin black pirate's mask with a dirk and a flintlock pistol crossed behind it.

That first issue of *The Black Mask* was dated April 1920, priced at twenty cents. It contained a dozen stories in its 128 pages and was subtitled: "An Illustrated Magazine of Detective, Mystery, Adventure, Romance and Spiritualism." (Through the years this subtitle was constantly revised as new genres of fiction were added or dropped.) Spiritualism as a cover subject was discarded after the first issue. Western fiction was eventually added, becoming a *Black Mask* staple (into the 1930s), along with adventure tales set in exotic locales around the world.

In the second issue (May 1920), an editorial headed "Five Magazines in One!" attempted to show readers that the *Mask* was open to almost any type of story:

> What we propose to do is to publish in every issue the best stories obtainable . . . of Adventure, the best Mystery and Detective Stories, the best Romances, the best Love stories, and the best stories of the Occult.

Published under the subsidiary name of Pro-Distributors, out of Warner Publications in New York, the editor of *Mask* was listed as F. M. Osborne. A woman. Miss Osborne used only her initials to project a masculine image, since the new magazine was aimed primarily at male readers. The main editorial chores were handled by Osborne and Wyndham Martyn (both of whom were associate editors on *The Smart Set*), but Mencken was soon complaining to Ernest Boyd: ". . . the thing has burdened both Nathan and me with disagreeable work."

Mencken made no secret of the fact that he cordially detested the *Mask,* calling it "a lousy magazine," adding that "reading manuscripts for it is a fearful job." But he also admitted, "It has kept us alive during a very bad year."

In November of 1920, just eight months after its first issue, Mencken and Nathan sold the *Mask* to Eltinge F. "Pop" Warner and Eugene Crowe, owner-publishers of *The Smart Set.* Since they had invested only $500 in the project, the Mencken-Nathan profit margin was a tidy one (at a reputed sale price of $12,250).*

---

*Some reports have placed the sum at $100,000, but this is obviously an overinflated figure.

Warner took over as business manager, retaining Miss Osborne as editor.

Within a year the magazine reached a very healthy circulation level, demonstrating that readers were starved for mysteries. Certainly, the early *Mask* displayed no hint of originality or literary merit.

Its writers supplied pale imitations of the fiction being printed in *Detective Story*. Early *Black Mask* crime solvers were dull and pretentious fellows, reflecting the overbaked melodramatic elements of the silent screen. They included foppish Inspector Des Moines, prim and proper Desmond Okewood, of the British Secret Service, and solemnly pompous criminal investigator F. Jackson Melville-Smith. Bores one and all.

> Shaking off the feeling of dread that had settled upon him like an incubus, Grimstead resolutely walked up the weed-encumbered walk that led to the front door, armed with a key that he had experienced no difficulty in securing from a cynical real-estate agent, who promptly offered to wager that he would not stay the night out, a wager that Grimstead as promptly accepted.

That is just *one* sentence of "Fingers From the Grave" by Edwin Carty Ranck in the September 1920 issue. Ranck indeed!

Dialogue could be truly incredible. Witness this exchange from a *Mask* story printed in October 1922:

> "My dear Inspector," protested the Professor. "You surely cannot expect me to believe that a mere monkey—"
>
> "That monkey threw Madame La Tourette into uncontrollable hysterics," Inspector Donaldson insisted. "Fifteen years ago, while on a hunting trip in Africa, her husband was crushed to death in the arms of a giant gorilla. Madame La Tourette is said to have recovered . . . yet, in her imagination, she could see re-enacted the tragedy of her husband's terrible end—even seem to hear the echo of the crunching of his bones and his agonized cries as a hairy monster of the jungle had squeezed the breath from him years before."

The awkward, heavy-handed titles of these early stories were in keeping with their outrageous plots and characters: "The Deviltry of Dr. Waugh," "The Strange Case of Nathaniel Broome," "The Uncanny Voice," "The House of the Fiend Who Laughs," "The Scar of the Gibbering Imp."

In a retrospective review of a late-1921 issue of *Mask* (which was then subtitled "A Magazine of Mystery, Thrills and Surprise"), pulp historian Robert Sampson brands the fiction as "inept drivel":

> It is sorry work to plod among the pages. Over all of the stories hangs the gray taint of inability. Not only are the authors [Bessie Dudley, J. Frederic Thorne, Ward Sterling, George Fayerweather, etc.] pretty condescending about mystery fiction, but they are unaware that they do not know how to write the stuff . . .
>
> In its early form *The Black Mask* was sterile. It existed without direction,

without self-respect . . . What ailed *Mask* was the baleful influence of *The Smart Set.* The lesser magazine aped the attitudes of the greater. . . . *Mask* disdained its own fiction, smirked at reader tastes, and [was] haughtily aloof from the field in which it would [within a decade] stand pre-eminent.

Advertising in these early issues was often more engaging than the fiction. In 1920 one might order a full "110-piece Dinner Set" for "$1.00 Down." Or, if you were feeling a bit under the weather, you could order a dozen "AK Tablets" for the relief of "Headaches, Neuralgias, Colds and La Grippe, Women's Ills, Rheumatic and Sciatic Pains." All for twenty-five cents a bottle. Or how about "Re-Mo-Vo," described as "the Daintily Perfumed Hair Remover." Or you could "Make People Like You" by sending five cents in stamps for a little booklet titled "Personal Power." If your nose was "ill shaped" you could send for "The Original [strap-on] Anita Nose-Adjuster." Or you could "Reduce Your Fat" by using "Cosi Obesity Cream."

By the October 1922 issue, the masthead listed a new editor, George W. Sutton, Jr.—with Harry C. North assisting him.

Sutton's first editorial was an odd one. Headed "How to Read Black Mask Stories," it implored readers "not to skip quickly over the pages" and warned them against a "jump to the end 'to see how it comes out.' . . . You cannot get the full force of these stories if you spoil your own pleasure by reading them the wrong end first."

Sutton immediately began to improve the *Mask.* In November he launched a series by ex-auto bandit Joe Taylor called "My Underworld," based on Taylor's life in crime. And in December of that year he printed the seminal work of two authors destined to reshape the genre, Carroll John Daly and Dashiell Hammett (then writing under the pseudonym of "Peter Collinson"). Daly's story, "The False Burton Combs," and Hammett's "The Road Home" were the forerunners of the *Black Mask* school of fiction.

That following year, 1923, provided the turning point, with the birth of the world's first tough private eye, Terry Mack, in Daly's "Three Gun Terry" in the May 15 issue. (In June, *Mask* featured the debut of Race Williams in "Knights of the Open Palm.") Hard on their heels, in the October 1 issue, Hammett's first Continental Op tale, "Arson Plus," was printed.

In publishing these stories, *The Black Mask* had made history; a revolution was under way, and the detective genre would never be the same.

Sutton, however, was not yet aware of what effect this new type of fiction would have, and in the same issue containing Hammett's first Op tale the editorial promised "stories of rugged Adventure, and real . . . Romance, rare Western yarns . . . weird, creepy mystery tales and the only convincing ghost stories to be found anywhere."

One thing *did* become clear to George Sutton—the value of issue-to-issue heroes. He began promoting series characters, including The Scarlet Fox (by Eustace Hale Ball) and detective T. McGuirk (by Ray Cummings). Soon, however,

Sutton's passion for motorboating began to replace his editorial interests. By April of 1924 he had resigned, and Philip C. Cody (who had been director of circulation) took over the editor's chair. North stayed on as Cody's associate.

Erle Stanley Gardner, who had been selling fiction to the *Mask* since 1923, appreciated Harry North's "patience and sense of humor." Gardner credited North with helping him to write "better stories [with his] coaching on the margin of rejection slips and in short personal letters."

Phil Cody, who always thought of himself as "primarily a businessman," proved to be a strong-minded, extremely capable editor; he saw what Sutton had failed to see—that the Hammett-Daly brand of tough, hard-edged storytelling represented a bold new step beyond the traditional deductive school of crime fiction. He began to feature Hammett's Op stories, and he also urged Daly to write more about Race Williams. (Cody recognized the fact that Daly's work was far inferior to Hammett's, but he was wise enough to know that content counted more than quality in establishing the popularity of this new brand of fiction.)

It was Cody who (in 1925) encouraged Gardner to develop his Ed Jenkins Phantom Crook series, and by the January 1926 issue, Cody felt confident enough to announce in an editorial that *"The Black Mask* has found its stride and is forging . . . to the front. Its circulation is increasing rapidly . . . [because] *The Black Mask* gives its readers more real, honest-to-Jasper, he-man stuff . . . than any other magazine . . ."

Cody also introduced (in 1925–1926) the work of four other highly influential writers: Nels Leroy Jorgensen, Tom Curry, Raoul Whitfield, and Frederick Nebel.

Jorgensen was a New Jersey motorcycle patrolman who moonlighted as a fiction-eer. His straight-shooting gambler from the Southwest, Stuart "Black" Burton, quickly earned reader approval—and Jorgensen continued Burton's adventures into 1938.

Curry also won favor with a series of yarns about Mac, a hard-knuckled New York police detective. Curry had been a police reporter for a major New York paper and claimed that his stories were "right out of life." Whenever he needed fresh plot material, he'd seek out one of his "detective pals" who would fill him in on the latest criminal cases.

Whitfield, who loved flying, provided Cody with aviation thrillers featuring pilot-hero Bill Scott—while Erle Stanley Gardner helped fill Cody's western fiction needs with the wild adventures of sagebrush bandit Black Barr.

Fred Nebel wrote just one story under Cody's editorship; his potential had yet to be realized.

According to Erle Stanley Gardner, Cody never received due credit for his formative role in editing *Mask:* "[He] had a keen appreciation of literature," Gardner declared. "And he didn't cater merely to one style of fiction . . . Under his regime, the new action type of detective story took a long stride forward." Gardner also pointed out that "Phil Cody was the first . . . to appreciate the real genius of Dashiell Hammett."

Gardner related a bizarre anecdote concerning himself, Cody, and Hammett.

Early in 1926 Hammett declared that he could not afford to continue writing for *Mask* unless he got a raise in his basic rate (which was probably three cents per word at that time).

Cody began sweating. He couldn't give Hammett a raise without doing the same for Daly and others. Yet if Hammett left, the magazine might fold without him. Cody contacted Gardner with his problem, and Gardner proposed that a penny per word be deducted from *his* rate and applied to Hammett's rate. That way Hammett would stay with *Mask* and Gardner would continue to have a ready market for Ed Jenkins.

Cody brought this proposal to Eltinge Warner. The publisher declared that Gardner "must be nuts" and that "it was a cockeyed offer and no good business-man would have made it." Besides, he'd never liked Hammett's work.

When Hammett failed to get his raise, he quit. And, indeed, the magazine suffered as a result. By the summer of 1926, circulation had dropped to 66,000—and Warner felt that *Mask* needed a new editor.

This suited Cody. He was unhappy with his editorial duties and wanted to return to the business end of publishing, as vice-president and circulation director. (In the 1930s he was promoted, replacing A. W. Sutton as president of the company.)

Warner contacted mystery writer Joel Townsley Rogers, who was then an editor with *Century* magazine, and offered him the editing job at *Mask*. Rogers wanted to say yes but could not extricate himself from his contract with *Century*.

Enter Joseph Thompson Shaw.

Historically, Shaw's name is directly linked with *Black Mask* as the man who shaped and perfected the hard-boiled genre of detective fiction. W. T. Ballard (who began writing for the magazine in 1933) recounted the story of how Shaw became editor: "Writing was what he most wanted to do . . . [and] he had a manuscript that he took to Phil Cody at Warner Publications. Shaw did *not* sell the story, but he so impressed Phil that Cody hired him to edit *Black Mask* on the spot."

Joseph Shaw's background was diverse and colorful. Born in 1874, he was a descendant of Roger Shaw, a New England immigrant of the 1630s.

From boyhood, Joe Shaw loved boats and sailing. A writer friend reported that "he always had a flair for adventure—which he humorously ascribed to the mar-riage of a Crusading ancestor and a Saracen princess."

Shaw attended venerable Bowdoin College, in Brunswick, Maine, where he edited the campus paper and specialized in athletics.

Following his graduation, he obtained a job with a New York paper, then took over the editorship of a semitrade weekly. In 1904, working for the American Woolen Company, he wrote his first book, *From Wool to Cloth,* and felt that he was on his way to becoming "a literary man."

After a trip to Spain, in 1909, his second book was published: *Spain of Today: A Narrative Guide to the Country of the Dons.*

He continued his interest in athletics and became a master of the sword, winning the national championship in sabers and the president's medal for his skill with foil, epée, and saber.

During the First World War, Shaw was a bayonet instructor, leaving the service as an army captain. (During his days with *Black Mask*, he was widely known as "Cap" Shaw.)

Following the war, for a period of five years, he functioned as chief of the Hoover relief mission in Czechoslovakia and Greece. He returned to the U.S. in the early 1920s, determined to make his living as a full-time writer—but as Raymond Chandler later stated, "[Shaw's work was] about the deadest writing I ever saw on a supposedly professional level."

In truth, Joe Shaw was a superb editor and a dreadful writer. He did manage to get four of his mystery novels into print during the 1930s (*Derelict, Danger Ahead, Blood on the Curb,* and *It Happened at the Lake*), but they were hopelessly flat and banal, betraying no evidence of his outstanding skills as an editor.

In 1926, when Shaw walked into the Warner offices at 25 West Forty-fifth Street, he knew absolutely nothing about pulps or pulp writing and had never read a single issue of the magazine he was hired to edit. He spent a full week poring over back numbers—and decided that Hammett was the writer whose work pointed in the direction Shaw wanted *Black Mask* to go.

But Hammett had, by then, quit writing pulp fiction. Shaw determined to lure him back and sent a letter to Hammett, suggesting that it was time to revive the Continental Op in a "longer form," in which situation and character could be fully explored. Shaw's ideas excited Hammett, and he returned to the fold with two long Op novelettes, forming a superb short novel, *Blood Money*.

Cap Shaw was off and running.

The first Shaw-edited issue (November 1926, subtitled "Western, DETEC-TIVE, and Adventure Stories") contained fiction by Daly, Whitfield, Nebel, and Gardner. Shaw continued to feature the work of these four writers, along with Curry and Nels Jorgensen. But he was actively seeking new talent.

For the June 1927 issue (which featured the opening installment of the first Race Williams serial), Shaw penned an editorial, "The Aim of Black Mask," in which he claimed that the publication now had "a definite purpose and a definite aim . . . [to] establish itself as the only magazine of its kind in the . . . world:"

> . . . detective fiction, as we view it, has only commenced to be developed.
> . . . all other fields have been worked and overworked [but detective fiction] has been barely scratched.
> . . . However, to be convincing . . . [such fiction] must be real in motive, character and action . . . must be plausible . . . clear and understandable . . . Therefore, word has gone out to writers of our requirements of plausibility, of truthfulness in details, of realism in . . . the portrayal of action and emotion . . . Slowly, but surely, we are moulding the contents of this magazine along the lines of our purpose.

Shaw was getting results. Several major new writers were to be developed under his editorship.

The first was Horace McCoy, who made his bow in the December 1927 issue (now subtitled "The He-Man's Magazine").

By 1928, Shaw was printing the team of Earl and Marion Scott (who created the Phil Craleigh series about a drunken lawyer trying to reform). Also in 1928, Fred Nebel began his popular MacBride-Kennedy police series for Shaw. And that year's December issue featured the debut of a new series character, Tex of the Border Service. Surprise: Tex carried a purse! Shaw was taking a gamble in bringing Katherine Brocklebank's secret-service heroine into the tough pages of the *Mask*. Yet, readers liked Tex, and Miss Brocklebank brought her back in three more adventures over the next seven months.*

Shaw also brought western writer Eugene Cunningham to the *Mask* and later helped him devise his series of Cleve Corby fighting-ranger shoot-em-ups. (It is not generally known that although Shaw emphasized detective fiction, he also strongly favored westerns—and *Mask* did not become an all-crime magazine until 1932. Many of its covers in the 1920s depicted gunslingers and outlaws. Eventually, by 1933, the magazine was subtitled "Gripping, Smashing Detective Stories," reflecting its specialized approach.)

In order to achieve greater impact and unity, Shaw used only *one* artist for all of the magazine's interior illustrations—Arthur Rodman Bowker. Boldly sketched and highly stylized, Bowker's work offered a perfect counterpart to *Mask's* hard-hitting fiction.

Beginning in 1927, Shaw had also tightened the magazine's title: *The Black Mask* was now simply *Black Mask*.

To Joe Shaw, the editor's job became very personal. From the outset, he functioned as a potent, ever-helpful father figure to his authors. He offered them practical advice and wise counsel, encouraged their goals, cheered them in times of stress, and sought, constantly, to bolster their confidence, to draw out their best work.

Shaw's credo included "simplicity for the sake of clarity, plausibility, and belief." He wanted action, but he felt that "action is meaningless unless it involves recognizable human character in three-dimensional form."

He hated the word "pulp." To him, it smacked of cheapness and vulgarity. He always referred to *Mask* as "a rough-paper book" and felt that he and his authors were fighting a war for quality in a market glutted with hasty, hack writing. It was "Cap and his boys" against the competition.

Shaw's editorials reflected the special pride he felt in *Black Mask*. Late in 1929, he wrote of "the change in the character of [crime] stories . . ." commenting that "this magazine has . . . been the pioneer in the development of the new type of detective story."

---

*At least thirty other women had fiction printed in *Black Mask*, but nearly all of their contributions fall into the magazine's early "Romance" category.

Series characters continued to dominate the *Mask*. Once Shaw was convinced of an author's talent, he would ask that writer to come up with a character strong enough to support a series. The ongoing success of Race Williams and the Continental Op proved that readers became emotionally addicted to continuing characters and would eagerly buy issues featuring their favorites. (Akin, today, to viewer addiction for series characters appearing weekly on television.)

In 1929, Shaw launched the Jerry Frost, Flying Ranger series by McCoy—and, in 1930, arranged for Whitfield to begin his Jo Gar, Island Detective stories under the suitably exotic pseudonym of "Ramon Decolta."

Mask continued to feature Dashiell Hammett as the "prime innovator in this field." Shaw was responsible for Hammett's mature development as a novelist, and it was in *Black Mask* that such all-time Hammett classics as *Red Harvest, The Dain Curse,* and *The Maltese Falcon* initially appeared.

"Hammett was the leader in the thought that finally brought the magazine its distinctive form . . ." declared Shaw. "[He] set character before situation and led . . . others along that path."

The February 1930 issue announced the results of a reader poll: "The leaders . . . are Dashiell Hammett, Carroll John Daly, Erle Stanley Gardner, Frederick Nebel, Raoul Whitfield, and the Scotts." McCoy was next.

The *Mask* lost one of its editors that year. In a December 1930 letter to McCoy, Shaw reported the death of George Sutton.

After delivering *The Glass Key* and a few more Op stories, Hammett left *Mask* at the close of 1930 for greener financial pastures. This was a blow to Shaw, who felt the loss keenly. However, Daly, Nebel, Whitfield, and Gardner continued to supply him with material—Daly with Race Williams, Nebel with his new Donahue series, Whitfield with Hollywood eye Ben Jardinn, and Gardner with stalwart Ed Jenkins.

The icy, diamond-hard Kells series (forming the novel *Fast One*) began in 1932, from Paul Cain; and in 1934, Norbert Davis created private eye Ben Shaley for *Mask*.

Davis had been a law student at Stanford when he sold his first story to Shaw in 1932. He obtained a law degree two years later but never took his bar exam, deciding that fiction writing was his proper profession. Davis became a frequent contributor to the pulps, later breaking into *The Saturday Evening Post* with his often humorous, well-crafted stories. But there was ultimate tragedy behind his humor, and at the age of forty, in 1949, depressed over the slow progress of his career, he died of carbon monoxide poisoning. A Cape Cod suicide.

Shaw introduced Theodore A. Tinsley to his readers late in 1932 with series character Jerry Tracy, a troubleshooting news columnist.

The following year proved to be Shaw's finest as he brought five powerful new writers into the *Mask:* Thomas Walsh, Roger Torrey, H. H. Stinson, W. T. Ballard, and (at the close of 1933) Raymond Chandler.

Walsh was unique in *not* creating a series hero.

Torrey contributed Mal Prentice, a ruggedly tough police detective. The toughness was genuine; Torrey had been an Oregon lumberjack in his younger days. He was a "heavy boozer," who worked evenings on his pulp fiction in a sleazy New York hotel room. Then, his work done, he would "drink the night away" in the bars of New Jersey (which remained open until 6:00 A.M.). When his doctor warned him that alcohol was destroying his liver, Torrey gave up drinking. For exactly one month.

Shaw liked Torrey's work; it represented precisely what he was after in editing *Mask*. From the September 1933 issue, a sample of tough Torrey:

> Bruner leaned over without warning and hit Prentice in the mouth, and Prentice tried to roll with the punch. . . . Locked to the bed frame, he jerked a foot up and kicked at Bruner, who stepped out of range and jeered: "Not even close." He knocked Prentice's guarding hand aside, stepped in and struck again.
>
> Prentice wiped blood from his face . . . "I'll remember that." . . . His eyes were hot. He was shaking so the cuff rattled where it was fastened to the bed.

H. H. Stinson's series hero was quick-fisted Ken O'Hara, of the *Los Angeles Tribune*. Again, a very tough cookie.

Tod Ballard began an extensive *Mask* series with Bill Lennox, a Hollywood trouble-chaser for Consolidated Films. The series grew out of Ballard's earlier screen experiences. He'd walked away from an electrical engineering career in Cleveland and had bummed his way west in the late 1920s to become a contract writer for Columbia Studios. For the Lennox stories, Columbia became Consolidated, with Ballard creating one of the first popular hard-boiled series characters based on the film industry. (At Shaw's suggestion, Ballard later devised another hit series for *Mask* concerning race-track detective Red Drake.)

Chandler wrote his first two stories for Shaw about a tough private eye named Mallory. He also turned out four series stories for Shaw about another "private dick" named Carmady. They were the same man. In truth, all of Chandler's knight-detectives, under whatever name he gave them, were prototypes for Philip Marlowe.

In 1933, Shaw presented his personal view of "the ideal *Black Mask* reader." In a blatantly melodramatic editorial he described this romanticized man of action:

> He is vigorous-minded . . . hating unfairness, trickery, injustice . . . responsive to the thrill of danger, the stirring exhilaration of clean, swift, hard action . . . [he is] a man who . . . knows the song of a bullet, the soft, slithering hiss of a swift-thrown knife, the feel of hard fists, the call of courage . . .

In the 1934–1935 period, Shaw brought three more star writers into the *Mask:* Dwight Babcock (with detective Maguire, and later G-man Chuck Thompson), John K. Butler (who wrote about hard-edged government agents), and George Harmon Coxe.

Coxe had been a newspaper reporter on the *Los Angeles Express*, and he had also worked for other papers in Florida and New York. Coxe wanted to utilize his newspaper background, but, as he declared, "there were already too many reporter-detectives in the pulps. So I came up with a guy who was a crime photographer. Called him 'Flashgun' Casey."

Casey worked out of Boston and became a big success for Coxe. Beyond the pages of *Black Mask,* Casey went on to star on radio, in novels, and in films and television.

Coxe's crime photographer mellowed considerably through the years, but there was nothing mild about his early adventures in *Mask.* From "Hot Delivery" (July 1934):

> Casey dropped behind the desk as the automatic roared. He scrambled around the side on hands and knees. Flip screamed in pain, fired again. Then Casey straightened, leaped forward. Flip was trying to get out of the chair. Blinded, he waved the gun wildly, one hand clasped to his blackened, charred face . . . He was nearly erect when Casey hit him.
>
> Flip went over backwards with the chair. Casey landed on top, his hand on the automatic. He wrenched it free, struck once, twice. Crushing, violent blows. Flip's body did not move after that, probably would never move.

Attempting to justify the violence in his magazine, Shaw bragged that *Mask* was being read by "clergymen, bankers, lawyers, doctors." Among his readership he also claimed judges, embassy officials, and "the heads of large businesses."

As a *Black Mask* writer of that period recalled: "It was important to Cap that the magazine be respected. He *needed* to believe that he was editing a publication of real importance, and he took his job very seriously."

However, by the middle 1930s, *Black Mask* was in trouble.

When Shaw had taken over in 1926, he had increased circulation from 66,000 to 80,000 in the first year. The climb continued, peaking in 1930 at 103,000— but by the close of 1935, as America was suffering through the Depression era, circulation slumped to 63,000.

Hammett had been out of *Mask* for five years. Now Whitfield was gone, along with Daly, McCoy, and Curry. Even a per-issue price reduction late in 1934 (from twenty cents to fifteen cents) had not helped.

Eltinge Warner told Shaw that he might have to make some salary cuts in 1936. Shaw made it clear that he would not abide by this. The situation became tense.

Meanwhile, Shaw brought another star talent to the *Mask* when he printed two stories about a treasure-hunting boat owner named Oscar Sail. These were written by Lester Dent, based on his own treasure-hunting adventures off the coast of Florida.

Best known under the pseudonym of "Kenneth Robeson," Dent was grinding out a 60,000-word Doc Savage novel every month for Street & Smith. (Eventually, he wrote more than 150 of these.) He lived aboard a forty-foot schooner in Miami and sidelined in professional photography. Originally a Teletype operator from the

Midwest, he'd been writing pulp fiction since 1929 and had sold work to dozens of editors, but Shaw was something special. Dent praised him as "the finest coachwhip I ever met in an editor's chair. *Mask*, in Cap Shaw's hands, was akin to a writer's shrine . . . When you went into his office and talked with Shaw, you felt you were doing fiction that was powerful. You had feelings of stature."

Dent was plotting a third Oscar Sail novelette in October of 1936 when he received a note from Shaw reporting a salary dispute. After ten years with the *Mask*, Joe Shaw had been relieved of his editorial duties.

A shock wave ran through the ranks of "Joe's boys" from New York to California. Dent quit the *Mask*, and Chandler switched to *Dime Detective*. Nebel also left, and Paul Cain did no more pulp writing.

Shaw's remarkable decade was over, but he had achieved his goal: He had shaped and guided dozens of writers toward a new form of objective realism within crime fiction.

His stable had included Ed Lybeck, Reuben Jennings Shay, J. J. des Ormeaux, Eric Taylor, Stewart Stirling, Donald Barr Chidsey, Norvell Page, Hugh Cave, and John Lawrence.

By the December 1936 issue, *Mask* had a new editor, listed on the masthead as F. Ellsworth. Another woman in disguise. As the guiding editor of *Ranch Romances* (also a Warner publication), Fanny Ellsworth seemed an odd choice to helm a hard-boiled detective magazine. Indeed, her ideas on crime fiction were much "softer" than Joe Shaw's; she intended to bring "a more humanistic" type of story into *Mask*, feeling that the strict hard-boiled approach was too limiting.

Ellsworth certainly made an impressive start at her new job. Within a space of just eight months, between January and September of 1937, she brought no less than nine impressive talents to the *Mask*. Among them: Cornell Woolrich, Max Brand, Frank Gruber, and Steve Fisher.

Woolrich (who also gained fame as "William Irish") was a prime example of the "softer, more nakedly-emotional approach" in crime writing favored by Ellsworth. His detectives were never hard-boiled; they were usually "little" men, trying to do a job within the dark, threatening universe of a big city.

Woolrich himself existed inside such a universe, living with his mother in a series of cramped, friendless New York hotels. Writing was his salvation; it kept him sane.

Frederick Faust (who wrote as "Max Brand") was also an emotionalist, who believed "in the prime essentials of truth and beauty." A Renaissance man who loved Italy, he lived for many years with his family and servants in a hillside villa near Florence, turning out more than a million words a year for the pulps. He contributed only two stories to *Mask*, but Max Brand's name on the cover meant an upsurge in sales.

Another prolific pulpster, Frank Gruber, now brought his quirky series hero, Oliver Quade, "the Human Encyclopedia," into *Mask*. Gruber recalled that he had made several attempts to sell his work to Shaw. "[He] was a charming man

. . . [who] encouraged revisions of revisions. When he rejected your story it was always with great regret. [He] wore me out with kindness."

Frank Gruber's pal, Steve Fisher, made his first *Mask* appearance just two months after Gruber. He, too, had been rejected by Shaw. As Fisher later commented: "[My] subjective style, mood and approach to a story was the antithesis of [a] Roger Torrey who, like Hammett, wrote objectively, with crisp, cold precision."

With Ellsworth, *Mask* had been opened to the subjective approach. Other authors she brought to the magazine during that first year included Baynard Kendrick, Donald Wandrei, Wyatt Blassingame, Lawrence Treat, and Dale Clark. Among them all, Shaw might have approved most of Clark's Mike O'Hanna—a tough "house dick" at a resort hotel.

Gruber described Fanny Ellsworth as strong-minded. "She was an extremely erudite woman. You would have thought she'd be more at home with a magazine like *Vogue* or *Harper's* . . . [but] she knew what she wanted."

Ellsworth's tenure at the *Mask* lasted until the spring of 1940. Circulation had taken another severe drop. Warner and his associates felt that it was time to get out.

They sold *Mask* to Popular Publications, whose *Dime Detective*, under the editorship of Kenneth S. White, had been *Black Mask*'s chief competitor. During the 1930s, Ken White had deliberately edited *Dime* in the Shaw tradition, luring several of "Cap's boys" into his magazine with a guarantee of higher word rates.

Now, ironically, in the summer of 1940, Ken White became editor of *Black Mask*. Immediately, he began injecting new life and vigor into its pages, reestablishing the magazine's tougher, hard-edged image.

Before the close of the year, White had printed work by Cleve Adams, D. L. Champion, and Robert Reeves.

Adams wrote in the direct hard-boiled Chandler manner, and Champion's Rex Sackler was a tough ex-cop operating as a private eye. With his offbeat detective, Cellini Smith, Reeves brought elements of wry humor into the magazine.

A major change was taking place in popular culture. Three emerging forms of entertainment—comic books, paperback mass-market editions, and television—were destined to wipe out the pulps. By 1940, the death knell had been sounded, and the pulp magazines began their inexorable slide toward oblivion.

Ken White fought to keep *Black Mask* solvent, but it was a losing battle. He utilized tough, wisecracking titles—"You're the Crime in My Coffin," "My Body Lies Over the Ocean," "Blood, Sweat and Biers," "Murder Had a Little Lamb," "Once Upon a Crime"—and he commissioned gaudy, sensationalistic covers by Raphael De Soto which portrayed scantily clad young ladies being threatened by unsavory thugs. White also brought in such diverse talents as Leslie Charteris (with The Saint) and Curt Siodmak (with his now classic science-fiction-suspense tale, "Donovan's Brain").

In the January 1941 issue, he printed stories featuring five series characters and appealed to reader loyalty with a strong editorial:

If any one thing can be said to be the main factor in *Black Mask's* success down through the years it is unquestionably the great parade of series characters who have marched through its pages bringing readers back issue after issue to renew old friendships.

In the early 1940s, White ran "timely" stories of government agents, Nazi villains, and espionage—but these efforts did little to increase circulation.

Finally, in 1944, White utilized the expert services of Joe Shaw as an adviser to new writers.* White also brought "Flashgun" Casey back to the *Mask* in book-length adventures by Coxe. He purchased new work from Carroll John Daly, and featured Gardner's popular Ed Jenkins. He also printed other *Black Mask* veterans—Ballard, Davis, and Torrey—along with an impressive roster of new names and characters: C. P. Donnel, Jr. (with Doc Rennie), Merle Constiner (with Luther McGavock), William Campbell Gault (with Mortimer Jones), and John D. MacDonald (with Sam Dermott).

Added to these were Fredric Brown, Bruno Fischer, and, in 1949 with a single story, Louis L'Amour.

But *Mask* now had dropped back to bimonthly publicaton; the overall page content had been cut; the magazine's size was also reduced and the cover price raised to twenty-five cents. Nothing worked; the downward plunge continued. By 1950, White had left the magazine, and *Mask* was under the emergency supervision of its publisher, Harry Steeger. Reprints began to be used to cut editorial costs and soon dominated the contents page.

The long battle ended in July of 1951. *Black Mask* printed its final issue that month after more than thirty-one years of publication.† The bare statistics are awesome. In its three decades, *Black Mask* printed some 2,500 stories by 640 authors. Total wordage for 340 issues: over 30 million.

Black Mask was dead, but its place in the history of modern detective literature was secure. It had pioneered and developed a vital new genre, and its "hard-boiled boys" had become the stuff of legend.

NOTE: Beyond the writers named in this history, there were others who also contributed their talents to the *Mask,* many of whom helped shape the magazine's unique image. Some appeared only once or twice in *Mask,* yet

---

*Shaw had been functioning as a New York literary agent. In 1946 he edited his famous collection of *Black Mask* stories, *The Hard-Boiled Omnibus.* By late 1951 he had opened his own literary agency, where he died at his desk in August of the following year. Among the writers paying him tribute was W. T. Ballard, who sadly reflected on Shaw's frustrations as a writer: "He could point the way for [others], contribute much to helping work out their problems with sympathy and understanding—but he could not do the same for himself, though writing was what he most wanted to do."

Chandler recalled Shaw as "a warm editor [who] always seemed to have time to write at length and to argue with you. To some of us, I think he was indeed a genuine inspiration in that . . . we wrote better for him than we could have written for anybody else."

†In the 1970s there was an abortive attempt to revive the magazine. Published by Adrian Lopez and edited by Keith Deutsch, it was aimed at bimonthly publication. Using mainly reprint material, the new *Black Mask* never got beyond its pilot issue, dated August 1974.

deserve to be listed. Each name is followed by the date of the author's first appearance in the magazine.

Robert Arthur   (1940)
S. Omar Barker   (1929)
William E. Barrett   (1933)
Maurice Beam   (1937)
H. Bedford-Jones   (1932)
Hal Murray Bonnett   (1938)
Charles G. Booth   (1923)
Anthony Boucher   (1945)
William Donald Bray   (1927)
Walter C. Brown   (1938)
Curtis Cluff   (1948)
Francis Cockrell   (1933)
Richard Connell   (1923)
William R. Cox   (1938)
Frederick C. Davis   (1922)
Richard Deming   (1948)
Robert C. Dennis   (1946)
James Duncan   (1934)
Allan Vaughan Elston   (1946)
Dean Evans   (1949)
Paul W. Fairman   (1948)
G. T. Fleming-Roberts   (1940)
J. S. Fletcher   (1922)
Richard E. Glendinning   (1950)
Jackson Gregory   (1939)
Brett Halliday   (1944)
Cutcliffe Hyne   (1926)
Francis James   (1922)
Norman Katkov   (1946)
Day Keene   (1943)
W. H. B. Kent   (1927)
Philip Ketchum   (1941)
Jim Kjelgaard   (1940)
C. M. Kornbluth   (1946)
Murray Leinster   (1922)
Maurice Level   (1920)
Julius Long   (1943)
William Colt MacDonald   (1926)
Carl L. Martin   (1927)
Robert Martin   (1946)
Raymond J. Moffatt   (1934)

James P. Olsen   (1930)
Peter Paige   (1939)
Edgar Pangborn   (1938)
Hugh Pentecost   (1942)
Herman Petersen   (1922)
Henry Wallace Phillips   (1927)
Talmage Powell   (1949)
E. Hoffman Price   (1945)
William Rollins, Jr.   (1923)
William Rough   (1942)
Richard Sale   (1942)
Hank Searls   (1950)
Robert E. Sherwood   (1922)
Bertrand W. Sinclair   (1930)
Charles Somerville   (1923)
Vincent Starrett   (1920)
Stewart Sterling   (1939)
J. Paul Suter   (1923)
Fergus Truslow   (1945)
Robert Turner   (1949)
Bryce Walton   (1950)
Edward Parrish Ware   (1923)
Henry S. Whitehead   (1925)
Edward S. Williams   (1936)
Sewell Peaslee Wright   (1928)

Behind the Mask:
Carroll John Daly

•

The first hard-boiled private detective novel was issued in 1927 from the small New York publishing firm of Edward J. Clode, Inc. Title: *The Snarl of the Beast.* Author: Carroll John Daly.

The tough detective was Race Williams, who introduced himself in the first chapter:

> . . . a sharp eye, a quick draw, and a steady trigger finger drove me into the game. Also you might add to that an aptitude for getting out of trouble almost as quickly as I get into it . . . I'm licensed as a private detective . . . My position is not exactly a healthy one. The police don't like me. The crooks don't like me. I'm just a halfway house between the law and crime; sort of working both ends against the middle . . . My ethics are my own . . . and I'll shoot it out with any gun in the city—any time, any place.

The writing was impossibly crude, the plotting labored and ridiculous, and Race Williams emerged as a swaggering illiterate with the emotional instability of a gun-crazed vigilante.

From the outset of his career in 1922, to the end of his productivity in the mid-1950s, Daly remained an artificial, awkward, self-conscious pulpster, endlessly repetitious, hopelessly melodramatic. He had absolutely no ability for three-dimensional characterization, nor did he possess a feel for language or mood. Additionally, he was cursed with a tin ear. His dialogue was impossibly stilted ("Oh, I ain't got any particular dislike to you . . .") and totally lacked the rhythm and bite of such gifted contemporaries as Hammett and Chandler.

35

Yet, despite all this, Carroll John Daly stands, historically, as the father of the hard-boiled private eye.

Although Race Williams was the first tough-guy detective to achieve book format, he was *not* Carroll John Daly's first genre protagonist. Actually, Daly created no less than three other tough-guy protagonists, two of them nameless, prior to the introduction of Race Williams.

The thirty-year-old narrator of "The False Burton Combs" (*Black Mask,* December 1922) is not a detective. He refers to himself as "a gentleman adventurer" and "a soldier of fortune," and makes his living by "working against the law breakers." For a fee, he takes on the job of protecting (and later impersonating) a rich man's son, Burton Combs, who is being pursued by several gangsters; he casually proceeds to kill three of them during the assignment. The story ends as he accepts a position with the Combs family, leaving his footloose life behind for a job and a wife.

The story is told in the first person, and the "my-ethics-are-my-own" code of the hero is identical to that of Race Williams.

Daly's second tough guy was also nameless. In "It's All in the Game" (*Black Mask,* April 15, 1923), he admits to using the profession of private detective as a "cover" for his illegal crime-fighting activities, declaring that "crooks is my meat." The sole support of his crippled sister, he talks about "gunning a skunk" and defends his quick-trigger method: "It may not be good morals or good ethics, but it's good common sense."

A few pages later he guns down a foe. Then, as Race Williams would later do in countless stories, our hero proudly describes the result of his single shot:

> There was a tiny hole in the center of his forehead and it was slowly turning a dull red. As I watched his eyes grew glassy . . . [and] he slid limply to the floor . . . Ed, the Killer, had gone out.

With "Three Gun Terry," the mold was fully cast. Daly's third tough-guy protagonist, Terry Mack (presented to *Black Mask* readers in May of 1923), became history's first full-fledged private eye. Mack was a direct prototype for Williams: a first-person narrator who was lawless, fast-shooting, hard-talking, and illiterate. (Daly invariably associated toughness with illiteracy.)

When Daly created Race Williams in the shadow of Terry Mack for "Knights of the Open Palm" (*Black Mask,* June 1, 1923), he utilized exactly the same language and approach—and there is little doubt that the lurid adventures of the supertough eye influenced many other pulp writers in the creation of a legion of gut-busting detectives.

In a 1924 *Mask* editorial, George Sutton urged frustrated readers to "fulfill that secret desire for an exciting life! Satisfy your craving for thrills! Let Race Williams and Terry Mack kill your enemies for you!"

Carroll John Daly was thirty-three when he created the Mack/Williams prototype "private dick," describing himself as "blue-eyed and brown-haired." At five feet nine inches, he once convinced Joe Shaw that he stood over six feet, since he knew that the editor favored six-footers in the *Mask*. The son of Mary L. (Brennan) Daly and Joseph F. Daly, he was born in Yonkers, New York, on September 14, 1889. He attended Yonkers High School, the De La Salle Institute, and the American Academy of Dramatic Arts.

He studied law ("a short stint") and stenography ("a longer one"), but gravitated toward theater work. Frank Gruber, who met Daly at a *Black Mask* Christmas party in 1937, later recalled that Daly was "first an usher, then an assistant manager in a motion picture house. He had tried acting, but didn't like it." Daly eventually owned and operated the first moving-picture theater on the boardwalk in Atlantic City.

In his 1967 memoir, *The Pulp Jungle,* Gruber recounts a "hilarious evening" when he listened to Daly "tell about his experiences as a 'receiver' for a bankrupt trunk company. Daly's uncle, a famous attorney who was very influential in New York politics, got him this political plum—[which is] what 'receiverships' were in the Tammany Hall days."

It was this same generous uncle who helped launch Daly's writing career by financing his early efforts at the typewriter. Daly had tried his hand at sales before he turned to writing; he later recalled that he'd been "a stock salesman and a real estate salesman." Neither job proved successful—and he did no better as "manager of a fire-alarm company."

Professional writing was his principal goal—and he sold his first story, "Dolly," to *Black Mask* in 1922.

In response to an editorial request for "colorful biographical data," Daly laid claim to having lived through several wild global adventures as a poverty-stricken youth: "I have been broke on the very edge of the Sahara Desert in Africa," he declared. "I have seen Paris on a thousand dollars a week and a week later seen London on eight dollars, and that eight borrowed from a friend."

In reviewing Daly's reclusive personality, one seriously questions the validity of such "colorful" recollections. In this instance, to please his readers, Daly was very likely stressing fancy over fact.

Factually, however, it *is* known that in 1913, at the age of twenty-four, he married Margaret G. Blakely, and that they had one son, John (who eventually became an actor).

The Dalys settled quietly into New York's suburban Westchester County, in White Plains. They lived in one of a row of identical houses. Returning home after one of his infrequent trips into New York City, Daly had trouble locating his house. He walked up to a door, rang the bell, and asked the woman who answered if she knew where Carroll John Daly lived. She stared at him. "But . . . *you're* Carroll John Daly!" With ruffled dignity, he replied: "I know who I am, madam. I am merely attempting to find out where I *live!*"

Erle Stanley Gardner, who knew him quite well in those pulp years, wrote with amused affection of Daly's hermitlike existence in White Plains. "I always felt that he used Race Williams as a means of satisfying subconscious impulses which he knew could never be gratified in real life. He . . . wanted no part of the rough and tumble. Only on rare occasions could he be tempted to go to New York. It was a major undertaking for him."

In winter, Daly would shut himself away for several months, making certain that the temperature inside the house did not vary by more than a single degree. When Gardner chided him about such habits, Daly replied: "You say I'm not an outdoor man . . . I'll have you know that when the sun shines I think nothing of going out and walking the full width of this lot—and it is a fifty-foot lot!"

Daly's world of crime and violence was purely imaginary; he had never had the slightest experience with actual crime or criminals, but he once made up his mind to buy a .45 automatic. Since Race Williams was always killing hoods with his two big .45s, Daly felt he should know what one was like. He purchased the gun and, on the way home, was arrested for carrying a concealed weapon. As one friend observed: "That was the end of Carroll's criminal research."

Race Williams laughed at pain and sustained many bullet wounds, cuts, and bruises in his savage career. ("The docs had plenty of work . . . in addition to the lead in me, there were two knife wounds . . . They used up nearly a spool of thread sewing me up.") In real-life contrast, Daly refused to have his teeth fixed due to his fear of dentists. His wife, according to Gruber, was continually after him about this, but Daly remained stubbornly and safely at home.

A photo from this period reveals him as a hesitant, mousy-looking man in oversize golf knickers who wore round, steel-rimmed spectacles above a wispy mustache. Yet he found emotional release by allowing his shy personality to be absorbed into the harsh toughness of Race Williams. Daly identified himself closely with his fictional creation and once admitted (in a 1927 issue of *Black Mask*) that he was "Carroll John Daly in the daytime and Race Williams at night." (Daly always did his pulp writing from midnight until six in the morning and claimed that it was as exhausting as "digging for coal in a mine.")

He spoke of Williams as one speaks of an alter ego:

> We live on the fat of the land or starve together . . . As for the opinions of Race Williams, they are his own and I make no apologies for his sentiments . . . He stands five feet eleven and a half, weighs 183 pounds. His hair is dark brown and his eyes are black . . . he admires a clever woman and respects a good one—when he finds her. There is nothing soft-boiled about him.

Indeed, there was not. Race was never weaponless. ("I don't shove a gun under my pillow [at night]—I sleep with one in my hand.") By day, he always packed his twin .45s, and he didn't mind who knew it: "I leaned slightly forward so . . . he got the flash of the two guns—one under each arm. Then I said simply, 'When you put Race Williams out of a rat trap like this, you'll put him out in a cloud of smoke.' "

But Race did more than bluff; he loved sending bullets into bad guys:

- When I fired his right eye disappeared, giving place to a gaping, vacant hole, [and] his huge body took a nose-dive down the stairs—his soul into hell. ("The Super-Devil")
- My bullet crashed home. There was a tiny black hole in the whiteness of his face . . . If hell wasn't all filled up here was another customer. ("Blind Alleys")
- I jerked my right hand down and fired . . . and he clicked his heels together and pitched forward on his face. ("The Death Trap")
- The masked figure never had a chance. I laid a bullet smack between his eyes. ("The Silver Eagle")
- I don't waste my lead—one shot was all I needed. The gold-rimmed glasses snapped right across the bridge of his nose . . . and he slipped to his knees, pitching forward . . . He'd passed out like a piece of boarding house soap on a Saturday night. ("Alias Buttercup")
- My left hand flashed up . . . His face was almost against my gun when I closed my finger and blasted away. ("Gunman's Gallows")
- Both my guns had spoken . . . and, so help me God, but a single hole appeared in Lutz's forehead. I've done a deal of shooting in my day—mighty fine shooting—but never anything like this. ("I'll Tell the World")

Since Williams killed at least one badman during each case, the trigger-happy detective's score, after more than three decades in the pulps, ran into the hundreds. He never had second thoughts about running up this incredible death toll. In fact, he was proud of his record. He was "cleaning out the rats."

In a 1927 interview in *Black Mask,* Daly commented on this vigilante approach to justice:

> I began to realize that there was a crying need for somebody to fight the crooks with their own weapons . . . the law is too cumbersome, too full of loopholes to be of much use. The only real answer to a lot of gunmen is the gun—someone a little quicker on the trigger than they are.

Many readers agreed. Typical of their reaction is this comment from an enthusiastic female: "Race appeals to me. If anything makes me tired, it is the milk and water blood of the modern hero as depicted by writers who are scared to admit that blood is *red.* You get me?"

The Daly popular appeal to readers kept him in the magazine. (At the height of his popularity, his name on the cover meant a 15 percent rise in sales for that issue.) In truth, *Black Mask* editors did not like his work, and Daly admitted that Joe Shaw would never have printed any Race Williams fiction were it not for reader demand.

Daly, however, was blissfully unconcerned with his shortcomings as a writer. He even bragged about some of them in the pages of *Writer's Digest* in 1947:

Punctuation . . . I find a matter of editorial opinion . . . Paragraphing, well, I simply paragraph when I begin to see too many black lines one after the other . . . About grammar. The answer is simple. I don't think anybody cares. About spelling. Well, I was once introduced to all the big editors at a dinner because of my poor spelling.

G. A. Finch, writing in *The Armchair Detective,* notes a pernicious influence in Daly's work:

Race Williams . . . had what no ordinary man had and every common man wanted to some degree: autonomy . . . to punish enemies without fear of reprisal. . . . One thing Williams especially took pride in was that he was "no brain" . . . In his . . . contempt for education and his overwhelming confidence in . . . fist and gun, Race Williams could ease the pangs of every young man who wasn't doing so well on the books. . . . What it comes down to is an acceptance of a state of mind which makes the demolition of other people a necessary and happy activity; associated with this are feelings of indifference and hostility, resistance to compassion, voyeuristic sadism, instant [justification] of dog-eat-dog attitudes, and an overpowering confidence in the efficacy of violence.

When Daly attempted to provide Williams with some feminine company, the result was ludicrous. During the same year that Hammett's masterwork, *The Maltese Falcon,* was serialized (in 1930), Daly also had a series running in the *Mask,* featuring one of his most overblown characters: Florence Drummond, called The Flame. She had a passionate yen for Williams, but poor Flo possessed "a criminal mind"—and Race kept rejecting her. She attempts to corrupt him in this incredibly stilted plea:

"Oh, I've used men . . . My mind guided me—that criminal mind . . . There's never been a man who held me in his arms and kissed me who hasn't come back and back and back. Moths! Moths! Moths! [to the Flame] . . . but my love for you has been . . . different. And now, Race, I can offer you . . . power. I can take the world's greatest racket and lay it at your feet. Me—a slip of a girl—The Flame . : . I want you. I love you . . . Race—Race."

But Williams will have no part of her offer:

"I don't want to love the woman who is The Flame."

Actually, Race didn't want to love *any* woman. He always steered clear of romantic and/or sexual engagements. ("Women mean nothing in my life.") The Flame never caught him—although she kept trying through the years in several heavily melodramatic novelettes and serials.

Race Williams remained popular with *Black Mask* readers into the 1930s, with Daly gunning him through seven novel-length adventures and twenty-seven shorter stories. However, by late 1934, Shaw and Daly had a falling-out, and he left the magazine and began to write regularly for *Dime Detective*. In the 1940s, Daly also took Race Williams into the pulp pages of *Clues, Detective Story,* and *Thrilling Detective.*

But Race Williams was not the only popular Daly character during this period. He created Frank "Satan" Hall for *Detective Fiction Weekly* and Vee Brown for *Dime Detective.*

In "Murder at Midnight," he described Brown as "a first-grade detective assigned to the district attorney's office, who was also the unknown Vivian, the Master of Melody, composer of music and lyrics for Tin Pan Alley's biggest song hits."

Brown was something of a softie compared to Race. He lived in a Park Avenue penthouse and glided around New York in a $15,000 car driven by a liveried chauffeur. But he could be just as deadly regarding thugs. ("Capollo never even closed a finger upon the trigger . . . He never had the chance. He died . . . shot through the top of the head by the gun in Vee Brown's hand.")

Like Williams, Brown never hesitated to blast down an enemy ("The lust to kill was in his eyes") and took the same pride in his crack marksmanship:

"Brown! . . . " I cried. "You killed him."

"Yes, I did . . . And if I do say it myself, it was damned pretty shooting."

Vee Brown was featured in two of Daly's luridly written books, *Murder Won't Wait* and *The Emperor of Evil,* but mainly he starred in *Dime Detective,* which now paid Daly four cents a word (a penny a word more than *Black Mask*). A 12,500-word novelette brought $500—excellent money in the Depression era.

Daly's other major crimefighter of the period was cast as a modern version of the devil himself. Frank Hall was called "Satan." A maverick New York police detective, (shades of Clint Eastwood's Dirty Harry), he was known as "the Lone Wolf of the Department," and, like Williams, carried two guns which he enjoyed using.

In each Satan Hall story, Daly described his slanted green eyes, sharp-tipped ears and pointed chin, and the V-shaped hair growing low across his forehead. (Actually, the satanic description Hammett supplied for Sam Spade in *The Maltese Falcon* could easily have provided the inspiration.)

Satan Hall achieved book publication in two novels, *The Mystery of the Smoking Gun* and *Ready to Burn*. (Daly also featured him in two post-Shaw *Mask* stories.)

As the harsh realities of World War II impelled the nation to mature, readers turned against Daly. They could no longer accept his hokey, simplistic approach; the better pulps began rejecting his work. In one such rejection letter, Mike Tilden (who edited *Detective Tales* and *Dime Mystery*) stated that he was attempting to upgrade the magazines, and that Daly's work was "a good deal too much along the old slam-bang, straight woodpulp formula."

It is ironic to note that, as Carroll John Daly began to fade from public favor, another hard-boiled crime writer was making a fortune from a character derived directly from Race Williams. That character was Mickey Spillane's sadistic private eye, Mike Hammer—first encountered in *I, the Jury* in 1947.

Robert Lowndes, the editor who printed Daly's final Race Williams tales in *Smashing Detective* (in the 1950s), recalled that Spillane wrote a letter "wherein [he] acknowledged Daly as the 'master' from whom he had learned everything . . . which had made for Mike Hammer's success."

In "The Book of the Dead" Daly had Williams declare: "When you're hunting the top guy you have to kick aside—or shoot aside—the gunmen he hires. You can't make hamburger without grinding up a little meat." Or, as Williams rephrased it in another story: "You can't make ketchup without busting up a few tomatoes."

Spillane adapted this brand of personalized gun justice in his gore-splattered novels. Hammer, like Williams, operated as a one-man judge and jury, a mobile killing machine. Readers purchased his books in the millions.

Daly was never happy about the Spillane situation. "I'm broke and this guy gets rich writing about *my* detective."

Of course, Daly overlooked the fact that Spillane had added the element of raw sexuality to his Hammer books. There is no doubt that Mike Hammer would have had The Flame stripped and bedded in the first chapter! And the Spillane style, while primitive in comparison to Chandler's, was swift and savage melodrama, craftily adapted to fit the postwar era.

During the 1950s, Daly was able to sell an average of just one Race Williams story per year; by the spring of 1955, the pulps had expired, and Williams with them.

In his long career, Daly had made more than 175 pulp sales—including thirty-eight non-*Mask* Williams stories—but his run was over. (Daly's last U.S. novel had been released in 1937; he was forced to sell his final four books outside the States. No American publisher wanted them.)

After the collapse of the pulps, Daly moved to California and attempted to break into television with the help of his Hollywood friend, Frank Gruber.

The attempt failed.

Gruber lived close to the Dalys and would drop over each week to play bridge with them. He recalled that "Daly talked [sadly] of the 'old days' when his stuff was in demand . . . He'd developed a style of writing he found hard to change. He couldn't adapt."

Gruber tried to convince Pocket Books to issue Daly's eight Race Williams novels in paperback, but they turned down the idea.

"He lived for a while in Santa Monica," recounted Gruber. "Then he and his wife moved to the desert. Toward the end of his life he was reduced to writing for comic books."

On January 16, 1958, Carroll John Daly died quietly at his home in California at the age of sixty-eight. No critical tributes marked his passing. Despite the fact that his work had appeared in seventy-two issues of *Black Mask,* and that he had published eighteen books, Daly died a forgotten man who had never been able to rise above the level of a pulpwood hack.

The father of the hard-boiled detective was ultimately defeated by his own severe limitations.

Three Gun Terry

We are all fascinated with "firsts." Who was the first pilot to break the sound barrier? What pitcher won the first World Series game? Who was the first driver to lap the Indianapolis Speedway at a hundred miles per hour?

"Three Gun Terry" represents a major "first" in the genre of crime fiction. It is the first tough detective story starring the world's first wisecracking, hard-boiled private investigator. It appeared in the May 15, 1923, issue of *Black Mask* and has never been reprinted in any form since that date.

Terry Mack is the prototype for ten thousand private eyes who have gunned, slugged, and wisecracked their way through ten thousand magazines, books, films, and TV episodes.

In this early, raw-pulp novelette, Daly produced what may be termed "instant clichés."

Example: "Something like a ton of bricks comes down and . . . after that . . . everything goes black."

Or: "I'm off dames; they don't go well with my business."

This pioneer private-eye tale is remarkable in that almost every cliché that was to plague the genre from the 1920s into the 1980s is evident in "Three Gun Terry."

Read it and see for yourself.

But whatever grievous faults this story possesses, it's the one that fathered Sam Spade and Philip Marlowe and Lew Archer and Travis McGee and . . .

First is first.

THREE GUN TERRY

Series character: Terry Mack

My life is my own, and the opinions of others don't interest me; so don't form any, or if you do, keep them to yourself. If you want to sneer at my tactics, why go ahead; but do it behind the pages—you'll find that healthier.

So for my line. I have a little office which says "Terry Mack, Private Investigator," on the door; which means whatever you wish to think it. I ain't a crook, and I ain't a dick; I play the game on the level, in my own way. I'm in the center of a triangle; between the crook and the police and the victim. The police have had an eye on me for some time, but only an eye, never a hand; they don't get my lay at all. The crooks; well, some is on, and some ain't; most of them don't know what to think, until I've put the hooks in them. Sometimes they gun for me, but that ain't a one-sided affair. When it comes to shooting, I don't have to waste time cleaning my gun. A little windy that; but you get my game.

Now, the city's big, and that ain't meant for no outburst of personal wisdom. It's fact. Sometimes things is slow and I go out looking for business. About the cabarets; in the big hotels and even along the streets I find it. It's always there. I just spot some well-known faces playing their suckers, and that's my chance. A bit of trailing; I corral the bird, offer my help, and then things get lively. Blackmail it is mostly, but it doesn't matter to me. And then the fee; a hard-earned but gladly paid fee—that's me! I'm there forty ways from the ace.

So it comes that things is slow, and I'm anxious to chase down and corner a little of the ready. I guess I blow in nearly twenty bucks, jumping from joint to joint; but it's expense money, so I just shrug my shoulders when nothing turns up. Oh, I see crooks galore, but they ain't having no more luck than I am; which ain't the usual run of things.

Along about one-thirty I start for home—I got a car, but I ain't using it—the subway is my ticket that night. I just come out of a high-class robbers' den over on Sixth Avenue, and start toward Broadway; it's Fifty-sixth Street that I trot down, and it strikes me a wonderful place to pull off a murder—dark and quiet.

Then, when I'm halfway down the block, a woman shoots out of a brownstone front and skips down the steps toward a waiting taxi. She's just about to pull open the door and jump in when I see her draw back suddenly, stand undecidedlike a second, and then, turning, make a sudden dash for the steps. But she's too late. Two chaps hop out of that taxi and go after her. Now, I don't say that she mightn't 'a made it, for she had a start on them, but another lad steps out of the basement way and heads her off.

And let me give those boys credit for working fast; they sure turned the trick like professionals; there ain't no more than a scream and a couple of kicks when them birds have whisked her up and run her into the taxi. A crank of the motor, and the car is speeding away. Is that young lady lost forever? Not so you could notice it, she ain't! If they worked fast, so did I. I couldn't stop them—not me —but I had run across the street and as the car shot past me, I made a grab and swung up on the spare tire.

As we turn into Sixth Avenue, I see a window go up in the brownstone house, and I think I catch a shout. Then we ride. Things weren't so dead after all, and it looked as if I might get some return on that twenty.

There's three men and a driver, and you think the best thing I can do is to holler at the first cop we pass. But not me! He might stop us, and then again he might not. Also, I might get shot off the back of that speeding car, which was not exactly my most cherished thought. Besides, at the best, the police could only make a capture and give me a vote of thanks, with a misspelling of my name at the bottom of the page of the evening papers. No, I'm not looking for honor—there would probably be jack in this for yours truly.

It ain't cold, and the ride ain't so bad; not so good either, but then I couldn't be particular. As far as being worried about the end of the trip—not much! There were four of them—all armed I guess—but then I had a couple of guns of my own, and I'd be the one with the drop.

At last the ride was over, and we pulled up on a lonely street in the Bronx. It was an empty street, but on the next block was a row of two-story frame houses. I guess they didn't want to attract attention by arriving in style and would hoof it the rest of the way. There is some delay about them getting out of the cab, and I drop off the tire, and stretch my legs, and shake out enough kinks to account for a fifty-mile trip in a lizzy; also I might make mention of the fact that I played with my automatics—being overfond of such toys on certain occasions—and this was one of them. Of course, those birds couldn't know I had come along with them; they was too busy with the struggling girl when I swung aboard. So everything was rosy.

At length, they opened the door, and after stalling around a bit, one of them got out and leaving the door open beat it up the street. I guess he was going to get things set before he took the girl in. Well, I give him a chance. I like to do things right, and I waited to see which house he went into. Then I stepped around from the back of that car and slipped in. Yep, just slid right in and took the empty portable seat which he had left.

I get a laugh yet when I think of the expression on them lads' faces—the two of them, with the girl bound and gagged between them. There in the pale light of a dull moon, she sat, every muscle tense—her eyes wide and frightened.

But the two lads—regular tough birds they were too—no, their muscles weren't tense, they just sat there loose and staring, their eyes near popping out of their heads. Prepared! Why one of them held a gat right on his knees, but he never made no move to use it. Not that he got the chance, for I had rapped his knuckles with the barrel of my gun—not the butt but the barrel—and his gun just slid down his feet, to the floor. Of course, it's a bit risky using the barrel for such things; once in every so often the gun goes off, 'specially a light shooter like mine; but then you can't really bother about such little accidents; you can see where it would be his hard luck, not mine.

Say, there wasn't a yip out of either of them—their hands went up with such a goodwill that I thought they'd stick them through the top of the car. Very obliging they were, and I hadn't said a word yet. I just grinned. As for the lad in the front—well—I had the other cannon poked so hard into his spine that he was sitting straighter than he ever sat before in his life.

"Young lady," I says to the girl. "You got to help, as I can't keep more than half an eye on the driver—so just please close your left eye if he don't keep his hands well up and empty. That's the girl," I added as she nodded. "If you wink the left, I'll plug him. And don't be overparticular—I'm not of a sentimental nature."

Now most of this was only for effect. I didn't really think that the girl was able to help much, but it would give the chap in the front something to think about and make him behave. I didn't need much time because I work fast. Even this kind of a situation wasn't new to me.

In thirty seconds, I had them gunmen standing on the sidewalk, their backs to the car and their hands stretched toward the heavens, like they were listening to Walter Camp.

"Now," I says to the driver. "Let the hands drop and we'll go—back to where you came from. And pray that nothing happens to your car. For the first time that she slows down, I'll drill a hole in the back of your neck and do a little driving myself."

I didn't have to shout at him—you see, the window was down, and his attention was perfect.

And now for the first time, one of the lads on the pavement got his wind back and opened up.

"Better stay out of this," he warned me. "It will mean death for you—sure."

He spoke in broken English and his voice trembled with rage.

"All right Mr. Wolf," I chirped cheerfulike. "But Little Red Riding Hood and me will trot along. If she wants to come back to you later—why, well and good." Then turning to the driver I said sharp, "Let her go!"

And the driver being a man of sound judgment, we went.

I let him drive along for about a mile, and then I stop him and frisk him for a gun; he only has one, which shows a poor eye to the necessity of his profession. After that, we shoot along real merrily, and I give my attention to the girl. I guess it took about ten minutes to get her all straightened out, for I had to keep an eye on the driver, and take a look behind every once in a while. By the time I was finished, we were well down in Harlem.

Say, but that girl was scared; why, she didn't do nothing but hang close to me and keep her head up against my chest as she clung to my coat. And she was mighty little and mighty young too, I think, though I couldn't tell much about her, there in the dark of the cab. Somehow I felt almost like a father as I patted her little dark head and ran my fingers through her soft black locks. I could 'a laughed, but somehow I didn't. It certainly did seem strange to find myself putting my arm about a kid again. I don't know when I did it last—if I ever did it. And there I was, telling her that she was all right, and that I'd take care of her and—and—oh—just acting like a regular nut. What I should 'a been doing was questioning her and finding out just what her old man was worth and how much there would be in it for me. But somehow I didn't do anything but just try to comfort her like she was a baby.

After a bit, she calms down and gets out her handkerchief and snuffles a bit, but she never says a word, just clings to me like some frightened animal.

And then, when I'm about to ask her a few questions, the car suddenly comes to stop and I see that we have turned into Fifty-seventh Street and have stopped around the corner from Sixth Avenue.

"What's this, my lad?" I hail the driver. "Your memory is sorta weak, but mine ain't—come shake a leg and drive us around the block."

"This is as far as I go," he says sulkylike.

But at the same time there seems to be a note of determination in his voice.

"Oh, is it?" And I lean over and tickle him with the gat. "Come, I'll count just ten, and if we ain't off, then I'll give you the surprise of your life—and your death too." And I ain't bluffing either. I never bluff. And not being a chap what wastes time I start in counting:

"One, two, three, four, five." I run them up fast. I ain't no moving-picture director looking for suspense.

Would I have plugged him—well, he didn't wait to find out; he wasn't curious.

"Wait a minute, boss," he says. "I want to say something."

"Make it snappy—and if you ain't inclined to do what you're told, make it prayers."

"There's a cop down the street," he chirps. "If you don't get out here I'll holler to him."

It sounded like he meant business, too, though I couldn't get his game. Also, his English is pretty good.

"Call a cop! You!" I laugh. "Ten to twenty years for kidnapping—that's what you'll get."

Then he turns around sudden and looks at me.

"You ain't no Italian," he says, after a long look.

I only laugh. I'm too old in the game to take offense at such slander. Besides, there is something deadly earnest in the way he speaks.

"I guess you ain't in on the game. If you was, you wouldn't ask me to drive to that house, and you wouldn't go within miles of it yourself," he says half aloud.

"I wanta go home—I wanta go home!" The girl suddenly flings both arms about my neck. "Just around the corner!" She points down the street. Her voice is low —hysterical—foreign.

I shake the girl off and give him the once-over, and then I poke him with the gun.

"Now drive," I says. "Or I'll find a way to make you and the car move so fast that it will surprise both of you. Six, seven, eight—" I start in where I left off. I'm mighty sore and mean business—besides, I can see the cop coming down the street.

And then the girl suddenly takes things out of my hands. She opens the door and slips out, and is around on Sixth Avenue before I know she's gone. That settles the argument with the driver—I'm out and after her. One last look at the car, and the number is firmly in my mind as it goes rapidly down the street.

I'm only about ten seconds behind as she turns into Sixth Avenue, and then I swing around the corner myself and stop dead. There ain't a person in sight; the street is quiet and deserted.

It didn't seem possible that she could have made the length of that block in that short time, but I took a run down to the corner of Fifty-sixth Street to make sure.

I could see well down the street—clean to Seventh Avenue—and there wasn't a soul in sight. I sure was stumped. She must be hiding in one of the hallways along the avenue. But why? Anyway, I'd take a look. And just then along came a cop. Now I ain't afraid of any cop—not me. But they sure ask embarrassing questions, and I don't stand in good with most of the dicks. I've made good when they have failed so many times. So I just loitered around and played safe. And this bull is a good-natured fellow, who smiles at me and says, it's a fine night, as he goes by. He's trying all the doors and is mightily slow about it, and all the time I'm expecting him to come across the girl. But I just stand there and stretch and look around; then I light a butt and walk slowly about.

But that cop was a gentle trusting soul, and pretty soon he shoots across the street and passes down the next block; and he's faster there because there ain't no one to see if he tries all the store doors. Things look good, and I decide to have a peek.

There were several dark entrances to the flats above the stores—dirty, ill-smelling hallways that I'd have to look into. I just come out of one of them when I hear a voice, and there she was, popping up from behind a newsstand that had been pushed flat up against the building for the night.

"What are you doing there?" I says, some relieved and some mad.

"Oh—has he gone? I was frightened," she whispered as she come timidly out and clutched me by the arm. My, but she was a slim, delicate little thing.

"Who went?" I asked. "The lad with the car—yes, he went, all right." I still felt a bit sore about that.

"Oh no—not him—the policeman."

"The policeman," I exclaimed. "Why, what would you be afraid of him for? He'd be a good friend of yours—anyway."

"Oh—no, no. Uncle says no. I have had a lot of trouble since I have been in America. At the convent, things were so different, and I was so happy."

"How long have you been over?" I asked, to try and get her mind working easy; she was beginning to tremble again.

"Over?"

"Yes—in America?"

"Oh!" she said. "Three weeks—nearly."

"Is that all? You speak mighty fine English—almost as good as mine."

Why, there wasn't hardly any accent at all, just enough to make it sound attractive.

"I always knew the English, I think—my mother was an American—she died when I was a little girl."

She kind of sniffled a little.

"Never mind," I said. "You'll be with your father in another few minutes. It's your father that lives here?"

I paused; we were in front of that same brownstone front again—the one she had run out of earlier in the evening.

"I have no father—he died—a little while ago—and I came here—to my uncle."
I looked down at her again as we mounted the steps; she seemed so young.
"How old are you?" I asked. Fourteen, I guessed.

"Nineteen—almost twenty," she told me.

I whistled softly. Well, we never can tell, and the next minute I was ringing the doorbell. A moment later, an electric light flashed on above us. I felt that someone was observing us from within, and then the door was flung open.

Two men, fully dressed, whom I took for servants, stood one on either side of the door, and a tough-looking pair of citizens they were. They looked like they'd cut your throat in a minute. But that didn't bother me; a minute would have been too long—I'd 'a got them both—besides, just at present it seemed to me that these birds would be on my side of the fence.

And then, as we stepped inside and the door closed behind us, a stout man of about fifty, all dolled up in a trick bathrobe that would knock your eye out for color display, came down the stairs.

"Nita!" he yells. Then both clinch, and everything is jake.

After that I'm forgotten, except for those two rough-looking lads who watch me mighty careful—and what's more, I'm watching them too. There's a lot of Italian flung back between uncle and niece, and then I guess he starts in to question her; then they clinch again, and she beats it up the stairs.

Then the fat lad takes a tumble to himself and comes across the hall and takes me by the hand.

"The señorita calls you friend—she has told me of your chivalry, and I cannot thank you enough."

With that, he drags me by his cold, clammy hand into his library, and we both sit.

For a couple of minutes he just sits and looks at me and his smile grows bigger and bigger, and then fades and comes again. But he ain't fooling me none. Of course, I'm the light-haired boy with him now. I can see that, but behind that smile I can also see that he's a tough egg. His smile is broad enough, but then, I've seen too much of life. This bird I spot for a bad actor. And he's a buck with uncertain age, one of them half-bald fronts; he might be ten years older than what I think him, and then again he might be ten years younger.

So he has me tell him the whole story of the night's events, and he smiles some more, and I gather that he's thinking up an explanation of some kind. Then I pull a wisecrack, and I see that he's puzzled.

"You don't have to explain to me," I tell him. "I ain't interested unless—unless I got to be."

Well, that took the smile clean off his slate, for I suppose he was hatching up a barrel of lies. Then he starts to walk up and down the room. After a bit, he stops and looks down at me.

"You don't want to know about this—why—and why?" was the best he could get out.

"Not a word. It came out all right and I'm satisfied, if you are."

That fetches him up fine, and the smile comes back, and I see that he's getting ready to dismiss me without a yip. But he don't yet; he rings a bell and orders some refreshments—which is some pretty fair wine and a half-dozen slim sandwiches.

"You are a remarkable man—a real gentleman," he starts in to make a speech. "It is not often today that we find young men, who for the love of adventure and for their pride in the strong for the weak, succor women in distress. I wish I could reward you, but a gentleman cannot—"

And that's where I bust in on him. I don't want him to commit himself, and I see no reason why he should waste all them flowery thoughts. So I up and give him another shock.

"My reward for tonight's services—now that you suggest it—is exactly two hundred and fifty dollars. Fifty for the night's work and two hundred for the successful finish. I generally charge a little more at the end, but seeing how I came in uninvited—"

But I didn't get any further.

"Am I to understand that you wish money—money for what you did?" And his eyes grew big, and his wine slopped over his glass a little. I had touched him this time, for the foreign accent crept into his voice for the first time, and I knew that he was the brother of Nita's father. Before that, I wasn't sure which side of the fence he was on.

"Sure," I said. "You don't take me for no Sir Lunchlot, do you? This is business with me." And to keep him from having a stroke of apoplexy, I tell him my trade.

At first, I think that he's trying to hold out on me, but then I see that he's just thinking. His eyes go up and down, and his mouth too, for that matter; then his eyes get small, and he looks closely at me. Whatever he sees don't start a row, for he turns and, ringing a bell, tells the chap that comes to the door to send the señorita down. I get that much even if it is Italian.

And in about five minutes she comes in, and she's a wow. I didn't get a good look at her before, and I tell you it's a lucky thing that I ain't romantic. She sure was one swell-looking dame. Even me, a hardened citizen like me—yep, I was nearly ready to take ten dollars off the bill if the fat lad had suggested it. She sure looked grand, all fixed up.

But he didn't make a crack about money; he just talked to her for a bit and they seemed to be having a bit of a row about me. At length he gives a wave of his hand that she shall go, but she don't—she just stays there. He says something, and she stamps her foot, so I see that she ain't so timid when she's in her own house. For a minute, I get the idea that they are arguing about the price, and she don't look so beautiful, for I can't tell which side she's taking.

At length the old bird gives in on some point and turns to me.

"We'll pay you what you ask and—perhaps much more."

Things are looking up. I just nod.

"Yes," he goes on. "There will be money for you if you are as brave as the señorita says you are—but you must be very brave."

Now he's hitting my gait and talking turkey. So I just smile and tell him:

"Show me the coin, and I'll make the boys at Valley Forge look like pikers."

Then his shrewd eyes went over me again, and his lips opened wide and his teeth showed, but no smile came this time—just a bit of a dental display—he couldn't make a go of the smile because he had forgotten to open his eyes wide enough. Then he took another drink and without further preliminaries opened up; yep, opened up considerable. But he talked so fast that I couldn't get for sure which was the bull and which was the real thing.

"It is this way," he makes a break. "The señorita, Nita Gretna, is my niece. She is my brother's child; Michel Gretna who, if he had lived, would have been recognized as the world's greatest scientist. Well, he made a formula—a formula of great value. The result of it will someday—I hope—startle the world. It is for his daughter—the glory, the honor and the money. To a friend who was his assistant, he entrusted this sheet of paper; this young man, Manual Sparo, brought it here to America. Certain things about it were not quite clear; Manual would work on it—perfect it before he married the señorita and turned it over to us. And when all was ready and the great moment at hand, enemies who desire this paper more than life—great powerful enemies—fell upon him and bore him away."

"Then they got the formula?" I said. Of course, I felt that they didn't, but he paused so long that it seemed up to me to show a little interest. And this talk of marriage was sudden.

"No—they got it not," he said backward. "Wild horses would not tear the secret from him, and the formula was hidden away. Tonight, the señorita went out in answer to a message which she thought came from him. She was indiscreet and should have consulted me, though she says she could not find me. What they would have done with her, I do not know; frighten her, perhaps."

"But they talked of torturing me to make him tell—" the girl started, but the uncle stopped her.

"Tut—tut," he said. "You were frightened and nervous." He turned to me again. "We will pay you much for that formula."

"Do you want me to know what the formula is about?" I got to admit I was curious; it's as well to know how valuable your services are. Besides, I didn't quite like the whole story—it sounded fishy, at least parts of it.

"I do not think that that is necessary. For the paper we will pay much money," he repeated.

"How much is that?"

I don't take much stock in promises.

He thinks a while.

"A thousand dollars," he says at length.

Well, he might have said ten thousand; it wouldn't 'a made no difference to me. I don't work on that kind of speck'. I draw a regular salary. So I up and give him an earful:

"That may be all right," I say, "but I have a regular charge. Fifty dollars a day, and five hundred bonus when I deliver the goods; also, I am willing to take all sorts of chances, but if I get pinched, it's up to you to hire the best lawyer that money can buy—also, I get thirty bucks a day for every day I spend in jail. And for every man I croak—mind you, I ain't a killer, but sometimes a chap's got to turn a gun —I get two hundred dollars flat. It ain't that I don't count this as part of my services, but there's a certain nervous shock to it—and besides, they're your enemies and should be cheap at that price. Also, your game must be strictly honest —I ain't no crook."

I tell you his eyes sure did open wide enough now—wide enough to pop out of his head, almost. He sure was hearing a trunkful, and I could tell that I wasn't falling none in his estimation. I generally let the killing business go by the boards until the time comes, but this time I didn't. You see, if I had to hunt around Italian joints, there was almost sure to be some gunplay and—and I got to protect my interests.

After a bit he says:

"You make this quite a business, but a man would be a fool to sign up to any such agreement."

"Oh, you don't have to sign nothing," I tell him. "When you agree, we just shake hands like a couple of gentlemen. And that's that."

His smile this time was a real one.

"But that protects you not at all," he twists up his English again.

"It gives me all the protection I want. It makes me feel that I've done the right thing."

"But if one don't play fair, what then?"

"Then . . ." I rubbed my chin. "That's the only point I forgot to tell you. You see, that only happened once and—but why go into unpleasant details; let's just say that they buried him anyway."

This time he actually rubbed his hands together, and chuckled. These foreign gents sure do have a real appreciation of art.

And then, when he's all set to agree to everything, the girl suddenly breaks in with an Italian marathon. I don't think he agrees with what she says, but she turns to me anyway and says:

"Uncle is doing all in his power to recover that paper of my father's, and now it is my turn. I will shake you by the hand, and I will pay you for this service; it is my turn to do something, Señor—" She pauses, and knowing the proper thing to do I get up and bow.

"Mack," I says. "Terry Mack."

And with that she puts out her little hand and mitts me.

It was near four when I got home, and nearer five before I got to bed. Yep, I sat up there in my big easy chair and killed nearly a double deck of butts; I had something to think about, you'll admit.

In the first place, even with the long talk I later had with the fat bird, whose whole moniker was Gustave Gretna, I didn't get any information worth a hill of beans. He made it clear enough that he didn't want the police to know anything about the game. He said if they did, why, the Italian government would mix up in it and make him turn over the formula for about one-tenth of what it was really worth, and he didn't want his niece to lose all that money. I also gathered that she was worth considerable change in her own name. But with real dope, that lad wasn't there at all. Oh, he talked a lot, but he didn't say anything, and of course it was my game to look wise and act like I could settle everything in no time, which was probably what I would do once I got started.

As for the girl, well, she puzzled me; yes, and bothered me some too. When the uncle went upstairs to get the two hundred and fifty bucks for me, which he kept in the house, she spilled out some conversation that even rattled me.

"I am not going to marry this Manual Sparo," she tells me lowlike. "I think I am going to marry someone else—oh—I hope I am. He is an American and—and I love him." With that, she kind of ducks her head and turns red.

"Good for you," was the best that I could pull off—I didn't quite like the way she looked up at me through them thick lashes of hers.

"Yes," she goes on. "But I don't know if he loves me—what do you think?" And she turns them big, black glims of hers full on me. "He's so brave and so handsome and—but I have known him such a short time." Then she breaks off sudden, for her uncle is coming down the stairs.

"Terry," she whispers, leaning over and laying a little hand upon my arm. "You are hired by me, you know, and I want you to promise that you'll see me once every day—without fail."

With that, her uncle trots into the room, and I must say he was a welcome sight.

Now, that's part of what I was thinking over, alone in my room along about four-thirty in the morning. She loved someone else—and that someone was an American—and was brave—and she lived in a convent all her life and had never been out of the house alone since she came to this country—and—and she had called me Terry. Well, I didn't need no more than three guesses. That dame had fallen for me, and fallen hard.

Of course, there wasn't nothing so terrible strange about that, except that I'm off dames—they don't go well with my business—good or bad—women don't have no place in my life. And yet as I stretched myself and looked my reflection over in the glass, something seemed to say: "Why not?" A home in sunny Italy, an open garden beneath—but rats—I snuffed out my last butt and climbed into bed. No more thinking then. I don't do nothing but sleep once I hit the covers; I used to plan then, but queer ideas come to you in bed—great and glorious ideas—but when you turn them over in the morning they ain't worth a thing—you just find them a waste of time.

But the next morning, when I have breakfast, I do a bit of real brain work. You see, Bud brings me my coffee and chops—Bud is my man, my valet, my chauffeur, my assistant—in fact, Bud is the whole works; not much of a thinker, but he can carry out instructions to the big T.

The first thing I figure on doing is having a talk with that taxi lad who drove me and the girl the night before; he was a real funny citizen, and the way he had acted bothered me some. Of course, you might think that would be a tough job, but not for me; it would be easy. I know the ropes in the underworld and the way to get my hooks on these lads. You see, I had the number of the car, a fake number to be sure, but then me and the bird what drove it would know and that was enough.

Along about two o'clock, which is about an hour after I finish breakfast, I trot down to Larkin's Saloon in the Thirties. Now, this Larkin sells booze, but he's also a dope peddler. I've done him more than one good turn because I can use him a lot, and he's always ready to turn a trick for me, if none of the boys—his boys, that's what he calls the crooks—suffer by it. Larkin has a suspicion that I'm a big gun in the dope traffic, and since it leaves a good impression on him, I let him have his think—yes, and help it along. And this same Larkin has got a system of communication that ain't been beat from here to Frisco. So I brace Larkin.

"Larkin," I says, leaning over the little desk in that tiny private room of his, just off the corner of the old bar, "Larkin, I'm looking for a gink what drove a car last night—number 19964—fake, I guess."

Larkin don't say nothing, but just screws up his face and wiggles his fingers, which I know is the sign to slip over the regular fee, so I dig and produce the ready.

"I can only do my part, Mr. Smith." Larkin makes it a point of calling everybody Smith—it don't make no difference how well he knows you. "The word will go about, and of course I can guarantee that no hurt will come to the—the boy?"

"Absolutely. I'm looking for information with money, not force—at least when I use your system, Larkin. I always play fair with you."

He just nods.

"You may expect him at eleven, if he's alive. In my little room, eh—that'll be ten dollars more." His palm is itchy, and though he keeps his hand by his side, his fingers go nervously back and forth.

"I'll pay now," I tell him. "You can give it back to me if he don't show up." I knew that old boy's weakness.

"Good," said he, and taking the money, we both walked out of the little room. He ain't much of a talker, is Larkin, but he's clever, or maybe just shrewd in his own way.

When I leave that joint about ten minutes later, I see the number 19964 in small figures over his cash register. But it was big enough to read, and I knew that that same number would be in more than a hundred places within the next two or three hours. It was so that Larkin worked his system; the chap what drove the car would see it and know what it meant. Larkin had called, and he would answer. Yes, there had been something in that chauffeur's eyes which told me he would come—I couldn't be mistaken about them same eyes.

After that, I take a bit of a walk, and then I beat it up to the brownstone house on Fifty-sixth, partly to keep my promise to the girl, and partly to see if I couldn't unbutton something of real value out of her Uncle Gus. And that bimbo meets me with a sure-enough startler. Señorita Nita had gone away!

Suspicious! I should say I was; if my face ever betrayed anything, it betrayed it then. But I like to think it didn't; I have a regular poker face and am mighty proud of it.

"Where has she gone?"

This seemed a natural enough question, and I put it to him suddenlike.

But he didn't show any more expression than an oyster.

"Off to Lake—but there, she's away for a rest—Manual and she are to be married soon. I might as well tell you that the gang of cutthroats who were after that formula took fright last night and Michel has returned. You believe me, of course."

And he pulled that last sentence louder than any of the rest; and to me it sounded like he was giving it as a signal or warning to someone listening. But he smiled all over as he watched me closely. I could see that he didn't expect me to believe him, and wouldn't believe me if I said I did.

"No—I don't get you," I says. "What's the lay?"

"It is enough that you should know that everything is now all right. The formula is back—your appearance of last night was of great value. Nita is pleased and has left this for you."

He brought forth a wad and counted a number of bills out on the table.

But I wasn't watching him. I was looking over his shoulder, and I was sure that the curtains moved behind him and that someone peered in. There was something intensive and strained in the whole atmosphere of that room, and I knew, just as well as if I had seen it, that a gun was behind that curtain.

"Ah—you don't believe." He stretched out the money toward me. "Will this five hundred make you believe and—and forget? Nita and I will not need you now —you understand—we are paying you this for silence."

The constant use of that plural "we" grated on my nerves. I guess it was done to hand me the impression that his niece and he were acting in consort, and that she was all right, but it hit me exactly opposite. But then the waving curtain with death probably lurking behind it! It was best to play the game into his hands.

"For five hundred dollars I'll believe anything," I chirped with a grin. "Trot over the coin. When I wish to be, I am as silent as the grave."

He fell for it, and why wouldn't he, after the way I had represented myself last night. I was nothing more than a gunman in his estimation. It was quite evident that he didn't see the ethics of my profession and the good that I did—but I made up my mind that he'd see it later. You see, he had forgotten one thing: I had been hired by the girl—not him. He'd change that grin of his when he seen how a real gentleman played the game.

Then he up and patted me on the back.

"I knew you for a sensible rascal," he said. "Someday we may use you again— Nita and I."

So he bid me good night, and it was all I could do to keep from backing out of the room. I tell you it took real nerve to turn and walk to the front door and then go carelessly down the steps. I sure had a longing to put a bullet through that curtain. But I had five hundred dollars, and a mighty mean suspicion—also, I knew for a certainty that I was going to do that girl some good yet. As for her Uncle Gus—well, of course I didn't believe a word that hummingbird told me.

There was plenty to think about as I went down the street; there were the girl's last words to me, of the previous night, about seeing her every day. Did that just mean that she had fallen for me, or did it mean more? Did it mean that she was growing suspicious about her uncle? Well, I like to think that it meant both.

And there was more than just a feeling of money, and a feeling of pride to make good to the girl who had hired me. For one thing, I never fail—for another thing —well, somehow I just seemed to want to know that that little girl was all right. If I had 'a been sure of my ground and really thought it would 'a done her any good, I'd 'a thought nothing of forcing the truth out of her uncle or—yes—of bumping him over the hurdles. And the gun behind the curtain wouldn't 'a made no difference neither. I knew the gun was there, just as well as I knew that that fat crooked Italian had lied to me.

For the first time in my life I'm worried, and what's more I'm followed. I look at my watch; it ain't but five o'clock and there won't be nothing doing until eleven. Of course, I could shake off the lad what's following me—there ain't nothing to that—but I think it will leave things clearer for me if I can send him back to Uncle Gus with a good report. There ain't really nothing for me to do. I could go and search the house in the Bronx, of course, but if I had thought there would be any chance in that direction, I'd 'a been up there before I went home in the morning. I know that's useless; that gang was out of the dump twenty minutes after I lit out in the taxi—any cluck would know that.

So I play a high-class joint for a feed and spot a dapper little foreigner, sitting over in one corner, as my meat. But I don't give him a tumble; just act like a lad who was out for a good time—blowing in Uncle Gus's jack. I gotta laugh when I think how snug they're feeling and I figure along about midnight I'll have my fingers in their pie up to my wrists. Yes—all I want is plenty of leeway, and then, when I get my earful, there sure is going to be some fireworks.

And I'm right; that lad ain't got the sticking power. He follows me home, and twenty minutes later, when I look out the window, that street is as deserted as a poetry graveyard.

It's near eleven when I slip out of my apartment window—which is on the ground floor for just such occasions—and Bud meets me with the car around the corner. Away we go to Larkin's, and pulling up about a block away, I hop out and beat it for the saloon.

My bird's there; Larkin gives me the high sign as soon as I bust in the door. Into his little private room I slide and shut the door. My man looks up—a little frightened, but smiling just the same.

"Good!" I says. "The system worked."

"Larkin wanted me to see you and—and here I am." I could see he wasn't going to be none too cordial.

"Know me?" I sit down.

He just shows his teeth and nods his head.

"How deep were you in last night?" I ask.

"Deep enough," he answers.

"Want to double-cross?" I ain't going to waste time if he seems agreeable.

"Not me," he grins.

Then I look at him close.

"Snowbird, ain't you?" I shoot at him sudden. Those eyes couldn't fool me. It was those same eyes which had told me he would answer Larkin's call—Larkin was pretty well looked up to by the hopheads.

"What's that to you?" His eyes blaze a bit and the smile does a fadeout.

"Hard guy, eh?"

"Dick, eh?" he retorts.

"Ask Larkin—you know better."

"Did!"

I see he's a man of few words and we ain't getting no place, so I open up on him, tell him what's under my hat; that if he don't give me the information I want, I'll see that Larkin cuts off his supply. The thing registers a bit, and I see him get white under the gills, so I guess Larkin has tipped him off that I'm a big gun in the traffic. But I don't get much out of him; I see that he's in deadly fear of this Uncle Gus.

"He'd kill me in a minute," he says, his eyes wide with terror. "All I'll say is that he used to run a fruit stand down in Mott Street—just before the girl come, he fixed up the house on Fifty-sixth Street and then—no! My God! No! He'd find out who told and—no—not another word."

He wasn't smiling no more now; his face had turned a chalky white, and his teeth were chattering. In another minute, he had gone all to pieces like his kind do— he was between the two fears: of Larkin cutting his supply and Uncle Gus cutting his throat. Changed? Why, you wouldn't know him for the same man—cringing and whining and kneeling at my feet. But nothing came out of him, and then he suddenly turns, and I see him roll up his sleeve and give his arm a long scratch with a safety pin; then into the blood went a few drops from a tiny bottle. Blooey! Just like that he was himself again—and any chance I had, which wasn't much, was gone. But I was working on another idea.

"A hundred dollars for the information—where is the girl?" I rip out quick.

"The girl—again—"

Then he stopped short, but he eyed the money which I held in my hand longingly. But he wouldn't open up, so I pulled my best and last card; time was passing and something was telling me that the girl needed me.

"I tell you how you can avoid all trouble—with the gang and with Larkin," I told him. "Give me the name of one of the gang. One that knows all, and one that I can reach tonight—now. I'll get the information out of him just the same as I would have gotten it out of you, if I hadn't passed my word to Larkin." Oh,

I felt like shoving my gun down his throat and getting the truth out of him. But my word had gone to Larkin and—well—I couldn't break it. I know that don't sound like common sense, but we'll call it my weakness. Terry Mack's word is good, and weak or not, it always will be good.

I see I had him interested, and I took out three hundred and offered it to him. Then I told him if this Gustave was sure to find out everything, why, he'd find out that it wasn't him that told, but the other fellow.

"Ain't there some fellow—just give me his name and address—just one who knows what's going on tonight—perhaps you have an enemy—someone what done you dirt." And that caught him.

He grabs the bankroll and spills a mouthful.

"Daggo Joe," he says, and gives me an address which is less than five blocks away. "He's there now alone—and will be there until six-thirty, when he goes on duty."

"Good," I eye him, "and if you have lied to me, why I'll hunt you up and make you eat every one of them bills and then—then I'll cut them out of you again." Which may sound like a lot of wind, but it was the kind that he would understand best, and I don't know but what I meant it.

With that, I beat it over to the Thirties and step up and down in front of Daggo Joe's for a few minutes. You can't fool these birds and give them a surprise visit; they have a way of knowing you're coming. And this Daggo Joe knew, for I seen a figure at the window which I spotted for his, and then the light went out in that window. But I want him to know that I'm coming and coming alone—he won't beat it—not him; he'll stay and play it foxy on me—kind of get revenge for the previous night. So eleven-thirty finds me entering the dusty old building and climbing the stairs to the third floor, where this Daggo Joe parks his noble person.

Of course, my electric flash covers every jump of them hallways; there ain't a chance for a lad to jump me in the dark—also, my gun is mighty convenient. When I reach his door, I tap lightly, and there ain't no answer, but I know that he's listening in there, and I know that he takes me for a soft one announcing myself like that.

I don't waste much time, but try the door—just a turn of the knob, and it gives —the door ain't even locked. Do you get the game—well, I do. He wants me to walk right in so he can croak me off. It nearly makes me laugh—the simplicity of the whole thing; why he's almost like a kid.

And I know just where he's standing, as if he told me so himself; he's behind that door, and he's got a blackjack or a knife in his mitt. And then I start to do what any dick would do, and just what Daggo Joe figures I'll do—push the door open slowly. That's what ninety-nine in a hundred would do—play the game very cautious.

So I push the door very softly, and this Joe waits behind it, all smiles, I guess. Then I suddenly up with my foot and give that door a kick—a real healthy kick. If I do say so myself, that's the only way to enter a room what you got your doubts on.

Bang! Crash! You could hear his head connect with that door in one heavy thud. After that, there was nothing to it. I had my flash out and my gun on him, and the door closed and locked before he knew what had happened. It was five minutes before he recovered enough to speak. He didn't fall to the floor—I guess his head was too thick for that—but he slumped up against the wall and stayed slumped while I lit the gas.

"Howdy, Joe," I says, as I took the blackjack from his useless fingers and chucked it under the bed. And then, while he was recovering his manners, I dumped some water from the pitcher over his head and watched him swim ashore.

"I kill you yet," he says in a feeble voice, as he clutched at his aching head.

I could have laughed, but I didn't; there wasn't time. I saw now that that duck was able to talk and understand me, which was more to the point. I wasn't there for any fooling—not me—he had information that I wanted, and I hadn't passed my word that there'd be no force used.

"Joe," I says, whipping my gun into his stomach. "I want you to blow the whole game—first, where's the girl—quick!"

There was nothing gentle about me then—I'm a different man when it comes to business—that's why I'm a success. I always play that the end justifies the means.

"I tell you nothing!" He pulls himself up straight and folds his arms across his chest. "Your girl, eh—pretty soon they be through with her—and she my girl— the—"

But he never finished that string of dirty epithets. I up with the butt of my gun and gave him a swipe across the face that made his lordly air look mighty cheap. And right here come the tactics that you may not agree with. You may question the ethics, but the results are good. Poor morals perhaps, but good, sound, common sense.

It ain't pretty to tell, so I'll skip over it. But I beat and choked the truth out of him, anyway.

His tongue was hanging out, and he was black in face and pretty near gone when he nodded he'd tell. And tell he did.

"You'd torture that girl," I said. "And I'll torture the whole truth out of you," and I thought of that poor little kid and meant what I said. I don't bluff, and that gink knew it when he opened up.

It was in spasmodic jerks, and between the real fear of me and the imaginary fear of Gustave, he give me the lay of the game. Here's what I get:

In the first place Gustave ain't her uncle at all—his real handle is Boro, and him and her uncle ran a fruit market together down on Mott Street. The uncle had already kicked off when the word came that Nita was coming to America. This Boro got hold of the letter, fixed up the house, and posed as the uncle, whom Nita had never seen. It wasn't hard; he used to write all the letters for her uncle—that bird couldn't read nor write, and didn't feel overproud about letting his family know that America hadn't done much for him.

Nita comes and falls heavy; then comes this Manual Sparo, and things ain't so good; he spots the game at once. But he's a bit of a crook himself and loves Nita, so he offers not to spill the beans if he can marry Nita and connect with half of the formula money with Boro, the fake uncle. The uncle agrees, but Nita ducks on the marriage, and Boro, getting frightened that Manual may cash in on the formula, kidnaps him and tortures him to tell where he's hidden the paper.

Enough of that—he won't tell, and Boro hits on the plan of torturing Nita—for deep down in his black heart, this Manual really loves the girl.

That would hold me for a while—Joe didn't know what the formula was about, but he knew there was much money in it. A final shake and he tells me where the girl is hid. And that stumped me—she was right in that house on Fifty-sixth Street, and they were dead set on getting the formula that night.

The dirty swine; I just looked down at him—if he'd 'a smiled then I'd—but I had seen to it that there wasn't enough left of his map to smile. So I just cracked him over the head once—one good one that would put him to sleep for the rest of the night. I didn't want him to come butting in on the grand finale. Leaving him lying on the floor, I beat it; locked the door on the outside and, slipping the key in my pocket, turned the corner and whistled for Bud.

We sure made time uptown. It would be too late to call for help, and besides, I didn't figure I'd want none. When I left the car on Sixth Avenue, about a block away, I said to Bud:

"Give me an hour, and then if you don't get word from me, why—send the police—tell them it's murder."

"Police! Police!" Bud's mouth opened wide.

"Yes—police," I says. "It's the first time you ever had that kind of an order, but obey it to the letter—let the police know and then beat it."

Not that I thought that there was a chance of failure—I never fail—but that girl was trusting me and I was— But I turned my back on Bud and beat it down Fifty-seventh Street. It was like I was a bit ashamed of showing weakness.

So I pick my distance and make my approach from the other street. I duck through an alleyway, hop a high fence and land in the backyard of the house next door to the gang's. I got to figure out the best way to make it. Oh, I'm going in all right if I have to bust straight through the big French windows in the front with a gun in either mitt. But that's my last stand. I ain't one that goes in for dramatics; not me. I got the two big guns and one little one—the little one I always have—it's a sleeve gun and is used in an emergency; also, I have my flash and am ready for business.

I guess I take about five minutes studying all of them rear windows: I want to make sure that there ain't anyone spying out the back; it don't seem likely, but then I don't take no chances. There are only two lights—one high up which you can hardly see—the other one comes from a window about seven foot from the ground. I think it's the kitchen. Now, there is a water pipe running up to the top light, but I ain't no acrobat. Another look around, and I jump the adjoining fence and land in the yard of the brownstone house.

Edging up close to the back of the house, where a lad at the upper windows couldn't see me without raising one and looking out, I try to peer in the kitchen window, and it's a success; the shade is up just enough to look in under. There's one man in there, a dirty-looking bird, and he's in his shirt-sleeves and fiddling around the coal stove.

Now, there ain't no trick ways of entering houses without people knowing it when they are awake—least I don't know of none. Open windows are nice, but you don't find them in a joint like this one. I'm good with a gun, and in my line that's near enough, but I might say that I have brains too and know how crooks think. For another thing, I ain't a lad what waits around all night for what is called an opening. I don't spend the rest of the night planning when some client's life is at stake, not me; I earn my money and act.

So—I just up with my fist and knock lightly on that kitchen window. If that boy goes for help, I'll be in that window before he ever comes back, for there ain't no bars on it. But if he ain't scared and uses his think box, he'll get to figuring that only a friend would knock. And that's what he done—he comes to the window and looks out.

It's dark, and he can't see nothing but my outline, which I stand there and let him see. Then I lift my hand cautiously like and signal him to lift the window. He stands undecided a minute, and then plays into my hand—he opens the window, but I ain't altogether in luck, for he don't stick his head out. He whispers something in Italian. I don't get what it is, but I make a sucking noise which he can take to keep quiet, and I hand him up a slip of paper which I pull out of my pocket. Out comes his hand to grasp it, and then—with all my strength I take hold of his wrist and pull. Say, there ain't a shout out of him as he comes out that window. But there is one unfortunate circumstance which I had hoped to avoid. I don't figure enough on the play of his heels—they crack that windowsill some wallop, but no glass breaks. He don't holler none as he lands; guess he's too surprised, but he sure did kick up the woodwork. One belt on the head, and the cry dies on his lips, and I'm up and over that sill and into the kitchen. Down comes the shade again; from an upper window someone might see the light and the shadow of the limp body on the ground below.

Just a jump and a brace and a swing, and I'm standing in that kitchen; believe me, I didn't waste no time. I wasn't going to get caught half in and half out of that window. Now, if any of them lads wanted to take a potshot at me, well and good—I was ready. Let them come. I was now in a position to return the compliment; in fact, I was perfectly willing to *start* the show. A fellow don't have to take a shot at me to arouse my interest; you don't have to give me a good moral reason to shoot. Show me the man, and if he's drawing on me and is a man what really needs a good killing, why, I'm the boy to do it.

Well, luck is with me or with them; you can take your choice, for I ain't dodging no gunplay, but there ain't a sound in the house. I'm inside, without anyone being the wiser.

I stand around for several minutes, though, to make sure, and then I hear a tap tap of feet in the room above me—just pounding on the ceiling—slow, like slippered feet that were treading heavily up and down in the same place. It would stop and then go on again, but listen as I would by the kitchen door, there was no other sound of life in the whole house. Still, that didn't mean so much. It was an old house and the walls were thick, and sound don't carry much—but it sure was a deathly stillness and that tap, tap, tap just above me.

I took a look around the kitchen to see if I could find out why that lad was down there, and I did—my heart missed a beat, which is something for my heart to do, I can tell you. What had I seen—well, I had seen two pokers flaming red hot, there in the open stove. Now, if it had 'a been one, it might have been there by accident, just dropped in when I knocked on the window. But two, I knew they were being heated for some purpose, and it was the realization of that purpose which made my heart give a sudden beat and a quick jump. The pokers were to be used to torture the girl and . . . A sudden scream—a woman's scream of terrible agony or fear came sharply through that heavy silence. I was out in the hall in a moment —it was Nita who had given that piercing shriek.

But I didn't lose my head none. Like a cat I went sneaking up the heavy wooden stairs, my sneakered feet making no sound there in the darkness. Oh, I had my flash, but I didn't use it. I ain't much stuck on suicide.

But the cry don't come again, and I reach the second-floor landing. I grope about in the darkness, following the banister along the hall, for that cry had come from someplace near the top of the house. Then, when I'm about to start that second flight, the tap, tap, tap comes again, and I stop dead listening. The sound is right behind me—just about in the middle of that hallway. Then I turn and catch a tiny speck of light creeping under a doorway. I sneak toward it carefully and listen again —the tapping stopped, but I hear a moaning now, and then a feeble foreign voice.

I push my hand along, feeling for the knob, and my fingers strike a panel—a sliding panel—just a tiny one, like they have in the speakeasies. I work it slowly just a crack and peer in. The room is only lit by a candle, which stands on an old table right in the center of the room; the rest of the place is bare, and then—came the groan again, and I see a figure laying on the hard boards, in one corner of the room.

There ain't a spot in the room for a cat to hide in, so I turn the knob; the door opens and I walk in, shutting it gently behind me. One look and a flash of light tells me that there ain't no cause to fear that gent lying in the corner—his hours are on the run; just another groan, and I don't need to be a doctor to know that that guy is going out.

Right off the bat I spot him as Manual Sparo, and I'm right. He half turns his head, and his eyes are glassy and he don't seem to be sure if there is someone in the room with him or not; then he mutters something, but I don't get him.

"Speak English," I says. I'm none too gentle because it won't do him any good now, and if he has anything to say I want to get it before he slips over.

"I'll tell—I'll tell," he says, in good English. "The girl don't know—I wouldn't tell her. The formula's in one of Boro's books—downstairs—third shelf—*Modern Italian Poets.* I tell you the girl don't know—spare her."

And his voice is getting louder with the final effort. Partly because I'm afraid he'll spill my chances all over the house, and partly because I fell sorry for the poor cuss, I up and tell him that I'm the rescue party.

At first he don't understand, but then things kind of get into his head and he grabs me by the hand. He knows I'm friendly, and he takes me for his brother back in Naples. So half in English and half in Italian, he gives me a lot of chatter. But I gather enough to learn this: They had carted him down from the Bronx early that morning, and they told him that they would torture the girl if he didn't tell. He wouldn't tell, and they sent the girl in to him; and he started to tell her where the formula was, and then he changed his mind. Some of the birds were trying to listen outside and got enough to make them think that he had told her—that was about two hours ago. He guessed that they were torturing her, and he had been knocking on the floor with his bare feet—he was ready to blow the game and save the girl, which I don't think would have helped her none.

And you should 'a seen him; his whole body had been hacked at, and his feet and hands burnt to the bone; he had grit, that boy—they didn't get nothing out of him, with all their deviltry. Yep, he had grit and bullheaded stupidity.

Now, you see, I just about did the right thing when I choked the truth out of that murdering villain a short while before—this was no crowd to fool with.

"How many are there in the house?" I said, lifting up his head so that he could breathe better. "How many?" I repeated again a bit louder, and then I look down at him.

There I'd been, listening to his story and trying to ease him up a bit and—well —he had gone out on me—living through all that he did, and then kicking off sudden like that. But I just shrug my shoulders—I can't expect all the luck—the poor devil was better off; he'd never have walked again anyway; that was certain. I let him down easy; he was a bad egg, but way down in his black heart he had loved the girl, and even if it was a selfish love, why—oh, well, I let him slip down to the boards easy.

I straightened up for one last look around that room, and then that shriek—that terrible cry—came again, a bit longer, more penetrating and piercing. This time I didn't wait to take things easy; I just dashed out of that room and up the stairs, my flash going full blast. And it was a good thing I had it, too, for it shines right on a lad sitting on the top of the stairs. Oh, he fired—yes—and I don't know what kind of a shot he was under ordinary circumstances. My light, a mighty powerful one, too, had struck him right between the eyes, and he didn't see none too well, or he shot in a hurry. Anyway, he only shot once—none never do shoot more than once at me. I guess our guns spoke together. I felt nothing and I didn't need to give a second look to him. When I fire, there ain't no guessing contest as to where that bullet is going. Often I poke for the heart, 'specially if there is any distance to cover; its surer. But this was shooting uphill like, and the light was directly on his face, so I let him have it there—someplace about the center of that ugly map of his.

There ain't much to that sort of shooting; you just kind of see a hole for a second; a tiny speck of red, and then the face fades out of the picture. So I just step over him as he rolls down the stairs.

Of course the shot is heard, and another bimbo ducks out of a side room, just as I make the landing. He don't do no shooting—he don't even get a look—just a spurt of flame and I get him. He falls pretty, blocking the doorway which someone is trying to close, but having no luck. And then for the fireworks!

I got the jump on them now; I've made a mighty good impression, and it'll have a good moral effect; there is nothing like following it up. Two of them dead—oh, they're dead all right—none ever come back and fire just one more shot after I plug them. Once I hit a lad, he stays put. So I jump to the door, kick it flying, and, dropping my flash, I stand there a gun in either fin.

And then things ain't so good; to this day I can't explain how they happened to be so well prepared. I just stand there like the avenging angel, with a smile of greeting, when something like a ton of brick comes down and cracks me on the head. I remember firing at a sneering brown face and muttering number three as the clouds come down—after that, curtains—everything goes black.

How long, I don't know, but I come to after a bit and sit up. I ain't tied or nothing—just dazed—I see near a million stars and then I see worse. Over in one corner of the room I see Nita, and she's bound hand and foot on a bare hard bed. There's Boro and another lad close beside him, and one stretched dead out in the center of the floor—so I figure that even with the weight on my head, my aim was good because he ain't dressed like the bird I copped in the doorway.

And Boro is playing the game hard now, and there ain't no smile on that mean, wicked kisser of his. He has a gat stuck close up against my chest, which don't give me much of a chance even if I did feel like pulling something—which I don't. It's a good thought, but my brains are dusty—hitting on one cylinder like. But there's one thing they overlooked, one thing what brings a gleam of hope. They got both my big guns, yes—but their search hadn't been a good one, or was it the way I was lying? Yep, tucked up my sleeve is still the little automatic twenty-five; it's little, yes, but as I get the feel of it there, it seems as big as a cannon. Just let me get my head clear and give me a chance to drop my hands, and those birds will receive a treat—a little treat what they won't enjoy long.

I can shoot in a split second on an open draw—none faster. I'll pull a gun with anyone, even if he comes from the cow country; and I'll beat him to the draw too —there ain't no two ways about that. But on the sleeve business—oh, I'm fast— like lightning—but it takes a second, a whole second, and that's some time in a matter of life and death. But to pull my arm down and shoot takes one full second; I know, I've timed it.

But Boro has that gun bored into my chest and my hands shoved up in the air;

through instinct, I guess, for there ain't no will to hold them there, for I don't hardly know what I'm doing. But I was trying to think—place exactly where I was —what was happening—and behind it all was the reassuring pressure of hard steel just below the elbow.

"Get up!" says Boro, and though his hand is steady, his voice trembles with rage.

And I get up. I can see he's mighty willing to shoot and wonder why he don't. Then he backs me up against the wall.

"You say everything is all clear downstairs, Pedro, and that no one heard the shots," he says to the only other lad left, but he keeps his gun and his eyes on me while he talks. I guess his English is for my benefit, though why he wants to shower me with happiness, I don't know.

"No one heard," Pedro answers, and his English is punk.

"Go fetch some rope," Boro chirps, "and we'll tie up this swine—but first—well, you shall see something amusing when you return, Pedro—and Pedro, another hot poker—very hot—it is for his eyes."

So Pedro beats it. Well, you don't need three guesses to tell you that I'm going to take chances at the first opportunity, or without any opportunity, for that matter.

Boro holds me, with his gun, against the wall a moment, and then he backs away about three paces.

"You are one who shoots well, but so do I," he sneers. "Watch—first I will cripple you. The arms and then the legs—a bullet for each; and then when Pedro returns, it will be the eyes, but that will not be so pleasant—you would play a game with Boro, eh?"

Get what he was up to; why, he'd just stand me against the wall and wing me, and then burn out my eyes. I tried to think. I said to myself, now or never, and did nothing. I was like a man in a dream, and a mighty bad dream—just acting mechanically.

Bang! He had fired. There was a sear of red hot flame just below the elbow, and my left arm dropped to my side. I heard Boro laugh and Nita give a little smothered cry—just the quick intake of breath.

As the blood streamed down onto my wrist, my head seemed to clear, and then my brain hit suddenly back to normal. I was Terry Mack again, and believe me that is something.

Bang! The report came again and I thought it was too late, but no—his bullet had jammed against the hard steel of my little twenty-five, without ever touching my arm.

I don't know if he saw me smile as my right hand started to slink to my side. I think he did, for he was suddenly raising his gun again when I fired. But he never used it; Boro had fired his last shot.

The tiny splash of red appeared for a moment between his eyes; he stood so, his great eyes bulging in surprise more than pain—the surprise of death—then without a groan or a cry he pitched his length upon the floor. He didn't roll over and give a last convulsive groan or a kick—some may do it—none that I ever hit at that range. Boro died standing; died before he fell, and when he fell, there was not so much as a wiggle of his fingers.

As he hit them boards, the door opened and Pedro appeared for a moment in the aperture—but only for a moment. Why I didn't wing him I don't know—but he was gone—whining like a dog as he ran down the stairs, and that was the last I ever heard of Pedro. Of course I bolted the door before I went over to the girl. And I spotted the weight, too, which had put me out of business—it was fixed so that the rope didn't loosen it from the ceiling until someone pressed a catch near the door. Oh, it was good stuff all right, and I admired the pretty way it was pulled off.

I guess I must have staggered across to the girl—my arm didn't bother me none, but my head had gotten about as big as a church again. But somehow I released her. It seemed like I was two persons, and I'd ask my other self what I'd do, and my other self would answer me. Like this it went:

"Any now, Terry, my boy, what's on the program—they've all gone, you know."
And then I'd answer:

"Get a knife, Mack—there's one in the corner there—and cut the rope."

And I did, and afterward Nita told me that I talked to myself like a man in a fever. It was then that I told her about Boro not being her uncle at all, and about Manual being dead, and all that I had learned from Daggo Joe. But I never mentioned the formula; somehow I kept that to myself. And she wasn't hurt at all. Her feet were all right, for they had only just started the torture and hardly touched her tender skin. She had cried out more in deadly fear than in pain—but her mental suffering must have been terrible just the same.

It was she who took the chances, while I just sat there on the floor and mumbled to myself; she went downstairs and got water and bathed my head and tied up my arm, which proved to be only a flesh wound, and not much to bother about at that.

And then, when I come about all right, she turned around and fainted on me. I tell you it was a tough proposition, there with her in that house of death. But I was as clear as a bell now; it's wonderful what water will do for a man, and I tell you it's been a good friend to me in many an emergency.

Water helped her, too, and just as I got her able to sit up and was thinking of helping her downstairs, there came a ringing at the doorbell, followed by a heavy pounding on the door. I left her a moment and, opening the door, listened. The rapping came again, louder than before; and then came the crash of an ax, and I remembered—the hour was more than up and Bud had sent for the police. Good old Bud—I felt like wringing his neck; I wanted to do some talking with a first-class lawyer before I paid my social obligations to the police.

I turned to the window and looked out—there was the lead pipe, the one I couldn't climb up, but I felt that even with my bad arm I could slide down it—especially now that I had the proper incentive behind me. You see, this was no kind of a situation for Terry Mack to be found in. The girl would be all right—they couldn't possibly suspect her of all that slaughter.

"It's the police," I told her in a hurry. "You'll be all right, but for me—a quick getaway. You can tell them about me, but I'll hang low till my lawyer has proven a case against this gang. If they got me, they'd frame me sure—they love me like poison—you'll be O.K. Nita—I'm going to duck."

And then she up and staggered across the room and threw her arms about my neck and hung there; in fact, I had to hold her—she was so weak that her hands couldn't even retain their grasp about my neck.

"Don't leave me, Terry—you're all I got—and the police—oh, Terry, I'll die if you leave me."

And that shows you what fear of the police the fake uncle had instilled in her.

And right there is another thing that I can't explain. Maybe it's weakness, but I like to think it ain't, though I can't account for it. You might think that I had done enough for this girl and earned my pay—well, perhaps I had. But there was soft little hands about my neck and silken hair against my cheek—great innocent, childish eyes looking through pools of water into mine—and—well, I stayed—yep, I just played the fool and stayed.

So it was I held her in my arms when half a dozen cops busted into the room. My cap is still sticking on my head, and I retain sense enough to pull it down close to my eyes.

Then there is questions and warnings and one thing and another. But I don't need no warning—my trap is shut tight—I'll have my mouthpiece when I do any talking, and he's a good lawyer, too. As for the girl, well, she opens up a bit but don't say nothing about the formula, which I think is wise but don't get her real reason for it; though I put it down to the money what's behind it, and her distrust of the police. And I tell you another thing—they are some surprised cops after they look that house over. I hear some of them in the backyard, where they have found the first lad what I socked.

Then in walks Detective Sergeant Quinn, and I know that things are going to get lively. This same Quinn has been trying to hook something on me since George Washington was a boy.

"And the story goes that this one man killed these four—pretty thin," he says, and then he walks over to me. "We'll just have a look at that mug of yours, my man."

With that he jerks off my cap, and me and Quinn look straight at each other.

"Good evening, Sergeant." I can't help but grin. Quinn's fizz is a scream.

"Terry Mack! Terry Mack!" he says twice as he steps back, but he can't hide the feeling of joy that comes over him. "Well, after all it does look like it might be a one-man job—with Mack that man," he says to one of his men. "Hooked at last!" His ugly face screws up in satisfaction. "We'll trot this pair out—separate them—you can keep the girl here until after the coroner comes. But keep your eye on her, and trot this fellow along."

Just as the cop comes up to me with the cuffs in his mitts, I turn to the girl!

"If you have any friends, know of anyone in the city that can help us—now's the time—we're in bad."

And I meant every word of it. I knew the police system, and knew that they'd put me through the jumps before I ever got my lawyer.

Nita seemed to recover somewhat.

"I know one who would help me—who would do anything that I ask. Can—how can I get him?" She was looking at the ceiling while she talked.

That's what I wanted; I wanted her request registered while all them cops were in the room. One of them would be looking for Quinn's job, and if Quinn did anything to hamper the cause of justice, one of them might be glad to blow it—secretly.

"Quick," I says. "Who do you know—who that can help us on the outside?"

"I know Mr. James Roland Williams," she said quietly, though her voice shook a bit. "I think he would do anything for me."

Quinn drew back; I gasped! And why not? James Roland Williams was the commissioner of police.

"Well—well—we'll see about that in the morning." But I noticed that Quinn's voice lacked its usual air of authority.

"How about it now—Quinn?" I chimed in. "This young lady is not used to being treated like a common crook, and from what I know of her friendship with Mr. Williams, it might cost you your shield."

Of course, I didn't know nothing about it, but it didn't strike me as a good time to show my ignorance.

Quinn just scowled at me and told me to hold my tongue, then he turned to the girl. Her honest, quiet air of refinement evidently impressed him.

"Do you know him very well—Miss?" He added the "Miss" after a moment's hesitation.

"Oh yes—I should say—oh, very well indeed." She nodded her head.

"Well enough to disturb him at this hour of the morning?" Quinn bent those hard, stern eyes of his full upon her. "You know, he only got back from a trip south last night."

"No—I did not know that. But it does not matter. He would be glad to come to me at any hour—he has told me so—told me—oh, please call him." Her voice broke.

Another glance, and Quinn turned toward the door. He paused undecided a moment, and then:

"Who shall I say—what name?" he said, and his manner was almost courteous.

"Sen—Miss Nita Gretna—Nita will be enough—he will come at once." There was a certain calm dignity in her manner.

One more close scrutinizing look, and Quinn turned again and left the room.

"And make it snappy, Quinn, even if you are getting a bit on for so many stairs."

I could not resist the temptation to call after him as he descended the stairs. I could see now that pretty soon everything would be jake, and I'd be the light-haired boy; a commissioner has a way of hushing up unpleasant events. Of course, I never doubted the girl—just one look at those clear, honest glims of hers was enough to convince anyone.

It was five minutes later when Quinn returned, and although he had run up the stairs his face was white—white with anger.

"Take them away!" he roared. "Keep them apart—watch that girl." He pointed a finger which shook with rage at Nita. "What do you mean by lying to me—Mr. Williams never heard of you. And he had other things to say to me, things that you'll pay for, my fine girl. Take them away!" he spoke to his men. "And keep an eye on that gunman—Terry Mack." With that, he showed us the width of his shoulders as he stamped viciously from the room.

As for me, I didn't look at the girl—she must'a felt pretty cheap, I thought. But what a superb bluff she had made! That innocent-appearing kid had looked the tough Quinn straight between the eyes and handed him out that earful of bull—and me—oh, I fell for it too.

But I shrugged my shoulders as they slipped on the bracelets and led me away.

"Holler for the best lawyer you can get," I called back over my shoulder to Nita. "We'll see it through together if they don't railroad me. And if you need any money, why—why, I got a bit saved up."

And that last line will pretty near show you that my head wasn't altogether clear yet.

And there you are; I spent the night behind bars. I didn't like the ride they give me neither. I should have been taken to an uptown station, but they booked me further downtown, which sure did look bad. You see, I had a sneaking fear that they might jump me through the hoop; there were several little things that the bulls would have liked to have gotten out of me. I ain't afraid of nothing, mind you, but I was a bit worried; this third degree which you hear so much about ain't all wind—not by a jugful it ain't. I know them birds.

Of course, I was searched all right, but there wasn't a thing on me. I had dropped that sleeve gun when the cops broke in the door, and frisking me was about as exciting as searching a Sunday school superintendent. But this Quinn was a lad who would railroad a bishop, if he felt like it, and—and I ain't no bishop.

A cop what knows something about medicine looks over my arms and sniffs at the wound and says it ain't nothing—so I don't even see a doctor. But I guess he's right, and although it smarts a bit, there ain't much to it as for my head—well, it's a pretty tough head, and I ain't looking for any sympathy, and what's more I don't get any.

I slept pretty well, though, for I felt they'd be too busy to put over any rough stuff that morning; just like a baby I sleep until breakfast. The turnkey was agreeable, and I got a pretty good breakfast. But I didn't like the idea of eating there—I should 'a been brought before a magistrate—the whole thing didn't look good.

At eleven o'clock a dick comes to my door and has it opened and smiles in at me:

"Come on Terry," he says. He's grinning from ear to ear and looks real friendly, which, of course, makes me suspicious. But he walks me right out of the side door of the jail and lands me on the street. Then he hands me out my things that they took from me when I was booked.

"You're sure in luck this time, Terry," he says. "You fitted in right last night, and Quinn is having forty fits—that car there is waiting for you." And he indicates a big touring car with the jerk of his thumb. "Good luck, Terry, you're a game boy, if a tough citizen, and I don't hold anything against you."

I take his outstretched fist and turn toward the car like I had expected it to be there; they ain't going to faze me.

"Good-bye and thanks—" I wave to the dick from the backseat.

"Casey's my name," he says, "Richard Casey!"

"Casey it is."

I shake again as the car speeds away. Then I look around a bit to get my breath; it's an expensive car all right, and there ain't no one but me and the driver. But the chauffeur don't seem to need any instructions, so I don't say anything. Just sit tight; that's my game.

Right up to the restaurant entrance of the Bolton Hotel we pull, and I hop out as live as life. I even start to enter the front door when a great big strapping boy of about twenty-five comes running out and grabs me by the hand.

"Mr. Mack—Mr. Terry Mack!" He smiles all over as he pump-handles me. "I'm James Williams—James Roland Williams, Jr. How's the arm?" he asks suddenly.

I almost forget myself for the moment:

"You're the police commissioner's son!" I guess I kind of gasp.

"That's it," he laughed. "Nita has told me all about you. She forgot the Junior last night when she rang up. You see, father was south when I returned from Italy, and I didn't get a chance to tell him the good news. Besides, there really wasn't any until this morning. Nita slipped away from me on the dock; she was to let me hear from her when she would say yes. She said it this morning."

He laughed again.

But I was to lunch with him and Nita, and there she was, waiting for us in a little private dining room upstairs. She didn't seem much the worse for last night. Young Williams said he wouldn't let her remember; he'd keep her going under high pressure until she forgot. Of course, his old man would see that everything was fixed up properly, and not a reporter had found out who had done the bumping off, nor that Nita was mixed up in it. The papers had just set it down for a general feeling of discontent among the Black-Handers.

And then I learned that he had met Nita on the boat, and that a wedding was all cooked up for the next day.

"It'll just be a quiet affair." Williams smiles all over his good-natured map. "Nita don't know anyone but you, so you'll have to show up." Then he tells me the church, and both of them get my promise to be on deck at eleven the next morning.

"Yes," she looks up at me from across the table, and I notice that there are dark rings under her eyes and that her fingers are twitching nervously. "We must have you Terry—it could not be a wedding without you and—oh—that old formula." She half closes her eyes. "I guess that it is gone forever."

And that's where I shine once again:

"Oh, is it?" I said. "Not so you could notice it—it ain't. Miss Nita, I was hired by you to get that formula, and I most generally get what I go after."

Then I turn to young Williams. I don't give him no information, but just make him promise to go and bring that copy of poems about them Italians to me, without opening the book, and I give him full instruction as to the lay of the book.

It ain't nothing to him, being the commissioner's son, to step right in and turn the trick, and in a half-hour or less he's back with the book. I open it, and there's the envelope. I guess I play the actor a bit when I hand it over to Nita, unopened. There sure was a certain air of satisfaction in that delivery.

Do their eyes open? Well, I should smile; Nita breaks the seal and opens it. She reads it a minute and then chirps:

"That is it." And leaning over the table she takes a match and lights the thin tissuey paper that she holds in her hand. We just sit and stare as she drops it in the plate—a burnt, blackened, unrecognizable mass.

At first I just scratch my head; it's like seeing all your good work literally going up in smoke. Then curiosity gets the better of me for once, and I break my rule about not asking questions.

"Would you mind telling me what it was?" I can't help but ask; you must remember that at least five met their deaths on account of that same piece of paper.

She gives a wan little smile:

"All I know is that it is a formula—a chemical for making poison gas—a gas far stronger and more deadly than any used in the last war, or ever invented. I understand that a small quantity dropped in a container, from a plane, would be enough to wipe out hundreds upon hundreds of people. It may be worth much money, and I do not doubt that it is—but—but it is worth more to humanity there in that dish." And she stirs up the ashes with her spoon.

Personally, I don't take much stock in such sentiment, and I look at Williams to see how he's taking it. But he's only looking at her, cowlike and grinning. Well, he's either dough-heavy or he's in love—or I guess both, for he looks like money and I think the car is his.

And then when I'm leaving them, Nita up and throws her arms about me and kisses me—yes, kisses me full on the lips.

"Oh, Terry, Terry," she says and her voice breaks a little, "you've been more than a father to me—much more."

More than a father! Grandfather, she must mean. But I don't say that. I look at Williams to see how he's taking it, but it seems that his only aim in life is to carry a perpetual grin, which he does to the queen's taste.

"There—there! Be a good girl," is all I say as I pat her on the back. And wasn't that a fool remark for a full-grown man with all his senses!

So I left them.

I guess it's near three o'clock when I see Bud and wrap myself into my easy chair. You see, my arm's all right, but I feel like taking it easy. And then along about eight that night Bud brings me in a envelope.

It's a check, and a good big one; I can see at a glance that everything has been taken into account, and she ain't forgotten the little matter of the four lads what got bumped off. And then the bonus—guess the extra was for Boro. But the check was big—very big—yet I can't honestly say that it was more than I was worth.

So I smoke and think; after all, it was an American that she loved and she hadn't fooled me none. Well, that little garden and the sunny sky of Italy had all gone blooey. I stood up and looked at myself in the glass—not a gray hair appeared— so she might have spared me that father scene. Did I feel bad—not me. I was mighty relieved; for a time, it looked like that dame was going to hook herself onto me for life. With a shrug of my shoulders, I picked up my hat and coat.

And how did I take it? Why, like the gentleman that I am. I just went out and bought her the very best wedding present that the swellest pawnshop in the city could produce. And believe me, that little gift, marked with the best wishes of Terry Mack, would hold its own alongside of anything that she got.

Daly in *Black Mask*

1922–1944

Series characters: Terry Mack   (TM)
Race Williams   (RW)
Satan Hall   (SH)
Pete Hines   (PH)

*—indicates use as basis for published novel
•—included in *The* Black Mask *Boys*

"Dolly"   October 1922
"Roarin' Jack" (as "John D. Carroll")   December 1922
"The False Burton Combs"   December 1922
"It's All in the Game"   15 April 1923
•"Three Gun Terry" (TM)   15 May 1923
"Knights of the Open Palm" (RW)   1 June 1923
"Three Thousand to the Good" (RW)   15 July 1923
"Kiss-the-Canvas Crowley"   1 September 1923
"Action! Action!" (TM)   1 January 1924
"The Brute"   15 January 1924
"One Night of Frenzy"   15 April 1924
"The Red Peril" (RW)   June 1924
"Them That Lives by Their Guns" (RW)   August 1924
"Devil Cat" (RW)   November 1924
"The Face Behind the Mask" (RW)   February 1925
"Conceited, Maybe" (RW)   April 1925

"Say It With Lead!" (RW)   June 1925
"I'll Tell the World" (RW)   August 1925
"Alias Buttercup" (RW)   October 1925
"Under Cover" (RW) Two-parter   December 1925, January 1926
"South Sea Steel" (RW)   May 1926
"The False Clara Burkhart" (RW)   July 1926
"The Super Devil" (RW)   August 1926
"Out of the Night"   October 1926
"Half-Breed" (RW)   November 1926
"Twenty Grand"   January 1927
"Blind Alleys" (RW)   April 1927
*"The Snarl of the Beast" (RW) Four-parter   June, July, August, September
    1927
"The Egyptian Lure" (RW)   March 1928
"The Law of Silence" Two-parter   April, May 1928
*"Creeping Death" (RW)   June 1928
*"Wanted for Murder" (RW)   July 1928
*"Rough Stuff" (RW)   August 1928
*"The Last Chance" (RW)   September 1928
*"The Last Shot" (RW)   October 1928
*"Tags of Death" (RW)   March 1929
*"A Pretty Bit of Shooting" (RW)   April 1929
*"Get Race Williams" (RW)   May 1929
*"Race Williams Never Bluffs" (RW)   June 1929
"The Silver Eagle" (RW)   October 1929
"The Death Trap" (RW)   November 1929
*"Tainted Power" (RW)   June 1930
*"Framed" (RW)   July 1930
*"The Final Shot" (RW)   August 1930
"Shooting Out of Turn" (RW)   October 1930
"Murder by Mail" (RW)   March 1931
*" 'The Flame' and Race Williams" (RW)   Three-parter   June, July, August
    1931
"Death for Two" (RW)   September 1931
*"The Amateur Murderer" (RW) Four-parter   April, May, June, July 1932
"Merger With Death" (RW)   December 1932
"The Death Drop" (RW)   May 1933
"If Death Is Respectable" (RW)   July 1933
"Murder in the Open" (RW)   October 1933
*"Six Have Died" (RW)   May 1934
*"Flaming Death" (RW)   June 1934
*"Murder Book" (RW)   August 1934
"The Eyes Have It" (RW)   November 1934

"I Am the Law" (SH)   March 1938
"Wrong Street" (SH)   May 1938
"Murder Made Easy"   May 1939
"No Sap for Murder" (PH)   November 1940
"Five Minutes for Murder" (PH)   January 1941
"Murder Theme"   July 1944

Published Daly Novels Derived from *Black Mask*

The Snarl of the Beast—New York: Clode, 1927
  (Derived from the four-part serial)
The Hidden Hand—New York: Clode, 1929
  (Derived from "Creeping Death," "Wanted for Murder," "Rough Stuff,"
  "The Last Chance," "The Last Shot")
The Tag Murders—New York: Clode, 1930
  (Derived from "Tags of Death," "A Pretty Bit of Shooting," "Get Race
  Williams," "Race Williams Never Bluffs")
The Third Murderer—New York: Farrar & Rinehart, 1931
  (Derived from the three-part serial, " 'The Flame' and Race Williams")
Tainted Power—New York: Clode, 1931
  (Derived from "Tainted Power," "Framed," "The Final Shot")
The Amateur Murderer—New York: Washburn, 1933
  (Derived from the four-part serial)
Murder From the East—New York: Stokes, 1935
  (Derived from "Six Have Died," "Flaming Death," "Murder Book")

NOTE: Daly's final Race Williams novel, *Better Corpses*, was published in
London by Hale in 1940, but it did not originate in *Black Mask*.

Behind the Mask:
Dashiell Hammett

•

Black Mask and Dashiell Hammett are inexorably linked. Hammett brought depth of character, realism, and literary values unmatched by any other writer to the pages of the *Mask*. It was here that he perfected the now classic "Hammett style" —swift, lean, objective, often cynical—a style that literally transformed the genre.

In his famous 1944 essay, "The Simple Art of Murder," Raymond Chandler openly acknowledged Hammett's influential position. He properly credited Hammett as the "ace performer"—the one writer responsible for the creation and development of the hard-boiled school of literature.

Joe Shaw viewed Hammett's work with near reverential awe and later cited him as the prime exemplar of the *Black Mask* school. He named Hammett as the strongest single force in shaping the magazine's special image in the years 1927 through 1930. With some justification, Erle Stanley Gardner accused Shaw of trying to "Hammettize" *Black Mask*.

Shaw recognized the gritty authenticity of Hammett's fiction. Unlike Carroll John Daly, who knew nothing about the real world of crime, Hammett used his own extensive background as a detective to construct a solid base for his novels and stories. During his on-and-off years as a Pinkerton operative (1915–1922), he was involved in the widest possible range of police work, from petty theft to murder.

Hammett exposed counterfeiters, investigated bank swindlers, trapped blackmailers, trailed jewel thieves, uncovered missing gold shipments, arrested forgers, tangled with gangsters and holdup men, gathered evidence for criminal trials, and performed services for Pinkerton as a guard, hotel detective, and strikebreaker.

Thus, when he turned from crime to professional writing, his colorful, action-filled experiences provided an inexhaustible, invaluable source of plots and characters.

As novelist Joe Gores aptly phrased it, "In the early 1920s, as he began working in the pulps, Hammett was not a writer learning about private detectives, he was a private detective learning about writing."

Hammett had joined Pinkerton's National Detective Agency in Baltimore, at the age of twenty-one, after a knockabout series of early jobs—as a railroad-freight handler, cannery worker, nail-machine operator, and stock-brokerage clerk. He had been on his own for seven years, forced to leave school at fourteen to help bring in money when his father became too ill to work.

His ancestors were Scottish and French. He was born Samuel Dashiell Hammett on May 27, 1894, in St. Mary's County, Maryland. In 1901 he moved to Baltimore with his family.

His father, Richard Thomas Hammett, was stern and unloving; his mother, Annie Bond Hammett, suffered from tuberculosis and was often bedridden.

Although he got on well enough with his sister, young Samuel was in constant conflict with his father and brother. He grew up feeling rebellious and alienated. Until he joined Pinkerton's in 1915, Hammett had never found an occupation that suited his roving temperament.

The cases he worked on as a Pinkerton operative fed his need for adventure and day-to-day challenge. Sam Hammett soon became known as one of the agency's top "shadows" (an expert at tailing subjects).

He left Pinkerton's in the summer of 1918 to enlist in the U.S. Army. Assigned to a motor ambulance company in Maryland, he soon contracted influenza, which damaged his lungs and heart.

After a partial recovery, Hammett left the service in 1919 to resume detective work with Pinkerton's. By November of 1920, however, he was hospitalized again —this time for tuberculosis—in Tacoma, Washington. During his Tacoma stay, Hammett began an intense love affair with an attractive young ward nurse, Josephine ("Jose") Anna Dolan. After returning to her Montana home, Jose discovered that she was pregnant with his child.

Hammett, now in San Francisco, sent for her, and they were married there on July 7, 1921. Hammett was once again working as a "Pink" (for the agency's San Francisco branch), but his health kept getting worse. He was forced to resign from the detective business permanently in mid-February 1922, following the birth of his first daughter, Mary Jane.

Aided by the Veterans' Bureau, Hammett enrolled in a vocational training course at Munson's Business College; he had decided to prepare himself for a career in advertising.

Always an avid reader (who had loved mysteries as a boy), Hammett had great respect for creative writing. Encouraged by Jose, he began to experiment with verse and short satiric pieces, selling one of these to H. L. Mencken at *The Smart Set.*

Mencken was no longer associated with *Black Mask;* he had sold his financial interest two years earlier, in 1920. But he may have suggested that Hammett look into *Mask* as a possible market.

Hammett submitted a short crime story, "The Road Home," to editor George Sutton. (Hammett was then using the pseudonym "Peter Collinson" for his short fiction, reserving his real byline for verse and essays.)

Sutton bought the Collinson submission and asked for more. After selling another three stories, Hammett decided that the work he was doing for *Mask* was good enough to rate the use of his real name. Throughout his life he had answered to "Sam" or Samuel D. Hammett. Now, for his fiction, he dropped the Samuel and became, simply, Dashiell Hammett. The name was stronger and looked better on a page.

In 1915, when he had joined Pinkerton's Baltimore branch, their offices were located in the Continental Building, which gave Hammett the name for his fictional detective agency. In 1923 he created the nameless "Man from Continental," sending "The Op" out to solve many of the same cases Hammett himself had worked on. (In letters to *Mask*, and later in interviews, he claimed that all of his characters were "based on people I'd known personally, or known about, when I was a Pink.")

The tough, tart Op stories generated growing enthusiasm from readers and quickly elevated Hammett to a top position among *Black Mask* writers.

But money had become a serious problem for the Hammett family. In 1926 his writing career was sidetracked when he quit the *Mask* to take a job as advertising manager for a San Francisco jeweler. With the birth of his second daughter, Josephine Rebecca, Hammett needed to increase his earnings. Advertising seemed to be the answer.

It wasn't. He collapsed at work, bleeding from the lungs; his health had failed once again and he was forced to abandon the new job. Now Hammett had to remain in bed for most of each day.

Joe Shaw had taken over the reins at *Black Mask*, and he very much wanted Hammett back in the magazine. Shaw promised higher word rates and a "free creative hand" if Hammett would develop the Op at novel length.

Hammett returned to the fold. By 1927 he had written the brilliant "Poisonville" series, linked novelettes which formed *Red Harvest*, his first published book. By the end of 1930 he had provided Shaw with *The Dain Curse*, *The Maltese Falcon*, and *The Glass Key*.

The crime story would never again be the same. Hammett's classic contributions to *Mask* had altered the basic form of the genre. No writer since Edgar Allan Poe had exerted a greater influence on mystery fiction.

Major changes were taking place in Hammett's personal life. By 1929 his tuberculosis was in total remission and his health had improved greatly, yet he was abusing it with heavy drinking, chain-smoking, and late nights on the town. Gambling had become a real addiction, and he was also seeing other women. The breakup of his marriage was inevitable.

Hammett left his family for Nell Martin (who was also a writer) at the close of 1929, and together they moved to New York. He obtained a job there as a crime-fiction reviewer for the *Evening Post*. (He had quit the pulps, including *Black Mask*.)

During his eight years with the *Mask*, Hammett's work had appeared in some half-hundred issues, and he had placed an additional dozen stories with other pulp magazines. (He had also made several sales to slick-paper magazines in this same period; these markets would claim the remainder of his prose work into early 1934, when he gave up writing short fiction altogether.)

Alone, Hammett moved to Hollywood where, beginning in the early 1930s, he quickly became one of the town's most sought-after script writers.

Although no less than *three* versions of *The Maltese Falcon* were produced, Hammett did not work on any of the film adaptations. Nevertheless, the final 1941 Bogart-as-Spade version, directed by John Huston, was (as one critic termed it) "100-proof Hammett." Dialogue and scenes were taken directly out of the novel for Huston's script; the result was a classic example of pure *Black Mask* prose brought to the screen.

In Hollywood, Hammett began a passionate relationship with Lillian Hellman, a young, aspiring writer who was a story analyst for MGM. To the twenty-five-year-old Hellman, Hammett was irresistible. Hugely successful, he was handsome, mature, well read and witty, and wore his clothes with style and flair. (One columnist called him "a Hollywood Dream Prince.")

As their relationship deepened, Hammett offered to help Hellman with her work. She wanted to write plays but needed professional guidance. Hammett provided it. Throughout almost three decades he served as her "mentor and literary conscience," criticizing each act, each scene, each page of the plays she wrote, from *The Children's Hour* in 1934 to *Toys in the Attic* in 1960.

They also shared a deep personal commitment to left-wing politics, which led to a five-month contempt-of-court prison term for Hammett in 1951. (He had refused to "name names" before a federal judge in New York.)

Hammett was sickened by the civic and political corruption he had encountered, first as a Pinkerton, later as a writer. His final published novel, *The Thin Man* (completed in 1933), appears to be a comedic crime thriller. Actually, it is a bitter and savage social portrait. Hammett no longer believed that a lone detective (such as the Op, or Spade, or Nick Charles) could make any impact on a corrupt society. In reaction, he abandoned crime fiction and turned instead to radical politics as a moral substitute.

In 1942, during World War II, he amazed his friends by enlisting in the Army Signal Corps at the advanced age of forty-eight—a direct result of his hatred of Fascism. Hammett served three years (into September of 1945) in the storm-blasted Aleutian Islands of Alaska. He spent a large part of this period editing *The Adakain*, an army newspaper printed daily for the troops along the remote island chain.

He attempted to resume his writing career after the war, but this time he aimed in a new literary direction. Hammett wanted to write "socially significant" novels, not more crime stories. He resented the label "mystery writer." A frustrating position, since comic strips, radio shows, and films based on his crime works were bringing him a small fortune each year. In self-disgust, he got rid of this money as fast as it arrived—gambling and drinking it away.

Earlier, during the time he had written a Thin Man film for MGM, he had leased the lavish Harold Lloyd multimillion-dollar, forty-four-room mansion as his personal living quarters. With formal gardens, a huge swimming pool, tennis courts, and an ice cream parlor in the basement, it was, as Hammett called it, "a great joint for parties."

Although they remained as close as ever emotionally, by the early 1940s the sexual aspect of his relationship with Lillian Hellman had ended; his drunken pursuit of other women, married or single, provided grist for numerous gossip columns.

Behind the high-living partygoer, the serious writer was blocked. Hammett was unable to get the novels inside his head onto paper. It was not until the 1950s, after several aborted efforts, that he made any real progress on another book. Hammett wrote 17,000 words on a work he called "Tulip" but was unable to finish the manuscript. Ironically, it was about a blocked writer who could not finish a novel.

At this point, ravaged by alcohol and emphysema, Dashiell Hammett was an extremely sick man. In 1955 he suffered a serious heart attack.

In addition to these physical problems, he was now totally without funds. His political activities and jail term had resulted in his being blacklisted. He was unemployable in Hollywood. All of his radio shows were off the air, and publishers refused to issue new collections of his fiction.

Finally, in a killing blow, the IRS levied a huge tax bill against him. As a result, Hammett was forced to exist as a virtual pauper for the last decade of his life.

Although he had given up drinking and cut down on his smoking, it was too late. In November of 1960 a medical examination revealed terminal lung cancer.

Dashiell Hammett died at Lenox Hill Hospital in New York on January 10, 1961, at the age of sixty-six. As requested in his will, he was buried at Arlington National Cemetery.

After publication of *The Thin Man*, in 1934, he had lived the remaining twenty-seven years of his life in creative despair, unable to complete the "important" novels he dreamed of writing.

Yet, in the final analysis, another Hammett novel was not required. With his brilliant, moody, trailblazing work in *Black Mask*, he had forged his own new brand of action literature. Although he had refused to acknowledge its importance, his position in history was secure.

Samuel Dashiell Hammett had nothing more to prove.

Bodies Piled Up

When this fast-paced adventure starring San Francisco's Man from Continental was printed late in 1923, editor George Sutton announced to his readers: "Mr. Hammett has suddenly become one of the most popular of *Black Mask* writers . . . His stories are always entertaining, full of action and very unusual situations. This is his best to date—a real detective yarn."

Hammett's popularity was indeed "suddenly" achieved. The Op's first case had been printed just two months earlier under the pseudonym "Peter Collinson," and this was only Hammett's fourth appearance in *Mask* under his real name.

"Bodies Piled Up" is not included in either of the main Hammett collections, *The Big Knockover* or *The Continental Op,* and has remained out of print since its first book appearance (as "House Dick") in the 1947 paperback, *Dead Yellow Women.*

Such obscurity is undeserved. This one is vintage Hammett, a clever and exciting tale from the master of the genre.

BODIES PILED UP

Series character: The Continental Op

The Montgomery Hotel's regular detective had taken his last week's rake-off from the hotel bootlegger in merchandise instead of cash, had drunk it down, had fallen asleep in the lobby, and had been fired. I happened to be the only idle operative in the Continental Detective Agency's San Francisco branch at the time, and thus it came about that I had three days of hotel-coppering while a man was being found to take the job permanently.

The Montgomery is a quiet hotel of the better sort, and so I had a very restful time of it—until the third and last day. Then things changed.

I came down into the lobby that afternoon to find Stacey, the assistant manager, hunting for me.

"One of the maids just phoned that there's something wrong up in 906," he said.

We went up to that room together. The door was open. In the center of the floor stood a maid, staring goggle-eyed at the closed door of the clothespress. From under it, extending perhaps a foot across the floor toward us, was a snake-shaped ribbon of blood.

I stepped past the maid and tried the door. It was unlocked. I opened it. Slowly, rigidly, a man pitched out into my arms—pitched out backward—and there was a six-inch slit down the back of his coat, and the coat was wet and sticky.

That wasn't altogether a surprise: the blood on the floor had prepared me for something of the sort. But when another followed him—facing me, this one, with a dark, distorted face—I dropped the one I had caught and jumped back.

And as I jumped, a third man came tumbling out after the others.

From behind me came a scream and a thud as the maid fainted. I wasn't feeling any too steady myself. I'm no sensitive plant, and I've looked at a lot of unlovely sights in my time, but for weeks afterward I could see those three dead men coming out of that clothespress to pile up at my feet: coming out slowly—almost deliberately—in a ghastly game of "follow your leader."

Seeing them, you couldn't doubt that they were really dead. Every detail of their falling, every detail of the heap in which they now lay, had a horrible certainty of lifelessness in it.

I turned to Stacey, who, deathly white himself, was keeping on his feet only by clinging to the foot of the brass bed.

"Get the woman out! Get doctors—police!"

I pulled the three dead bodies apart, laying them out in a grim row, faces up. Then I made a hasty examination of the room.

A soft hat, which fitted one of the dead men, lay in the center of the unruffled bed. The room key was in the door, on the inside. There was no blood in the room except what had leaked out of the clothespress, and the room showed no signs of having been the scene of a struggle.

The door to the bathroom was open. In the bottom of the bathtub was a shattered gin bottle, which, from the strength of the odor and the dampness of the tub, had been nearly full when broken. In one corner of the bathroom I found a small whiskey glass, and another under the tub. Both were dry, clean, and odorless.

The inside of the clothespress door was stained with blood from the height of my shoulder to the floor, and two hats lay in the puddle of blood on the closet floor. Each of the hats fitted one of the dead men.

That was all. Three dead men, a broken gin bottle, blood.

Stacey returned presently with a doctor, and while the doctor was examining the dead men, the police detectives arrived.

The doctor's work was soon done.

"This man," he said, pointing to one of them, "was struck on the back of the head with a small blunt instrument, and then strangled. This one," pointing to another, "was simply strangled. And the third was stabbed in the back with a blade perhaps five inches long. They have been dead for about two hours—since noon or a little after."

The assistant manager identified two of the bodies. The man who had been stabbed—the first to fall out of the clothespress—had arrived at the hotel three days before, registering as Tudor Ingraham of Washington, D.C., and had occupied room 915, three doors away.

The last man to fall out—the one who had been simply choked—was the occupant of this room. His name was Vincent Develyn. He was an insurance broker and had made the hotel his home since his wife's death, some four years before.

The third man had been seen in Develyn's company frequently, and one of the clerks remembered that they had come into the hotel together at about five minutes after twelve this day. Cards and letters in his pockets told us that he was Homer Ansley, a member of the law firm of Lankershim and Ansley, whose offices were in the Miles Building—next door to Develyn's office.

Develyn's pockets held between $150 and $200; Ansley's wallet contained more than $100; Ingraham's pockets yielded nearly $300, and in a money belt around his waist we found $2,200 and two medium-sized unset diamonds. All three had watches—Develyn's was a valuable one—in their pockets, and Ingraham wore two rings, both of which were expensive ones. Ingraham's room key was in his pocket.

Beyond this money—whose presence would seem to indicate that robbery hadn't been the motive behind the three killings—we found nothing on any of the persons to throw the slightest light on the crime. Nor did the most thorough examination of both Ingraham's and Develyn's rooms teach us anything.

In Ingraham's room we found a dozen or more packs of carefully marked cards, some crooked dice, and an immense amount of data on racehorses. Also we found that he had a wife who lived on East Delavan Avenue in Buffalo, and a brother on Crutcher Street in Dallas; as well as a list of names and addresses that we carried off to investigate later. But nothing in either room pointed, even indirectly, at murder.

Phels, the police department Bertillon man, found a number of fingerprints in Develyn's room, but we couldn't tell whether they would be of any value or not until he had worked them up. Though Develyn and Ansley had apparently been strangled by hands, Phels was unable to get prints from either their necks or their collars.

The maid who had discovered the blood said that she had straightened up Develyn's room between ten and eleven that morning but had not put fresh towels in the bathroom. It was for this purpose that she had gone to the room in the afternoon. She had found the door unlocked, with the key on the inside, and, as soon as she entered, had seen the blood, and telephoned Stacey.

She had straightened up Ingraham's room, she said, at a few minutes after one. She had gone there earlier—between 10:20 and 10:45—for that purpose, but Ingraham had not then left it.

The elevator man who had carried Ansley and Develyn up from the lobby at a few minutes after twelve remembered that they had been laughingly discussing their golf scores of the previous day during the ride. No one had seen anything suspicious in the hotel around the time at which the doctor had placed the murders. But that was to be expected.

The murderer could have left the room, closing the door behind him, and walked away secure in the knowledge that at noon a man in the corridors of the Montgomery would attract little attention. If he was staying at the hotel he would simply have gone to his room; if not, he would have either walked all the way down to the street, or down a floor or two and then caught an elevator.

None of the hotel employees had ever seen Ingraham and Develyn together. There was nothing to show that they had even the slightest acquaintance. Ingraham habitually stayed in his room until noon, and did not return to it until late at night. Nothing was known of his affairs.

At the Miles Building we—that is, Marty O'Hara and George Dean of the police department homicide detail and I—questioned Ansley's partner and Develyn's employees. Both Develyn and Ansley, it seemed, were ordinary men who led ordinary lives: lives that held neither dark spots nor queer kinks. Ansley was married and had two children; he lived on Lake Street. Both men had a sprinkling of relatives and friends scattered here and there through the country; and, so far as we could learn, their affairs were in perfect order.

They had left their offices this day to go to luncheon together, intending to visit Develyn's room first for a drink apiece from a bottle of gin someone coming from Australia had smuggled in to him.

"Well," O'Hara said, when we were on the street again, "this much is clear. If they went up to Develyn's room for a drink, it's a cinch that they were killed almost as soon as they got in the room. Those whiskey glasses you found were dry and clean. Whoever turned the trick must have been waiting for them. I wonder about this fellow Ingraham."

"I'm wondering, too," I said. "Figuring it out from the positions I found them in when I opened the closet door, Ingraham sizes up as the key to the whole thing. Develyn was back against the wall, with Ansley in front of him, both facing the door. Ingraham was facing them, with his back to the door. The clothespress was just large enough for them to be packed in it—too small for them to slip down while the door was closed.

"Then there was no blood in the room except what had come from the clothespress. Ingraham, with that gaping slit in his back, couldn't have been stabbed until he was inside the closet, or he'd have bled elsewhere. He was standing close to the other men when he was knifed, and whoever knifed him closed the door quickly afterward.

"Now, why should he have been standing in such a position? Do you dope it out that he and another killed the two friends, and that while he was stowing their bodies in the closet his accomplice finished him off?"

"Maybe," Dean said.

And that "maybe" was still as far as we had gone three days later.

We had sent and received bales of telegrams, having relatives and acquaintances of the dead men interviewed; and we had found nothing that seemed to have any bearing upon their deaths. Nor had we found the slightest connecting link between Ingraham and the other two. We had traced those other two back, step by step, almost to their cradles. We had accounted for every minute of their time since Ingraham had arrived in San Francisco—thoroughly enough to convince us that neither of them had met Ingraham.

Ingraham, we had learned, was a bookmaker and all-around crooked gambler. His wife and he had separated, but were on good terms. Some fifteen years before, he had been convicted of "assault with intent to kill" in Newark, N.J., and had served two years in the state prison. But the man he had assaulted had died of pneumonia in Omaha.

Ingraham had come to San Francisco for the purpose of opening a gambling club, and all our investigations had tended to show that his activities while in the city had been toward that end alone.

The fingerprints Phels had secured had all turned out to belong to Stacey, the maid, the police detectives, or myself. In short, we had found nothing!

So much for our attempts to learn the motive behind the three murders.

We now dropped that angle and settled down to the detail-studying, patience-taxing grind of picking up the murderer's trail. From any crime to its author there is a trail. It may be—as in this case—obscure; but, since matter cannot move without disturbing other matter along its path, there always is—there must be—a trail of some sort. And finding and following such trails is what a detective is paid to do.

In the case of a murder it is possible sometimes to take a shortcut to the end of the trail, by first finding the motive. A knowledge of the motive often reduces the field of possibilities; sometimes points directly to the guilty one.

So far, all we knew about the motive in the particular case we were dealing with was that it hadn't been robbery; unless something we didn't know about had been stolen—something of sufficient value to make the murderer scorn the money in his victims' pockets.

We hadn't altogether neglected the search for the murderer's trail, of course, but—being human—we had devoted most of our attention to trying to find a shortcut. Now we set out to find our man, or men, regardless of what had urged him or them to commit the crimes.

Of the people who had been registered at the hotel on the day of the killing there were nine men of whose innocence we hadn't found a reasonable amount of proof. Four of these were still at the hotel, and only one of that four interested us very strongly. That one—a big, rawboned man of forty-five or fifty, who had registered as J. J. Cooper of Anaconda, Montana—wasn't, we had definitely established, really a mining man, as he pretended to be. And our telegraphic communications with Anaconda failed to show that he was known there. Therefore we were having him shadowed—with few results.

Five men of the nine had departed since the murders—three of them leaving forwarding addresses with the mail clerk. Gilbert Jacquemart had occupied room 946 and had ordered his mail forwarded to him at a Los Angeles hotel. W. F. Salway, who had occupied room 1022, had given instructions that his mail be readdressed to a number on Clark Street in Chicago. Ross Orrett, room 609, had asked to have his mail sent to him care of General Delivery at the local post office.

Jacquemart had arrived at the hotel two days before and had left on the afternoon of the murders. Salway had arrived the day before the murders and had left
the day after them. Orrett had arrived the day of the murders and had left the
following day.

Sending telegrams to have the first two found and investigated, I went after
Orrett myself. A musical comedy named *What For?* was being widely advertised
just then with gaily printed plum-colored handbills. I got one of them and, at a
stationery store, an envelope to match, and mailed it to Orrett at the Montgomery
Hotel. There are concerns that make a practice of securing the names of arrivals
at the principal hotels and mailing them advertisements. I trusted that Orrett,
knowing this, wouldn't be suspicious when my gaudy envelope, forwarded from the
hotel, reached him through the General Delivery window.

Dick Foley—the agency's shadow specialist—planted himself in the post office,
to loiter around with an eye on the "O" window until he saw my plum-colored
envelope passed out, and then to shadow the receiver.

I spent the next day trying to solve the mysterious J. J. Cooper's game, but he
was still a puzzle when I knocked off that night.

At a little before five the following morning Dick Foley dropped into my room
on his way home to wake me up and tell me what he had done.

"This Orrett baby is our meat!" he said. "Picked him up when he got his mail
yesterday afternoon. Got another letter besides yours. Got an apartment on Van
Ness Avenue. Took it the day after the killing, under the name of B. T. Quinn.
Packing a gun under his left arm—there's that sort of a bulge there. Just went
home to bed. Been visiting all the dives in North Beach. Who do you think he's
hunting for?"

"Who?"

"Guy Cudner."

That was news! This Guy Cudner, alias "The Darkman," was the most dangerous bird on the Coast, if not in the country. He had only been nailed once, but
if he had been convicted of all the crimes that everybody knew he had committed,
he'd have needed half a dozen lives to crowd his sentences into, besides another
half-dozen to carry to the gallows. However, he had decidedly the right sort of
backing—enough to buy him everything he needed in the way of witnesses, alibis,
even juries, and an occasional judge.

I don't know what went wrong with his support that one time he was convicted
up north and sent over for a one-to-fourteen-year hitch; but it adjusted itself
promptly, for the ink was hardly dry on the press notices of his conviction before
he was loose again on parole.

"Is Cudner in town?"

"Don't know," Dick said, "but this Orrett, or Quinn, or whatever his name is,
is surely hunting for him. In Rick's place, at 'Wop' Healey's, and at Pigatti's.
'Porky' Grout tipped me off. Says Orrett doesn't know Cudner by sight but is
trying to find him. Porky didn't know what he wants with him."

This Porky Grout was a dirty little rat who would sell out his family—if he ever had one—for the price of a flop. But with these lads who play both sides of the game, it's always a question of which side they're playing when you think they're playing yours.

"Think Porky was coming clean?" I asked.

"Chances are—but you can't gamble on him."

"Is Orrett acquainted here?"

"Doesn't seem to be. Knows where he wants to go but has to ask how to get there. Hasn't spoken to anybody that seemed to know him."

"What's he like?"

"Not the kind of egg you'd want to tangle with offhand, if you ask me. He and Cudner would make a good pair. They don't look alike. This egg is tall and slim, but he's built right—those fast, smooth muscles. Face is sharp without being thin, if you get me. I mean all the lines in it are straight. No curves. Chin, nose, mouth, eyes—all straight, sharp lines and angles. Looks like the kind of egg we know Cudner is. Make a good pair. Dresses well and doesn't look like a rowdy—but harder than hell! A big-game hunter! Our meat, I bet you!"

"It doesn't look bad," I agreed. "He came to the hotel the morning of the day the men were killed and checked out the next morning. He packs a rod and changed his name after he left. And now he's paired off with The Darkman. It doesn't look bad at all!"

"I'm telling you," Dick said, "this fellow looks like three killings wouldn't disturb his rest any. I wonder where Cudner fits in."

"I can't guess. But if he and Orrett haven't connected yet, then Cudner wasn't in on the murders; but he may give us the answer."

Then I jumped out of bed. "I'm going to gamble on Porky's dope being on the level! How would you describe Cudner?"

"You know him better than I do."

"Yes, but how would you describe him to me if I didn't know him?"

"A little fat guy with a red, forked scar on his left cheek. What's the idea?"

"It's a good one," I admitted. "That scar makes all the difference in the world. If he didn't have it and you were to describe him you'd go into all the details of his appearance. But he has it, so you simply say, 'A little fat guy with a red, forked scar on his left cheek.' It's a ten to one that that's just how he has been described to Orrett. I don't look like Cudner, but I'm his size and build, and with a scar on my face Orrett will fall for me."

"What then?"

"There's no telling, but I ought to be able to learn a lot if I can get Orrett talking to me as Cudner. It's worth a try anyway."

"You can't get away with it—not in San Francisco. Cudner is too well known."

"What difference does that make, Dick? Orrett is the only one I want to fool. If he takes me for Cudner, well and good. If he doesn't, still well and good. I won't force myself on him."

"How are you going to fake the scar?"

"Easy! We have pictures of Cudner, showing the scar, in the criminal gallery. I'll get some collodion—it's sold in drugstores under several trade names for putting on cuts and scratches—color it, and imitate Cudner's scar on my cheek. It dries with a shiny surface and, put on thick, will stand out enough to look like an old scar."

It was a little after eleven the following night when Dick telephoned me that Orrett was in Pigatti's place, on Pacific Street, and apparently settled there for some little while. My scar already painted on, I jumped into a taxi and within a few minutes was talking to Dick, around the corner from Pigatti's.

"He's sitting at the last table back on the left side. And he was alone when I came out. You can't miss him. He's the only egg in the joint with a clean collar."

"You better stick outside—half a block or so away—with the taxi," I told Dick. "Maybe brother Orrett and I will leave together, and I'd just as soon have you standing by in case things break wrong."

Pigatti's place is a long, narrow, low-ceilinged cellar, always dim with smoke. Down the middle runs a narrow strip of bare floor for dancing. The rest of the floor is covered with closely packed tables, whose cloths are always soiled.

Most of the tables were occupied when I came in, and half a dozen couples were dancing. Few of the faces to be seen were strangers to the morning "lineup" at police headquarters.

Peering through the smoke, I saw Orrett at once, seated alone in a far corner, looking at the dancers with the set, blank face of one who masks an all-seeing watchfulness. I walked down the other side of the room and crossed the strip of dance floor directly under a light, so that the scar might be clearly visible to him. Then I selected a vacant table not far from his, and sat down facing him.

Ten minutes passed while he pretended an interest in the dancers and I affected a thoughtful stare at the dirty cloth on my table, but neither of us missed so much as a flicker of the other's lids.

His eyes—gray eyes that were pale without being shallow, with black need-lepoint pupils—met mine after a while in a cold, steady, inscrutable stare; and, very slowly, he got to his feet. One hand—his right—in a side pocket of his dark coat, he walked straight across to my table and sat down.

"Cudner?"

"Looking for me, I hear," I replied, trying to match the icy smoothness of his voice, as I was matching the steadiness of his gaze.

He had sat down with his left side turned slightly toward me, which put his right arm in not too cramped a position for straight shooting from the pocket that still held his hand.

"You were looking for me, too."

I didn't know what the correct answer to that would be, so I just grinned. But the grin didn't come from my heart. I had, I realized, made a mistake—one that might cost me something before we were done. This bird wasn't hunting for Cudner as a friend, as I had carelessly assumed, but was on the warpath.

I saw those three dead men falling out of the closet in room 906!

My gun was inside the waistband of my trousers, where I could get it quickly, but his was in his hand. So I was careful to keep my own hands motionless on the edge of the table, while I widened my grin.

His eyes were changing now, and the more I looked at them the less I liked them. The gray in them had darkened and grown duller, and the pupils were larger, and white crescents were showing beneath the gray. Twice before I had looked into eyes such as these—and I hadn't forgotten what they meant—the eyes of the congenital killer!

"Suppose you speak your piece," I suggested after a while.

But he wasn't to be beguiled into conversation. He shook his head a mere fraction of an inch and the corners of his compressed mouth dropped down a trifle. The white crescents of eyeballs were growing broader, pushing the gray circles up under the upper lids.

It was coming! And there was no use waiting for it!

I drove a foot at his shins under the table, and at the same time pushed the table into his lap and threw myself across it. The bullet from his gun went off to one side. Another bullet—not from his gun—thudded into the table that was upended between us.

I had him by the shoulders when the second shot from behind took him in the left arm, just below my hand. I let go then and fell away, rolling over against the wall and twisting around to face the direction from which the bullets were coming.

I twisted around just in time to see—jerking out of sight behind a corner of the passage that gave to a small dining room—Guy Cudner's scarred face. And as it disappeared, a bullet from Orrett's gun splattered the plaster from the wall where it had been.

I grinned at the thought of what must be going on in Orrett's head as he lay sprawled out on the floor confronted by two Cudners. But he took a shot at me just then and I stopped grinning. Luckily, he had to twist around to fire at me, putting his weight on his wounded arm, and the pain made him wince, spoiling his aim.

Before he had adjusted himself more comfortably I had scrambled on hands and knees to Pigatti's kitchen door—only a few feet away—and had myself safely tucked out of range around an angle in the wall; all but my eyes and the top of my head, which I risked so that I might see what went on.

Orrett was now ten or twelve feet from me, lying flat on the floor, facing Cudner, with a gun in his hand and another on the floor beside him.

Across the room, perhaps thirty feet away, Cudner was showing himself around his protecting corner at brief intervals to exchange shots with the man on the floor, occasionally sending one my way. We had the place to ourselves. There were four exits, and the rest of Pigatti's customers had used them all.

I had my gun out, but I was playing a waiting game. Cudner, I figured, had been tipped off to Orrett's search for him and had arrived on the scene with no mistaken idea of the other's attitude. Just what there was between them and what bearing it had on the Montgomery murders was a mystery to me, but I didn't try to solve it now.

They were firing in unison. Cudner would show around his corner, both men's weapons would spit, and he would duck out of sight again. Orrett was bleeding about the head now and one of his legs sprawled crookedly behind him. I couldn't determine whether Cudner had been hit or not.

Each had fired eight, or perhaps nine, shots when Cudner suddenly jumped out into full view, pumping the gun in his left hand as fast as its mechanism would go, the gun in his right hand hanging at his side. Orrett had changed guns and was on his knees now, his fresh weapon keeping pace with his enemy's.

That couldn't last!

Cudner dropped his left-hand gun, and, as he raised the other, he sagged forward and went down on one knee. Orrett stopped firing abruptly and fell over on his back—spread out full-length. Cudner fired once more—wildly, into the ceiling—and pitched down on his face.

I sprang to Orrett's side and kicked both of his guns away. He was lying still, but his eyes were open.

"Are you Cudner, or was he?"

"He."

"Good!" he said, and closed his eyes.

I crossed to where Cudner lay and turned him over on his back. His chest was literally shot to pieces.

His thick lips worked, and I put my ear down to them. "I get him?"

"Yes," I lied, "he's already cold."

His dying face twisted into a grin.

"Sorry—three in hotel—" he gasped hoarsely. "Mistake—wrong room—got one —had to—other two—protect myself—I—" He shuddered and died.

A week later the hospital people let me talk to Orrett. I told him what Cudner had said before he died.

"That's the way I doped it out," Orrett said from out of the depths of the bandages in which he was swathed. "That's why I moved and changed my name the next day.

"I suppose you've got it nearly figured out by now," he said after a while.

"No," I confessed, "I haven't. I've an idea what it was all about, but I could stand having a few details cleared up."

"I'm sorry I can't clear them up for you, but I've got to cover myself. I'll tell you a story, though, and it may help you. Once upon a time there was a high-class crook—what the newspapers call a Mastermind. Came a day when he found he had accumulated enough money to give up the game and settle down as an honest man.

"But he had two lieutenants—one in New York and one in San Francisco—and they were the only men in the world who knew he was a crook. And, besides that, he was afraid of both of them. So he thought he'd rest easier if they were out of the way. And it happened that neither of these lieutenants had ever seen the other.

"So this Mastermind convinced each of them that the other was double-crossing him and would have to be bumped off for the safety of all concerned. And both of them fell for it. The New Yorker went to San Francisco to get the other, and the San Franciscan was told that the New Yorker would arrive on such-and-such a day and would stay at such-and-such a hotel.

"The Mastermind figured that there was an even chance of both men passing out when they met—and he was nearly right at that. But he was sure that one would die, and then, even if the other missed hanging, there would only be one man left for him to dispose of later."

There weren't as many details in the story as I would have liked to have, but it explained a lot.

"How do you figure out Cudner's getting the wrong room?" I asked.

"That was funny! Maybe it happened like this: My room was 609 and the killing was done in 906. Suppose Cudner went to the hotel on the day he knew I was due and took a quick slant at the register. He wouldn't want to be seen looking at it if he could avoid it, so he didn't turn it around but flashed a look at it as it lay —facing the desk.

"When you read numbers of three figures upside-down you have to transpose them in your head to get them straight. Like 1-2-3. You'd get that 3-2-1, and then turn them around in your head. That's what Cudner did with mine. He was keyed up, of course, thinking of the job ahead of him, and he overlooked the fact that 609 upside-down still reads 609 just the same. So he turned it around and made it 906—Develyn's room."

"That's how I doped it," I said, "and I reckon it's about right. And then he looked at the key rack and saw that 906 wasn't there. So he thought he might just as well get his job done right then, when he could roam the hotel corridors without attracting attention. Of course, he may have gone up to the room before Ansley and Develyn came in and waited for them, but I doubt it.

"I think it more likely that he simply happened to arrive at the hotel a few minutes after they had come in. Ansley was probably alone in the room when Cudner opened the unlocked door and came in—Develyn being in the bathroom getting the glasses.

"Ansley was about your size and age, and close enough in appearance to fit a rough description of you. Cudner went for him, and then Develyn, hearing the scuffle, dropped the bottle and glasses, rushed out, and got his.

"Cudner, being the sort he was, would figure that two murders were no worse than one, and he wouldn't want to leave any witnesses around.

"And that is probably how Ingraham got into it. He was passing on his way from his room to the elevator and perhaps heard the racket and investigated. And Cudner put a gun in his face and made him stow the two bodies in the clothespress. And then he stuck his knife in Ingraham's back and slammed the door on him. That's about the—"

An indignant nurse descended on me, from behind and ordered me out of the room, accusing me of getting her patient excited.

Orrett stopped me as I turned to go.

"Keep your eye on the New York dispatches," he said, "and maybe you'll get the rest of the story. It's not over yet. Nobody has anything on me out here. That shooting in Pigatti's was self-defense so far as I'm concerned. And as soon as I'm on my feet again and can get back East there's going to be a Mastermind holding a lot of lead. That's a promise!"

I believed him.

Hammett in *Black Mask*

1922–1930

Series characters: The Continental Op (CO)
Ned Beaumont (NB)

*—indicates use as basis for published novel
•—included in *The* Black Mask *Boys*

"The Road Home" (as "Peter Collinson") December 1922
"The Vicious Circle" (as "Collinson") 15 June 1923
"Arson Plus" (as "Collinson") (CO) 1 October 1923
"Slippery Fingers" (as "Collinson") (CO) 15 October 1923
"Crooked Souls" (CO) 15 October 1923
"It" (CO) 1 November 1923
"The Second-Story Angel" 15 November 1923
•"Bodies Piled Up" (CO) 1 December 1923
"The Tenth Clew" (CO) 1 January 1924
"The Man Who Killed Dan Odams" 15 January 1924
"Night Shots" (CO) 1 February 1924
"The New Racket" 15 February 1924
"Afraid of a Gun" 1 March 1924
"Zigzags of Treachery" (CO) 1 March 1924
"One Hour" (CO) 1 April 1924
"The House in Turk Street" (CO) 15 April 1924
"The Girl With the Silver Eyes" (CO) June 1924
"Women, Politics and Murder" (CO) September 1924
"The Golden Horseshoe" (CO) November 1924
"Mike or Alec or Rufus" (CO) January 1925
"The Whosis Kid" (CO) March 1925

"The Scorched Face" (CO)   May 1925
"Finger-Prints" (nonfiction)   June 1925
"Corkscrew" (CO)   September 1925
"Dead Yellow Women" (CO)   November 1925
"The Gutting of Couffignal" (CO)   December 1925
"The Nails in Mr. Cayterer"   January 1926
"The Assistant Murderer"   February 1926
"Creeping Siamese" (CO)   March 1926
*"The Big Knock-Over" (CO)   February 1927
*"$106,000 Blood Money" (CO)   May 1927
"The Main Death" (CO)   June 1927
*"The Cleansing of Poisonville" (CO)   November 1927
*"Crime Wanted—Male or Female" (CO)   December 1927
*"Dynamite" (CO)   January 1928
*"The 19th Murder" (CO)   February 1928
*"Black Lives" (CO)   November 1928
*"The Hollow Temple" (CO)   December 1928
*"Black Honeymoon" (CO)   January 1929
*"Black Riddle" (CO)   February 1929
"Fly Paper" (CO)   August 1929
*"The Maltese Falcon" Five-parter   September, October, November, December 1929, January 1930
"The Farewell Murder" (CO)   February 1930
*"The Glass Key" (NB)   March 1930
*"The Cyclone Shot" (NB)   April 1930
*"Dagger Point" (NB)   May 1930
*"The Shattered Key" (NB)   June 1930
"Death and Company" (CO)   November 1930

Published Hammett Novels Derived from *Black Mask*

Red Harvest—New York: Knopf, 1929
   (Derived from "The Cleansing of Poisonville," "Crime Wanted—Male or Female," "Dynamite," "The 19th Murder")
The Dain Curse—New York: Knopf, 1929
   (Derived from "Black Lives," "The Hollow Temple," "Black Honeymoon," "Black Riddle")
The Maltese Falcon—New York: Knopf, 1930

(Derived from the five-part serial)

The Glass Key—New York: Knopf, 1931
(Derived from "The Glass Key," "The Cyclone Shot," "Dagger Point," "The Shattered Key")

Blood Money—New York: World, 1943
(Derived from "The Big Knock-Over," "$106,000 Blood Money")

Behind the Mask:
Erle Stanley Gardner

•

His friends called him "Uncle Erle." Short and stocky, Gardner radiated virile, restless energy. Throughout his long professional career, he thought of himself as "a lawyer who wrote" rather than as a writer who had practiced law. Perry Mason was his fictional alter ego, once described by Gardner as "a fighter . . . possessed of infinite patience."

This description precisely fits Erle Stanley Gardner. Few writers ever fought harder to succeed; none surpassed Gardner's ingenuity and determination in building a career that would eventually see him outsell every writer in the world, certainly every mystery writer. Readers have purchased well over 315 million of Gardner's books, and they have been translated into thirty-two languages. Erle Stanley Gardner was far more than a popular writer; he was a phenomenon.

"On my father's side I am descended from hardy New England stock," he declared. "My forebears were the captains of windjammers, whalers . . . out of Nantucket . . . clippers which . . . sailed the Seven Seas."

He was born on July 17, 1889, in Malden, Massachusetts, to Grace Waugh and Charles W. Gardner. Erle was the second of three sons. His father took the family to Portland, Oregon, when the boy was ten, where the elder Gardner worked as a civil engineer. After three years there, they headed into the Klondike, where Charles Gardner was employed as a mining engineer. Then it was California, with the family settling into the small gold-mining town of Oroville. Charles Gardner practiced his trade there as young Erle entered high school.

Erle later described himself as "the family black sheep," and his school record certainly verified his restlessness. As Alva Johnston describes him in *The Case of Erle Stanley Gardner*: "He wouldn't take any nonsense from the school authorities and was expelled for spending too much time cartooning a long-chinned disciplinarian."

He was finally suspended from Oroville High School. (Among other pranks, he had helped organize unlicensed boxing matches in the area.)

Charles sent him to school in Palo Alto, in the Bay Area, where Erle managed to graduate. Things seemed calmer—until he entered Indiana's Valparaiso University to study law in the autumn of 1909. He lasted less than a month. The reason for his abrupt departure involved a boxing fiasco in his dormitory, during which a professor was "knocked flat." A warrant was issued by the university for Gardner's arrest. Erle skipped town, as he put it, "just one jump ahead of the sheriff."

He worked in a railroad construction camp in Eugene, Oregon, that year, but his fascination with the law drew him back to California. He obtained work as a clerk in the office of E. E. Keech in Santa Ana. After work he devoted his free time to preparation for the bar exam, spending fifty hours a week studying law.

"In those days you didn't need a college degree to become a lawyer," he stated. "I was admitted to the bar at twenty-one—and recall that I had two black eyes [from boxing] the day I was admitted."

By 1911 Erle had moved to Ventura County, "where I hung out my shingle with the corporation law firm of I. W. Stewart in Oxnard." Although just twelve miles from the county seat of Ventura, Oxnard was a wide-open, brawling town of saloons and brothels—with its own bustling Chinatown district.

Always the maverick, Gardner decided that the Chinese were not getting proper representation in court. After winning an important case for them, he became— to the chagrin of his colleagues—*the* lawyer for the entire Chinese community of Oxnard. Erle vigorously defended and won acquittals for Chinatown clients who were, as he put it, "only guilty of a little gambling among themselves." He claimed at the time that gambling was common within the town's leading white fraternal organizations, "but the police leave *them* alone."

In Oxnard, Gardner was now considered to be a legal pariah, and he took a perverse delight in having alienated the district attorney, the local police, and the city council.

A lifelong pattern was forming: his willingness to fight for the underdog against superior legal odds.

In 1912 Erle fell in love with Natalie Talbert, who worked in the same law office. They were married in early April, and a year later their daughter (Grace) was born. A father at twenty-three, Gardner decided that he should provide "some solid security" for his family. The small fees he'd been earning from the Chinese community in Oxnard were no longer adequate.

Therefore, in 1915, he entered into a law partnership with Frank Orr in Ventura (some seventy-five miles north of Los Angeles). The two men became lifelong friends—and Orr later declared that "Erle was an amazing lawyer":

> In behalf of his clients, he nosed about in forgotten statutes . . . to find just the right precedents to fit his needs . . . It got so he won all his court cases

[and] no one who had known him as a lawyer ever had to look far . . . **to** find where Perry Mason came from.

After two years with Orr, Gardner took "an extended leave" to try his hand as president of a sales organization, a roving salesman, supplying parts to manufacturing plants in several states west of the Rockies. He gained valuable sales technique, which he later used in dealing with editors and publishers.

However, by 1921, the Depression hit the Consolidated Sales Company and Erle was "dead broke." He hastily resumed his law practice with Frank Orr.

In court, Gardner's exceptional memory helped him win. "I almost never forgot the point made in a legal decision I had read, and I could listen to the testimony of witnesses by the hour and recall almost verbatim what each witness had said."

Still looking for a way to earn additional money, Gardner became aware of the burgeoning pulp field. Fiction magazines of every variety were crowding the newsstands. He thought he might "try producing a few stories." At thirty-one, he approached the job of writing as "just another branch of the sales game." A story was a commodity, a piece of goods to be offered in the marketplace.

He began by selling two "racy" fiction tales to *Breezy Stories* (racy only by 1921 standards). Gardner delightedly reported that his mother, a devout Methodist, had been deeply shocked by the title of one of these, "Nellie's Naughty Nightie."

After this brisk beginning, Gardner was unable to make another sale for the next two years. Professional fiction writing was far more difficult than he had anticipated. Gardner later declared that in this early stage of his career "my stories were terrible . . . I didn't know how to plot [and] I had no natural aptitude as a writer."

Since he was still practicing law under his own name, he decided to utilize the pseudonym of "Charles M. Green" for his fiction. In mid-1923 Gardner submitted a novelette to *Black Mask* under this pen name. "It was dreadful," recalled Gardner. "Even the *title* was dreadful. I called it 'The Shrieking Skeleton.' "

Phil Cody read Gardner's novelette and wrote a strong note to editor George Sutton listing all the things wrong with it. The story was rejected. However, Cody's note was accidentally returned with the manuscript. Gardner studied Cody's comments, then spent three nights revising the story. Sutton bought the revised draft, and "The Shrieking Skeleton" was printed in *Black Mask*. Gardner figured he had "cracked a new market."

But when Sutton stepped aside and Cody became editor of the *Mask*, he began rejecting all Gardner stories. It was Harry North who took a personal interest in the new writer; the associate editor supplied editorial tips for story revisions and suggested that the Charles Green pseudonym be dropped. Gardner soon began appearing regularly in *Mask* under his own name and credited North with "expert guidance."

As a friend of that period declared: "It was Harry North who launched Erle's career. Without North, he might have given up fiction."

In his fifth story for *Mask*, Gardner created his first pulp-series character, Bob Larkin, an amateur juggler who used a billiard cue as a weapon against villains. During this same period, for *Top Notch*, he was also writing about Speed Dash, a character known as "The Human Fly," since he was able to climb tall buildings with ease.

In all, during the years he wrote for the pulps, Gardner created three dozen separate series characters, including gunslinger Black Barr (for *Black Mask*), gentleman thief Lester Leith (for *Detective Fiction Weekly*), and confidence man Paul Pry (for *Gang World*). Gardner enjoyed thinking up offbeat names for his characters. Among his favorites: Fish Mouth McGinnis; Go Get 'Em Garver; Sidney Zoom; and Ed Migrane, the Headache.

His most enduring pulp character was Ed Jenkins, known as "The Phantom Crook," who first appeared in *Black Mask* during January of 1925. Jenkins was a social outcast, working beyond the law, pursued by police *and* criminals. Gardner kept him running through *Black Mask* for eighteen years, into 1943. Rated as one of the magazine's top favorites in reader polls, Jenkins was featured in seventy-three adventures.

Gardner was a tireless worker, turning out reams of material for a staggering variety of pulps. "It's a wonder I didn't kill myself with overwork," he later admitted. "Under my own name, and a dozen others, I [averaged] a full novelette every third day. . . . For ten years I kept up this pace of a hundred thousand words a month."

He did it on just three hours' sleep each night, working at his law profession by day, reading in the law library each evening, then typing into the dawn on his pulp fiction. It is doubtful that any writer in history ever matched this incredible ten-year performance.

Gardner and Phil Cody eventually became good friends, and it was Cody who suggested that Gardner contact a New York agent, Robert Hardy, in 1925. "I've never been mediocre in anything I've done," Gardner wrote to Hardy that year. "I want to either go to the top in the fiction game or quit it altogether."

Hardy responded by selling a million words of Gardner in 1926—a total of ninety-seven sales, twenty-six of them to *Black Mask*.

Now Joe Shaw had entered the scene as Gardner's new editor at the *Mask*. He valued the reader popularity that Gardner's fiction had earned and regularly featured the Ed Jenkins stories.

In the tradition of his adventurous ancestors, Gardner loved to travel, and a trip to China, in 1931, resulted in the creation of a new world-roving series hero, Major Brane, for *Argosy*.

But despite his enormous success in the pulps, Gardner, at forty-three, was becoming frustrated. Seeking a wider market for his fiction, he tackled his first full-length novel. Its protagonist was a tough young troubleshooting lawyer.

The novel didn't sell. Even Joe Shaw turned it down for *Mask*. Stubbornly, Gardner wrote a second novel featuring the same character. In November of 1932, both novels were purchased for book publication by William Morrow and Company. With this sale, Gardner acquired a new editor and a lifelong friend in Morrow president Thayer Hobson.

The tough young lawyer in Gardner's first two novels had originally been called Stark, then Keene, but these names didn't satisfy Hobson. By publication of the first Gardner novel (in March of 1933), the problem had been solved, and the public was introduced to Perry Mason in *The Case of the Velvet Claws*.

Actually, Mason's direct prototype was born in the pages of *Black Mask* in 1932 —when Gardner created a young fighting attorney from New York named Ken Corning. But by the summer of 1933, Corning's career was over and Perry Mason's was just beginning.

The second Mason novel, *The Case of the Sulky Girl*, was released that September—and Gardner knew he had struck gold. Over the next thirty-seven years he wrote another eighty Mason novels, establishing the fighting lawyer as a household word around the globe.

In 1970 social historian Russell Nye declared that Gardner was "the most widely read of all American writers." He reported that the first Mason novel had sold 28 million copies in its first fifteen years, and that "he is the most widely translated author in the world."

Perry Mason worked out of a modest law office in downtown Los Angeles with his ever-loyal secretary, Della Street. Based in part on Gardner's own real-life secretary, Jean Bethell, Street was the ideal companion for Mason. But she was all business. On occasion, during the series, Perry asked her to become his wife, but she always refused. Love and law didn't mix.

The Mason book titles evolved out of Gardner's pulp writing; in 1925 he had used the title "The Case of the Misplaced Thumbs" on a Speed Dash novelette. When the first two Perry Mason titles proved successful, Gardner decided to follow the same title format with each new book.

Perry Mason began as a tough guy. Mystery expert Francis Nevins claims that the first nine Mason novels were "steeped in the hard-boiled tradition of *Black Mask*" and that the early Mason was "a tiger . . . willing to take any risk for a client." He quotes Mason as saying, "I am a paid gladiator."

Gardner himself saw his early Masons as being firmly in the *Mask* tradition, and was actually concerned that he was suffering from "the Hammett influence." Regarding his third novel, *The Case of the Lucky Legs*, he declared that it "carries on the . . . idea of smash-bang action which is really the basis of Perry Mason's exploits."

In these early novels Mason was much closer to a typical *Black Mask* private eye than to the settled court lawyer he later became. Frank Robbins in "The World of Perry Mason" wrote, "Perry is constantly placing himself in jeopardy of disbarment or even criminal prosecution. His irregularities are many and various." From his exploits in these novels, Mason *could* have been convicted of withholding and destroying evidence, breaking and entering, reckless driving, etc.

By the close of 1933, after twenty-two years of active practice, Gardner had all but abandoned law. He needed the time to pursue his new career as a novelist, since Thayer Hobson was projecting an ambitious schedule of four books per year.

Perry Mason entered the motion-picture arena in the mid-1930s with the Warner Bros. release of a series of films starring Warren William in the title role.

Gardner was quite upset with Hollywood over these productions. "They ruined Mason. He had an acre of office and Della was so dazzling I couldn't see her for diamonds. Everybody drank a lot." However, Warner produced only six pictures.

In order to "gain a working knowledge of the film industry," Gardner purchased a home in Hollywood early in 1935. By then, his wife Natalie was living in Oakland; the couple had separated permanently.

A year later Gardner needed money. He responded to this financial crisis by creating another new series character for *Country Gentleman* magazine, a small-town district attorney named Doug Selby (writing the first of nine Selby novels in 1936).

In 1937 the *Saturday Evening Post* provided a welcome influx of cash with its serialization of *The Case of the Lame Canary*. Gardner was jubilant; he had been trying to break into the *Post* "in a big way" for years. Now he'd achieved this major breakthrough.

Beyond his love for writing and law, Erle Gardner was an enthusiastic outdoorsman, seriously involved with archery as a sport. He was also a vigorous tennis player, horseman, golfer, and wild-life photographer. In a camp wagon of his own design, he was constantly "on the prod," exploring remote parts of the Southwest.

In the autumn of 1937, roaming through the back country of California, Gardner discovered his personal dream ranch, 150 acres of wilderness at Temecula, framed by the San Bernardino mountains, some 100 miles southeast of Los Angeles.

"It was love at first sight," he later recalled. "I'd been looking for a place to work —far away from everything and everybody."

He named it Rancho del Paisano and immediately began improving the property. (Eventually, Gardner would expand the ranch to 3,000 acres.)

Gardner's biographer, Dorothy B. Hughes, summed up some of the many changes:

> The Rancho began to grow, as did all Erle's projects. He built a study for his books and papers . . . an office building was next. In time there were houses for permanent residents, houses for guests, any number of [new] buildings for trucks and cars and ranch equipment . . . fireproof vaults for Erle's papers . . . [and an] electric light plant . . .

In all, twenty-seven new buildings were added during the years Gardner lived there, yet, incredibly, he refused to allow a telephone to be installed until 1951. He resented the "damned annoyance" of incoming calls.

Gardner's "stalwart right arm" was his secretary-companion, Jean Bethell, who had been working with him for many years. Jean and her two sisters, Ruth and Peggy, transcribed hours of Gardner's dictation, typing his manuscripts and answering the heavy volume of mail. A reporter once asked Gardner when and why he switched from the typewriter to the Dictaphone. "To save time, I was dictating all my court cases," he replied. "Then I realized I could do the same thing with fiction. Worked like a charm. Now I can dictate a whole Mason novel in four days."

Gardner was criticized by book reviewers for his lack of in-depth characterization and for his heavy dependence on dialogue. The Perry Mason novels are almost entirely devoid of descriptive writing.

Francis Nevins came to Gardner's defense in his analysis of the series:

> What vivifies these novels is [their] sheer readability, breakneck pacing, the involuted plots, firework displays of courtroom tactics, (many based on gimmicks Gardner used in his own law practice) and the dialogue, when each line is a jab in a complex form of oral combat.

Gardner enjoyed setting new creative challenges for himself. When he wrote *The Bigger They Come,* in 1938, he launched yet another book series under the name of "A. A. Fair"—featuring the adventures of Cool and Lam, a pair of offbeat private detectives.

Bertha Cool was a hefty 165-pound widow in her sixties who joined forces with disbarred lawyer Donald Lam, an energetic little man weighing in at a wispy 127 pounds. (From 1939 through 1970, Gardner produced twenty-nine books concerning this bizarre detective team.) A. A. Fair soon earned his own loyal readership, and the novels sold briskly.

Despite his success with published books, Gardner had not yet abandoned pulp writing. In the late 1930s, for *Black Mask,* he created a new series character, Pete Wennick. A combination of clerk and detective, Wennick worked in a law office (a job directly out of Gardner's past) and solved crimes in his off hours.

By December of 1938, Gardner had been hired by MGM Studios to write a Nick Carter film at a salary of $1,500 per week. When the film was scrapped, Gardner happily returned to his prose. He didn't like screenwriting and vowed he would do no more scripting. Luckily, he didn't have to.

America entered the mass-market paperback era in 1940, and a new financial door was opened for popular authors. Gardner's easy-to-read, fast-paced mystery novels were ideal for the vast, waiting paperback audience, and they sold so rapidly that Erle Stanley Gardner's financial future was assured.

Pulp magazines were slowly dying under the onslaught of the rapidly proliferating paperbacks, and by 1943 Gardner had abandoned the pulps entirely. His last "rough-paper" tale appeared in *Black Mask* in September of that year. With better than one hundred stories in *Mask,* he had written more fiction for the magazine than any other author. In fact, Gardner's sales record in the pulp market over his twenty-two-year span was nothing short of phenomenal: 550 stories (most of them novelettes) to more than three dozen magazines.

Radio now offered another rich source of income. The Perry Mason radio show made its debut for CBS in October of 1943 (and remained on the air for twelve years). Gardner functioned as an active adviser as he listened to each half-hour show, monitoring the entire series from his ranch in Temecula.

This steady inflow of cash allowed Gardner to indulge his passion for travel and exploration. In 1947 he began a series of expeditions into the interior of Baja California, a wild and beautiful area stretching along the Gulf of California for 1,200 miles. Based on his trip into this primitive land of rock, sand, and mountains, Gardner wrote his first travel book, *The Land of Shorter Shadows*, published the following year.

He would write a dozen others, four of which chronicled subsequent trips into the Baja peninsula and the California desert.

As his income increased, Gardner began acquiring an impressive variety of properties—houses at Oceanside and Palm Springs, a place at Lake Shasta, a small date ranch in the desert, and another home near the mountain village of Idyllwild. Plus five house trailers, a cruiser, and two houseboats!

Added to all these were Gardner's beloved animals: birds, dogs, horses, a chipmunk—even a baby coyote named Bravo which he tamed as a pet.

During the 1948–1958 decade an important new project began to dominate Gardner's life. He established what he called "The Court of Last Resort." Its purpose was to reopen criminal cases in which innocent men and women had been wrongly convicted.

Gardner formed his "court" from a volunteer selection of outstanding talents, all of them legal, forensic, and penal experts. They agreed to review special cases involving an apparent miscarriage of justice—and their work resulted in the release of many unjustly imprisoned individuals.

For Erle Gardner, it was a personal crusade. He wrote more than seventy-five articles based on these cases for *Argosy* magazine, becoming a self-taught authority in scientific methods of crime detection.

As Dorothy Hughes observed:

He studied forensic medicine, polygraph work, and criminal psychology [and could] hold his own in discussions of the subjects with professionals in the field. . . . The impact Gardner made [in this decade] on the administration of justice cannot be overemphasized . . . [and] what he accomplished in the area of prison reform was notable.

By the mid-1950s the popularity of Gardner's Perry Mason novels convinced network executives that a Mason television show could be a winner. (At their height, his books were selling at the rate of 20,000 copies a day!)

Inquiries were made. Would Mr. Gardner accept a flat price of one million dollars for television rights to Perry Mason? No, Mr. Gardner would not. Mr. Gardner intended to produce his own TV show.

This intense network interest in Mason had inspired Gardner to form Paisano Productions, in partnership with "the secretaries who had been with me for thirty-five years and who knew the characters intimately, and Cornwell and Gail Patrick Jackson, who also knew the characters over a period of some fifteen or twenty years."

Gail Patrick Jackson negotiated an unbelievable contract which resulted in the phenomenal Perry Mason series which is still being rerun here and abroad.

Writers were hired to provide sample scripts. When Gardner read these he fired off an angry letter regarding TV writers to his editor pal Thayer Hobson: "Each and every one of them wants to change Perry Mason. [They call it] 'adapting the character to television.' . . . It is the god-damndest assortment of crap ever witnessed. Mason becomes a smart aleck, a wisecracker, a man who looks upon murder only as an opportunity for a new quip."

It took Gardner and his partners a full year to "whip the thing into shape." By then, Gardner had personally chosen Raymond Burr for the title role; Barbara Hale would portray Della Street, with William Talman as the luckless D.A. who always lost to Mason in court.

The show made its debut over CBS in late September of 1957. A solid hit, it ran for nine years—271 episodes—with Gardner as "watchdog" on every script. There were many shouted arguments during the life of the show, with Gardner and Gail Patrick holding ground against a host of proposed "improvements." Gardner would angrily inform network executives: "I know something about what the public wants—and a hell of a lot about what the public *doesn't* want!"

When this hugely successful series finally ended, in the spring of 1966, Gardner took off for another Baja adventure. At seventy-seven, he refused to slow down. "Erle was determined not to be shaken up by the fact that he was getting old," said a friend. "He just *ignored* his age."

However, Gardner *was* deeply shaken by the news of Thayer Hobson's death a year later. And in February of 1968, Natalie Gardner succumbed to a heart attack.

Although his health was failing, on August 7, 1968, Erle and Jean were wed in Carson City, Nevada. The man who called himself "the Fiction Factory" was dying. Erle was suffering from terminal cancer, a disease he'd been careful to hide from his friends. Cobalt treatment had failed to halt the cancer's growth.

By late February of 1970 the end was clearly in sight. Doctors told him that they could do nothing more to prolong his life.

"I don't want to die in a damn hospital," Gardner complained. "I want to go home—to my ranch."

The arrangements were made.

On March 11, 1970, Erle Stanley Gardner died at his ranch in Temecula, with his wife beside him. He was eighty years old.

Jean had his ashes scattered over Baja California.

Hell's Kettle

In a 1927 issue of the *Mask*, editor Joe Shaw described Ed Jenkins to his readers as "a real he-man, with human weaknesses and strength. For earlier misdeeds, Ed is branded as a crook and the fetters of his former reputation still hang about him . . . [He is] suspected by the police and, apparently, is an easy mark for the Underworld."

"Hell's Kettle" was the centerpiece in a linked trilogy of stories showing how the Phantom Crook smashed a local crime ring, using his wits and a specialized talent for disguise.

The story's explosion-filled climax proves that Erle Stanley Gardner was capable of descriptive action-adventure writing at its most graphic. This slam-bang narrative will surprise readers who know Gardner only for his later, more cerebral Perry Mason novels, in which description is practically nonexistent and action is generally confined to explosive dialogue in a courtroom.

Gardner related directly to Jenkins and once described him as "five feet seven and a quarter inches tall"—which was Erle Gardner's exact height! The author was, in fact, so fond of his popular *Black Mask* character that long after he had quit writing for the magazine (and a full decade after its expiration) he brought Jenkins back for a final bow in the slick pages of *Argosy* in 1961. (This was thirty-six years after Gardner had introduced Jenkins in the *Mask*.)

Here then, for the first time anywhere since it was printed in a 1930 issue, is "Hell's Kettle," a rousing, bullet-blasted adventure of the Phantom Crook at his toughest.

HELL'S KETTLE

Series character: Ed Jenkins

The morning sun struggled through the cobweb-covered window. The sickly yellow oblong that fell upon the bare floor was a jaundiced imitation of sunlight.

I was cold. My limbs were cramped from a night on the bare floor. My bones ached. My nostrils rebelled at the stench of the place, at the smell of my own clothing.

For I was disguised as a Chinaman of the lower class, and the building was an abandoned, condemned community house, given over to rats, cockroaches, cobwebs, smells.

I was wanted for first degree murder. As far as the police knew, Ed Jenkins, the Phantom Crook, arrested for murder, had escaped after being arrested. They didn't know of a confidential conversation I had had with the district attorney in which that official had told me he knew I was innocent, but that he had important work for me. Because he had found corruption in his own force and knew not whom to trust, he asked me to escape from the police and undertake a dangerous mission.

That mission was for me to go into the underworld as a fugitive from justice and prevent gangdom from organizing. I was not to detect crime. I was to prevent it. My weapons were to be my own wits. Pitted against me were the police who didn't know the secret, on the one hand, the underworld on the other.

It was not a happy situation.

I had made my first step the night before—my escape from the police—and it was spectacular enough to be convincing. Therefore the hideout.

I descended the rickety stairs, shuffled along the sidewalks, slapping my feet with the shuffling gait of a Chinaman. No one accosted me.

Money I had in plenty, and one can do much with money if one knows the ropes. Years of bitter experience had taught me the ropes.

By noon I had leased a rambling old house which had been cut up into two flats. As Doctor Chew, a Chinese herb doctor and fortune-teller, I had the lower floor. As Colonel Grayson I had the upper floor. There was a connecting stairway. I could shift instantly from one personality to another.

I chose the personality of Doctor Chew with which to start my work against the organized criminals. An ability to speak the Cantonese dialect like a native, strips of adhesive tape under a skullcap, drawing my eyes in a slant, a quickly removable face stain, Chinese silk clothes, all made me feel reasonably certain "Doctor" Chew would never be suspected by the police as being Ed Jenkins, the Phantom Crook.

The flats were furnished. They were on the outskirts of the business district, a neighborhood of cheap stores and unrepaired dwellings. Another year and the residences would be torn down for apartment houses or stores. In the meantime no one cared to make repairs or lease except with a cancellation clause. All of which suited my purpose. I had only to sign for water, gas, electricity and telephone service, move in, and I was ready to go to work.

Generally, I knew the criminal hookup of the city. There were three powerful gangsters. The Full Dress Kid was the most dramatic, the most dangerous. "Slick" Williams came next. Harry "the Hun" was third.

Rumor had it that The Full Dress Kid planned a coup.

I looked up the telephone number of the Quaker Candy Kitchen. An underworld tip had whispered that this was merely another name for Lena Skison, the consort of Slick Williams. She was known throughout gangdom as "Lean Lena."

I gave the number a ring.

"Lena?"

"Yeah. Who's talkin'?"

"Doctor Chew."

"Doctor Chew? Never heard of you. How'd you get this number, an' what d'you want?"

"I called," I said, speaking in the lilting singsong with which an educated Chinaman masters the English language, "to warn of evil. The day is evil. The night will be evil. Your soul have much misfortune upon this day. One you love walks into danger. Much treachery. Death come very close. You be wise trust nobody today—"

And I gave a half strangled cry in the middle of the sentence, and slammed the receiver back on the hook.

I knew she would trace the call through the name I had given her. I was playing with dynamite, but one cannot blast mountains without touching gunpowder.

I sat and racked my brains for underworld gossip, and thought of Police Captain Arthur Fuller. He had been shaking down the gangsters. Recently it was whispered that he and The Full Dress Kid were negotiating a treaty.

I wrote a letter to Fuller, and I signed that letter with the picture of a human eye done in red ink. It was a type of letter well calculated to cause uneasiness to a crooked police captain. It was just another monkey wrench in the machinery of gang activities. If I dropped enough monkey wrenches I'd get action.

I mailed the letter personally, then spent three hours talking with a nitwitted attendant of a parking station across from the house I had leased. That talk enabled me to lay a foundation for future visits, and from the parking station I could watch the front door of my house.

I expected Lena. No one came. At dusk I gave it up, disappointed. I would have to try some other method of establishing connections.

I bid my parking station friend good-bye, promised to bring him some herbs for a complaint he had described to me at great length, shuffled across the street, and entered my flat.

There was the rustle of motion. A figure glided through the half darkness as a trout glides through the shadow of a deep pool. I reached for the light switch, pressed the button.

Lights flared.

The girl who looked at me over the blued steel of a heavy-caliber revolver was rather young. Under other circumstances she might have been pretty. Now her face was distorted with various emotions.

I stood still, hands upraised. My respect for Lean Lena went up a notch.

"Don't start anything!" she warned.

"You want see Doctor Chew?"

"Never mind what I want. Keep your mitts up in the air or you'll get perforated like a bank check."

I raised my hands higher.

"There is about you," I intoned, "a cloud of misfortune."

"Horsefeathers!"

"You should not have come," I said, making my voice the soft singsong of a better class of Chinese, one who talks good English, yet retains the soft accent of his native race. "Today unfortunate one for you."

She snarled, and the thin lips twisted back from her teeth.

"Applesauce!"

"For you and people you love," I went on. "Today much misfortune. Today much treachery."

"Boloney!"

"Evil spirits come close. Black cloud above your head. Much trouble, heap much trouble. I see death. . . . You drink tea with me. We talk."

And I reached calmly for the alcohol stove, the teapot, took some herbs from a rack.

She laughed in my face.

"Yeah, I'd be a sap to drink the stuff you concocted. Get your hands up, damn you! Let's see who you are!"

This was more than I had bargained for.

If her hands shifted that skullcap, my secret would be exposed. What would she do with The Phantom Crook, self-confessed murderer, dabbler into the affairs of gangdom?

I tensed my muscles.

But she did not touch me. She kept just out of my reach, her icy blue eyes blazing into my features.

"What in hell do you know about what's going on?"

I made a gesture with my palms.

"I know you not. I do not know your name. Yet much I can see. Can see black clouds of evil over you. Can see treachery. Can see . . ."

"Well, you can see too damn much. Get your feet under you, because you're going for a ride."

Those icy eyes meant business.

I got to my feet.

Lena indicated the way toward the door, came in behind me with the gun.

An automobile had come up and was waiting in front.

There were two men in the back, well-dressed young men who might have been staid businessmen, but weren't. They were typical gangsters, quick of eye and motion, almost conservative in their dress, well tailored, ominously quiet in their manners.

One of them stepped to the curb and held the door open. His empty hands were in sight. But the other man kept both of his hands just below the edge of the car frame, just out of sight. From the angle of his shoulders, I knew that each hand held a gun.

Nor did I care to resist. I wanted to get in touch with Slick Williams. After that I'd trust to my wits to see me through.

I entered the automobile. Twin guns jammed into my sides. The girl started the motor and did the driving. We went rapidly, apparently to some predetermined destination. There was not a word said.

The car came to a stop in an alley.

There was no one within sight. The man on my right gave a tug at my arm. I stepped out. It was dark now, and I made a single swift survey of the alley, planning a way of escape, should escape seem advisable.

The girl slid out from behind the steering wheel.

A door banged open behind her.

"They got Slick," said a voice from the shadows.

The girl stiffened.

"What're you talkin' about?"

But her voice broke in spite of herself.

"Sure, Lena, I'm givin' it to you straight. They got Slick, an' they got Harry the Hun. How it happened we don't know, but a pinch was made by four harness bulls. They drove Slick and Harry away with 'em. Then there was some noises heard in a vacant garage. A guy that happened to be passing saw something suspicious. Harry the Hun and Slick Williams were in there."

She swayed back against a fender of the car. I could see her mouth writhing in grief, but her eyes were steady. For perhaps ten seconds the little group was motionless. Then she turned back to the car.

"Pile in," she said to me.

One of the men muttered a question.

"Back to his joint," she said, and her voice was tigerish in its fierce intensity. "This bird has got something, and I'm going through his place with a fine-toothed comb."

"Will the beautiful white lady permit me to talk?"

"Shut up!"

The car clattered into motion. Her driving showed she was nervous, but she said never a word. Guns continued to bore into my back and side. I sat very still.

Back at the house I had leased the woman got out. One of the men remained in the car. The other one escorted me to the door.

"Open it," said Lena.

I unlocked the door.

"Frisk the joint from cellar to garret, Bob."

I started to protest.

"Shut up!"

She led me into the study I had fitted up that afternoon. It was a riot of soft silks, incense smoke, a crystal, a few statues.

She looked around the place.

"Moved in today."

I listened.

"Thought you'd be pretty slick, telephoning me and then hanging up. But I traced you. Doctor Chew, eh? Well, I went to the electric light company, and their records showed me that you'd signed up today and gave me the address. And now you'll tell me just how you got that tip of yours, and how you happened to know where to telephone it."

To tell her I had been playing a bluff just to establish a point of contact would have done no good. Fate had taken a hand in the game, and I had prophesied not wisely but too well.

I pointed to the glass crystal.

"Horseradish!" she said.

The gangster glanced at her, she at him. Of a sudden, decision flashed over her features.

"All right then, Doctor Chew. Sit down there and take a peek in your glass ball again, and see something that's goin' to happen. An' do it damn quick, or you're goin' out like a light. This is the best place to have it happen."

The gangster got his weapon in sight.

"Wait a second, Bob. Let's see what sort of a line he has."

Perhaps they were bluffing. I doubted it. My prophecy had been too accurate, too gruesomely fulfilled. They were going to sift things to the bottom. But, after all, knowing what I knew, considering what I had heard, I should be able to make a fairly accurate guess as to the future. There had been treachery. That meant a plan.

I drew the crystal ball toward me and started my brain working, contemplating the simultaneous wiping out of the two leaders who had been alone in their opposition to The Full Dress Kid.

"I see great much confusion," I said, placing my face closer to the glass, as though to peer through a fog.

And I hooked my right hand so that I could scoop the heavy glass ball in a single swift gesture and send it crashing into the face of the man who held the gun on me, should it become necessary to fight it out.

"Yeah. That's boloney. See something else?"

Lena's voice was pitched high.

"Bottles," I said, "many bottles. Bottles in sacks. Many men move sacks. Men run. Men whisper. Men laugh."

The indrawing of her breath cut the silence of the incense-laden atmosphere of the room. The man who held the gun on me glanced from me to her, from her to me.

"Somebody shoot gun—one shot," I said.

"Just one?" she asked, and her words were dripping with venom and incredulity. "One is probably all you'll hear, anyway," she added, with a swift, flashing glance at the gangster.

"Just one," I intoned. "Then man who fired that shot stops shooting. He goes to others. They talk. They shake hands. Sacks are brought out. Lots sacks. Sacks different places. Some men start fight, but they quit. They laugh, shake hands, get new boss."

"Say," raged the girl, "do you s'pose The Full Dress Kid would start a hijacking expedition and our men would go over to him?"

She asked the question of the fellow who held the gun, and I noticed that he hesitated before he answered.

"Naw," he said, but his negative was all that was needed to clinch the affirmative.

She was on her feet, pacing the floor with long strides.

"This damned Chink's a fake, but he may not be making a bad guess at that. With Slick gone, the boys may figure I'm not strong enough to hold the gang together—Maybe they'd sold out before they bumped Slick. I wonder—"

She stopped.

The gangster edged toward the door.

"Wait'll I see what Bill says," he mumbled, and strode from the room.

A moment later there was the sound of an automobile slipping away from the curb. Lena made a swift spring, caught the window curtain, snatched it aside.

The taillight of the car in which the two gangsters were riding showed for a moment, then was gone.

"Well, the dirty—"

The words the girl said would have singed the silken hangings of the room had those hangings had ears. The foulest terms of abuse which the gutter could command came to the girl's lips, rasped the softly lighted atmosphere of the room.

Then she finished, sank into a chair.

The incense from the open-mouthed dragon sifted upward in smoky spirals. The light shone down upon the crystal globe.

I pushed my advantage to the limit, certain of my ground now.

"Can see traitors all about you," I intoned. "Can see boys who serve you start serve somebody else. Can see enemies instead of friends. Can see automobile. Automobile in which traitors want you ride. You go ride that car, you no come back."

I saw in her features that her world was crashing about her ears. It had only needed the treachery of the two gangsters who had come with her to my place to tell her the whole story.

"Good God!" she exclaimed, and never have I heard so much human soul-agony packed into two words.

"Much trouble," I intoned. "Yesterday many friends. Today many enemies. Yesterday you speak, many listen. Today you speak, many laugh."

"Who's the guy that's engineering the party?" she asked.

"I see man in full-dress suit. He is young; he got thin mouth, big nose. His eyes very cold."

She said nothing for a few minutes. I could see she was thinking.

"Say, listen, you," she blurted, after a moment. "You savvy Ed Jenkins? They call him Phantom Crook?"

I held my face motionless, let my eyes blink into hers with the blandness of the character I impersonated, a Chinese herb doctor of the better class.

"No savvy," I said.

"You should read the papers. He's a crook. He escaped from the police."

"No savvy."

"Well, damn it, look in that glass ball and do some savvying."

"What you want?"

"I want to get in touch with that Ed Jenkins. Listen here, Doc." She moved forward, gripped my arm with cold, taut fingers. "That guy knows more about crooks than any man in the city. And he ain't got much use for 'em.

"Now here's what happened.

"There was a gangster named Kelaney. He was going to turn state's evidence. He wrote out a confession and was to meet the district attorney. There was a leak and the big shots got tipped off.

"He blows into a Chink café with a broad. The jane gets him to hold a match to her cigarette. The lights go off. Somebody makes a sieve outa him. The broad flops, kisses his face and frisks him.

"But she doesn't get the confession. Somebody'd beat her to it. But she leaves red lipstick all over the stiff's face. Then a hophead gets the works, and he's got lipstick smeared all over *his* face.

"The bulls pick up Jenkins out at the hophead's. Jenkins was in the café when Kelaney got his. They third-degree Jenkins, and he confesses. Then he pulls one of his stunts and slips the bulls.

"Now I'm betting coin Jenkins has got that confession. The Full Dress Kid is going to wipe me out. But if I get that confession and put it where the district attorney could get it if anything happened to me I'd be good for a hundred years if my health lasted. Get me?"

I blinked at her some more.

"Maybe Jenkins no help you, then what?"

She laughed, a grim, metallic laugh.

"Listen, you. I want to find Jenkins. After that I'll either get the breaks or make 'em. That bird may slip through the fingers of the bulls, but when Lena fastens her claws on him it'll be a different story. I don't need Jenkins. I need that confession. If he holds out I'll . . ."

She raised her pointed forefinger, worked her thumb like the hammer of a gun and clicked her tongue six times.

I looked in the crystal.

"He hide," I said.

She laughed again, and that laugh did things to my spine.

"Of course he hides, you yellow-bellied fool! With the whole damned underworld on his tail and the cops with a two-time murder rap on him, he's gotta hide. If you're any damn good tell me where he is now."

I put my mouth to the glass crystal, blew my breath upon it, wiped off the moisture with the flap of my embroidered silk jacket, grunted thoughtfully.

"Sometime quick you see him. Maybe tonight," I said.

She sighed.

"Doc, I'm takin' your word for a lot. Somehow I believe you know your stuff. You've sure said a few mouthfuls. I know too much to live. They'll wipe me out.

A croaked gangster's frail is always taken for a ride—unless she switches to the other camp and Lena don't switch."

I looked into the steely glitter of her eyes and knew she spoke the truth. Lena wouldn't switch.

"You walk plenty careful," I warned.

She nodded, laughed grimly.

"Don't worry none about me, Doc. But wait till I get my claws on that confession. Then they'll be coming to me on their knees."

And she slammed the door.

I heard her steps pounding the rickety board porch, going down the stairs, thumping along the cement sidewalk. Then I locked the door and sat down to think.

I smoked a couple of cigarettes, and half decided to copy the confession and let her have the original. Lena was the only card I had left to play against The Full Dress Kid.

I thought it over for a while, decided to sleep on it. Lena should be good for at least one night, now that she was warned. In the meantime Doctor Chew had attracted enough attention for one day's work.

I walked to the back of the flat, took off the Chinese clothes, climbed the stairs, unlocked a door, adjusted my spectacles and mustache, put on a suit of tweeds that were distinctive, picked up my cane and broad-brimmed hat, and became Colonel Grayson.

A taxicab took me to the Union Depot. There, in the men's room, I did things to my disguise. When I emerged I was black mustached, dark rings under my eyes, my nose a trifle florid.

While my clothes were the same, I looked different. I was like a man in town to beat the eighteenth amendment and wanting action.

The place I picked to look for what I wanted was the Green Mill Café. That was the favorite hangout of The Full Dress Kid. I doubted if he'd be there tonight, but others might.

The orchestra was more or less out of tune. Waiters were nervous. This was a gang restaurant, and gangdom had gone far that day. Too far, perhaps.

The killing had broken the backs of the two gangs. The two leaders had lieutenants; and those lieutenants had made their arrangements previously and in secret. It only remained to remove the leaders. There had been the crash of pistol shots in that locked garage, and then action had started.

Lieutenants openly swung their allegiance. Dazed followers vacillated, considered the situation with a gun pointed at midriff, and changed their minds. The Full Dress Kid had swept all before him. Great stocks of liquor had changed hands. It had been orderly enough. The little resistance which had been made at first dissolved before the rapid shift of developments. By sundown it was all over.

Only Lena remained.

And all the underworld knew what would happen with Lean Lena. It had happened before with the women of gangsters who had been double-crossed. Those women knew too much. The spirit of resentment which is only natural in the female when her mate is escorted over the great divide by the bullet of a gangster's gun sometimes prompts a woman to talk too much. It is for the best interests of the whole underworld that such women join their mates.

The crowd in the restaurant looked up when I came in.

The part I had elected to play was that of an out-of-town "sport" who had blundered into the café.

I followed a waiter to a table, dropped into a chair, and ordered loudly that a cocktail be brought.

The waiter leaned forward, whispered. I laughed loud and long, and then the gaze of the diners shifted from me toward the door.

This time there was a slight gasp which ran around the room. It was an almost imperceptible hissing of excitement, that swift intake of breath which comes with tautened nerves.

The figure that stood in the doorway was consciously capitalizing the full dramatic value of the situation.

He was young, barely thirty. His hair was slicked back and glistened like the coat of a wet seal. He was, of course, in full evening dress. It was the boast of the Kid that he wore nothing else in the evening. He posed as a gentleman.

Knives and forks clattered, then resumed a clicking against plates. The music, which had blared into a discordant screech of timeless noise, straightened itself out and became again music to which one could dance—if one's ears were not particular.

The Full Dress Kid came in and sat down.

He was alone, ostensibly. Yet those in the know realized that the two men who preceded him, as well as the three who followed, were bodyguards. And they sat where they could watch every nook and corner of the room.

I watched the Kid.

In a little while one of the guards casually extended a hand toward him. The Kid picked a note from it, read, slowly crumpled the paper and smiled.

His eyes flickered upward for a swift instant. Then he nodded his head. The bodyguard leaned forward and growled something to the others.

As for myself, I looked in the direction in which the Kid's eyes had flickered.

I saw a table. At that table sat a woman. She had been there when I came in, and she was eating leisurely. Now I gave her a second look, and the second look led to a third.

The white hair was a wig. Those lines in the forehead were not placed there by nature. The grim look was natural. The mouth . . . It was Lena, having the temerity to come to this gaudy café on the one night when she should have been in hiding.

And, of course, for a purpose. Nor did it need a mind reader to tell what that purpose was!

Would she dare to shoot before she had a path of escape?

The bodyguards were between her and the man she sought. Could she draw a weapon and fire before they acted? Hardly, even if they had not been looking for such a move. But they were looking. They had her spotted. The end would be . . .

It was my task to break up the organization of gangdom. The Full Dress Kid had grabbed the reins. It looked as though he'd made a good job of it. This Lena, the widowed mate of a gangster, was the only opposition that remained. I needed her alive. She would be a disturbing influence. To befriend Lena would be to hamper the Kid. To hamper the Kid would be to keep gangdom away from such close organization that one man would really control all the criminal activities of the underworld.

I searched my pockets for a pencil, had none.

A bit of lipstick, evidently dropped from some vanity case, was on an adjoining table. I picked it up, used my napkin upon which to scrawl a message.

"They're wise. Beat it!"

And for signature, because I could think of nothing better, I inscribed a rude sketch of an eye, a red eye that gazed with unwinking fire from the white napkin.

I summoned a waiter, and did what I knew might be a fatal mistake. I tipped him and instructed him to slip the napkin into the hand of the white-haired lady.

He was willing enough, gullible enough; but how about the eyes that were watching him? The napkin might get by. A paper would have been fatal. I had no alternative. The situation demanded speed.

The waiter went to the table. He moved the salt, fiddled with the spoons, pretended to observe that she had no napkin, fluttered out the one I had given him, laid it in her hands and walked away.

She lowered her eyes to the napkin, read my message.

The gray eyes were filled with panic now as she raised them for a swift look around the room. Who had sent her the warning? How had they known? . . . Like every amateur, the girl thought her disguise was impenetrable. She did not realize that the art of disguise is the art of submerging personality.

She scraped back her chair, got to her feet.

Her hand shot to the inside of her dress. I realized she was going to chance a shot. She had determined to go out fighting, trying to avenge herself, knowing that her own life was doomed.

A man hulked at her back. A strong hand grasped her arm. Another came to the side. Two more walked from a table near the entrance.

She looked at them with eyes that were as coldly unwavering as those with which the captured hawk faces death.

One of the men said something to her.

She nodded, turned. There was a side door, and she slipped through that side door, a man holding either arm. She went willingly, and she went rapidly. Could I help? Were they watching me? Had anyone seen the episode of the napkin?

It had fluttered to the floor.

One of the men picked it up, looked at it, moved over toward the Kid. The music crashed up into a jazzy dance. I was alone and unarmed, but the girl who was leaving the restaurant was going to her death. And it was to my interest to prolong her life if possible.

I got to my feet, felt that strange sense which warns us when someone is looking at us, and turned to confront a pair of gray eyes, rather large, almost expressionless. The eyes were surmounted by jet black hair. The skin was as pale as a field of virgin snow.

It was the girl whom I had christened "The Lady of Death." She was the one who had sat with Al Kelaney, who, at the deadly instant, had asked him for a light. While his cigarette lighter had been held at her lips the lights had gone out, leaving the room in darkness save for the field of illumination cast by the lighter. And, into that field had crashed a fusillade of shots.*

She had been rated as an accomplice, by both press and police. There was a warrant out for her arrest on the charge of murder. The police sought her, and the police sought me. They thought I had fired the shots. They thought she was an accomplice.

And now the Lady of Death was smiling her incarnadined lips at me.

The mouth was as vividly red as it had been that night when she kissed the expiring gangster, while her white hands had made vain search of his clothing, seeking for that which I had later found, the signed confession which was to have gone to the ditrict attorney.

I confronted her with a questioning gaze which I did my best to maintain as a blank of unrecognition, yet filled with just that receptive leer which the character I impersonated would have used under such circumstances.

"Lookin' for someone?"

Her cold eyes took in each detail of my features.

"For you."

What was my duty? To expose her? Or should I cultivate her, try to find out what she knew about Al Kelaney, about the crime?

I had no time to waste on indecision. Lena was being led to her death. And I was no detective. The district attorney had told me not to concern myself with individual crimes, but to carry my fight along bigger, broader lines.

I bowed to her.

"Just a minute," I said. "Sit down. I'll come back."

I turned and made for the door through which Lena had gone. I had a glimpse of fluttering silks. The Lady of Death was at my side.

"I wouldn't go out—there!"

I wasted no time with further words. I turned my back to the girl. My hand grabbed the knob, wrenched the door open.

---

*Gardner here refers to a character and scene from the first of this trilogy of stories, "The Crime Crusher," *Black Mask*, May 1930.

There was a passage, a single light, a couple of doors which were closed, the sucking fingers of cold night air blowing in from some window.

The fingers of the Lady of Death were on my arm.

"Don't!" she said.

A flashlight stabbed squarely into my eyes. I tried to duck. The clinging body of the Death Lady wrapped itself about my back and hampered my motions. Something crashed upon my forehead and darkness rushed up to engulf me. . . .

I was dimly conscious. I could not move, could not restrain the nausea which tugged at my senses. But I knew that the thing which banged into my face was the floor. I knew that men's voices sounded in the corridor, and I knew that the Lady of Death bent over me, as she had bent over Al Kelaney the night before.

I knew that her lips were sobbing words of endearment.

"My sweetheart!" she groaned. "Light of my life! Speak to me, dearest. Oh, God!"

And then her crimsoned lips sought my face, kissed me with sticky caresses, just as they had kissed the dying features of Al Kelaney and left telltale imprints on the clammy skin.

I stirred, opened my eyes.

They caught hers, and I saw a look of puzzled bewilderment. Then she was crooning terms of endearment again. Her eyes were as emotionlessly hard as twin agates. Her lips were busy; and her hands were fluttering about my pockets.

A man's foot came to the floor, scarcely an inch from my ear. I could see the well-creased trouser leg, could see the cloth wrinkle as he stooped.

"Get the hell away from here!" he said, and there was the sound of a blow thudding upon skin, the half-muffled scream of a woman.

Hands grabbed my shoulders. Something fell upon me, an inert weight that slumped to my solar plexus, completing the job the slungshot had commenced. I became completely unconscious.

I felt that some one was pounding the top of my head with a hammer. It seemed those head poundings had gone back into the dim depths of antiquity. Ever since time had been, had been those poundings. My soul was sick of them. My brain was jellied. My stomach revolted.

"He's comin' to."

The words came from some limbo of outer darkness that held no location for me.

"Crack 'm again."

Something landed against my jaw. There was a wave of engulfing darkness interspersed with shooting lights, and then unconsciousness again.

Later on I again became aware of the poundings of my brain.

This time my senses returned more swiftly, with less nausea. I realized the poundings came from the jolting of an automobile as it took little irregularities in the road. I was lying upon the floor and the men had their feet over me, in my back, on my neck.

The roar of the motor and the swiftness with which the jolts were sent through the frame of the car indicated high speed.

I remained perfectly quiet.

The car slowed, swung to a dirt road. There was an agony of jolting. After a few hundred yards we swung again. A searchlight stabbed through the night and blasted full upon the car. There was a challenge, a hail, the searchlight sputtered into darkness. Hands grasped me, jerked me to the ground.

A boot caught my ribs.

"Get up and walk."

I got up and staggered.

I could see the silhouette of a house, outlined against the moon-filled heavens. Off to the left was a stable, converted into an open garage. In that garage was a fleet of heavy-duty trucks. Their big noses, huge tires, silvered headlights, showed as grim, silent faces, staring wide eyed in silent survey.

A girl's voice tinkled across the darkness between the house and the machine.

"Use the right-hand door."

They pushed me forward. A short flight of stairs caught my clogged feet and tripped me.

A hand gripped the back of my coat, jerked me up the stairs.

"Who is it?"

The voice was that of the woman.

The man behind me answered.

"The guy that wrote the Red Eye letter to Cap. Fuller. He tried to butt in with Lena. We'll shake 'm down."

And then I shot across a threshold, a door slammed and light tortured my eyeballs.

I was in a room that had once been a kitchen. Now it was a storehouse for all sorts of contraband. There were stacks of whiskey cases, barrels, bottles, boxes.

A man stood on guard, a holstered weapon at his hip. He looked at me with casual curiosity. A girl, whose voice I had heard, stood at an inner doorway. She was trim, short-skirted, and her face was as much of a mystery as the face of a young woman always is.

She looked a coy, respectable little lady. Perhaps there was a little too much pout to the lips, perhaps her eyes were just a shade too bold. Certain it was that her skirts were several inches too short. But I would have defied anyone to pick her face out of a crowd of modern girls as being any different from the rest.

She eyed me in frank appraisal.

"Where do they want this guy?"

"Upstairs," she said.

A hand lodged between my shoulder blades, gave me a forward push. The girl stood aside as I stumbled and staggered past, seeking to regain my balance.

Behind me, someone laughed.

The next room was vacant. Apparently there had been a meal served here. A table held some dishes, a couple of bottles, half a loaf of bread, part of a roll of butter. Stairs showed beyond the door.

"Better grab 'm an' see he don't get foxy," remarked one of the men.

Hands grasped my elbows. I was escorted to the stairs, given a kick to start me going in the right direction.

A door from the top corridor gave me a swift glimpse of the front room on the upper floor. It was a veritable arsenal. I saw a machine gun, mounted on a tripod, pointed at the window. Back of it were some hand grenades in a box. A rack contained some sawed-off shotguns.

I knew then where I was. It was one of the unloading depots of a rum-running gang. These depots are heavily armed, not against prohibition officers, but against hijackers.

The modern boozester fears the law but little. As a rule, he has arranged for immunity in advance. The officers have been bribed. In the event of a raid he is tipped off. In the event of an arrest he pays a small fine. But the hijacker is a different problem.

Stocks of booze run into thousands of dollars, sometimes into hundreds of thousands of dollars. The owner cannot complain in the event of its loss. Hence, those gangs of hard-bitten booze pirates who come swooping down upon supply depots, load captured booze into trucks and vanish into the night. Hence, those elaborate preparations which booze smugglers have taken for protection.

This house was probably an important unloading place, as witnessed by the fleet of trucks, the number of men housed there. And it was well protected. There were probably half a dozen machine guns about the place. A powerful searchlight could flood the approach to the house with brilliant light. Hand grenades could be thrown out upon the trucks of hijackers.

And all this equipment was ready for use at a moment's notice . . . small chance that the friends of one who had been taken to that house as a captive would try to make a rescue. Even if Lean Lena retained any loyal followers, it was unlikely that they would come to this house for her. And I felt certain that Lena would be taken here—after that, she would be "taken for a ride," grim slang of the underworld for a murder party.

My glimpse of that arsenal was only fleeting. I was propelled past that door, down the corridor, into another room.

"Sit down," rasped one of my captors, and shoved me into a chair.

The room was furnished mainly with chairs. Several doors opened from it. A spindle-legged table was in the center of the room. Some of the doors had been recently cut through the wall. A single light in the ceiling furnished sufficient illumination to make my head ache.

I took a swift look at the men who had brought me here. I had seen them before, the "bodyguards" of The Full Dress Kid.

"So you're the Red Eye?" remarked one, leaning against the doorjamb, lighting a cigarette.

"Whatcha talkin' about?" I demanded.

He laughed.

"Stuck a red eye on the letter you sent Cap. Fuller, an' you stuck a red eye on the napkin you used to tip off Lean Lena. Guess you an' the Kid'll have quite a chat."

I snorted.

"Guess again. You'll be arrested for kidnapping if you don't turn me loose."

He laughed at that, and it was a sincere laugh. He choked, gasped, chortled. The other two men shared in his mirth.

"The hell you say," remarked one, finally.

I started to make some remark that would lead to further comment when there was the sound of commotion from below, and a woman's scream came up the stairs, knifing the air with the shrillness of a locomotive's whistle.

"That'll be Lena," remarked one of my guards, and laughed.

"That'll be Lena," agreed the other.

There was a swaying, shuffling, banging noise on the stairs. Feet stamped, staggered and were silent. Then I could hear them in the upper corridor. They came in, carrying the form of a woman.

It was Lena, stiff as a board at times, then doubling, kicking, cursing, screaming.

A man swung his fist, a crashing blow to the temple, sent her reeling onto the floor. He followed her swiftly and sent his right crashing to her face.

"Sit there," he said as the thin body, staggering back from the force of the blow, caught against a chair, spilled into it.

The men laughed, then formed in chatting groups. Lena collapsed in the chair. Blood smeared over her lips. Her face was deathly pale. Once I thought her eyes flickered to me in swift appraisal, but I was not certain. The lethargy of death seemed to have gripped her.

I heard the sound of a motor. A girl's voice sounded, muffled by walls, yet clear.

"Take the left-hand door."

The sound of doors opening and closing, steps, masculine voices, the ripple of feminine laughter, the noise of a kiss. Then the steps came down the corridor which evidently lay just back of those newly made doors. I could hear a deep voice, laughing some jesting comment to the girl, catch her quick intake of breath, hear the steps stop, the rustle of motion, the sound of another kiss, then steps again.

A man thrust his head into the room, took a swift look about, then closed the door as he stepped back into the corridor.

I could hear the words he spoke.

"They're there."

"All three of 'em?"

"Just two. The other one'll be along in a minute."

There was some comment made to that, but I couldn't get the words. There was another commotion on the stairs up which I had come. Two men came to the door. Walking between them, head held high, eyes as expressionless as fleecy gray clouds against a mountainside, was the girl whom I had seen kissing Al Kelaney as he lay dying, the girl I had christened The Lady of Death.

She stalked with queenly dignity to a chair, sat down.

The room was now half filled with men, rough characters for the most part, with, here and there, one who had some of the dapper swagger of the professional gangster. But these men were mostly truck drivers, rum smugglers, bootleggers, the dregs of the underworld pressed into the service of King Whiskey.

We three were the only ones sitting, the two women and myself. The rest of the men stood about, smoking, chatting, waiting, eyeing their prisoners.

Steps again, then a booming voice.

I knew that voice. It belonged to Bull Clancey, the plainclothes man, who had risen to distinction in the detective service. Hop Haggerty had been his stool pigeon, and Hop Haggerty had tipped Clancey off to Kelaney's confession.

Now Clancey's voice was booming with some demand.

". . . and I don't mean maybe!" he roared.

The light, sardonic laugh that greeted his words could have come from none other than a leader, arrogant, sure of himself and his ground.

"Well, go to hell, then."

It was the voice of The Full Dress Kid.

The door opened. The Kid walked into the room. His lips were smiling. His eyes were hard. From behind him came Clancey's voice. It had lost its defiance now.

"Hell, Kid, you gotta stand back o' me."

The Kid terminated the sentence by deliberately closing the door in the face of the speaker.

"Well this *is* a collection!" he said.

The girl who had dined with Al Kelaney the night of his death, who had stooped to kiss me when the blackjack of a gangster had crashed me to the floor, surveyed him with cool emotionless eyes. Lena looked up and her face twisted in a spasm of hate.

The Kid caught that flicker of expression, and came over to her, standing by her chair.

"Lena, I ain't got anything in particular against you except that you know too damned much, and you're getting ready to squeal. You hate me an' you always will. That leaves me only one way to make sure you won't squeal— You've got to go for a ride, Lena."

She looked him straight in the eyes, spat at his face.

He took a handkerchief from his pocket. His eyes blazed as he wiped his distorted features.

"That won't buy you anything," he snarled.

She darted a hand toward her dress. One of the men sprang forward, grabbed the arm, twisted it.

"What the hell? You guys let her hold out a rod?"

The voice of the Kid was ominous.

"She ain't got nothing," said one of the men, and, to prove it, hooked his hand in the front of her waist, gave a tug. There was the sound of tearing cloth, and the girl's clothes fell on either side of her shoulders, disclosing a leather holster, empty.

"See?"

The Kid nodded, turned to me.

"And you're the observing Red Eye that sees everything and writes letters, eh?"

I said nothing.

He moved a step closer, his features darkening.

"Well, you're goin' to get writer's paralysis. You can't start gumming my game and make it stick. But first I'm going to know how much you know and how you found it out. That Fuller letter was dangerous, you know that."

Lean Lena made a sudden rush. Her hand went to the front of her torn garments, groped in the silk. A man stepped to her, measured the distance, swung, sent her sprawling.

The Kid turned, impatient at the interruption.

"Take her out," he said. "Take her *for a ride*! And, after that, we'll take the other two."

Two of the men jerked the thin woman to her feet. She began to curse, struggle. The three formed into a struggling group, swaying this way and that.

The gray-eyed girl sat motionless.

The Kid waited for the racket to die down. Little flames were dancing in his dark eyes. The corners of his mouth twitched, and I could see the gleam of a thin trickle of saliva oozing from the twitching lips.

I knew that Lena would be gone forever once she left that room. I knew, also, that it was on the cards that I should be taken for a ride. As to the gray-eyed girl I knew nothing. She might be one of the gang, or she might be the scout for a gang of hijackers.

It was all or nothing, any play to gain time, give me a break. I determined to disclose that which they would find out, sooner or later, of their own accord.

My hands went to my features. Bit by bit I picked off the disguise, smoothed the grease paint wrinkles.

"Yeah, disguised," said the Kid. "Knew that all the time, of course, after I saw you in a good light."

"But you didn't know *who* I was," I replied, as the last of the disguise came off.

He didn't know me even then, but one of his henchmen did.

"Ed Jenkins!" he yelled. "The Phantom Crook."

The Kid started, leaned closer.

The men who had been pushing Lena toward the door came to a sudden stop. The gray-eyed girl sat rigidly erect.

"So?" whistled the Kid. "Well, Jenkins, you can't horn in on *my* game. You're going out like a light."

A crafty look came across his features, twisted his mouth into a leering smile.

"Walk in there an' tell Bull Clancey I got a job for him," he told one of the men.

But from the manner in which the door popped open and Bull Clancey thrust a wide-eyed face into the room, it was apparent the plainclothes man had been listening through the keyhole.

"Bull," drawled the Kid, "this here's Ed Jenkins. You're going to arrest him. With his well known reputation for escaping, it won't cause any comment if you bring him into the station on a stretcher with a lot of lead in him. You'll get a promotion . . . and use plenty of lead."

Bull Clancey let his mouth open, then snapped it closed.

"You talk different when you want somethin', don't you?"

The Kid's eyes narrowed.

"Bull, you've been pretty lucky. Some guys in your place wouldn't have got by so easy."

Bull wetted his lips.

"Well, listen to this. I got some hot dope on this guy Jenkins that you want. I'll spill you the info, and I'll croak him, but you gotta do somethin' for me."

The Kid surveyed him with eyes that were cold and appraising.

"Well?"

Bull Clancey jerked his thumb toward the gray-eyed girl.

"Croak her," he said, and his voice was husky with hatred.

If the Kid was surprised he gave no sign.

"And this information of yours?"

Bull Clancey leaned forward.

"Listen," he said, swaggering, impressive. "Jenkins shook Hop Haggerty down for some info. Hop spilled the beans about Al Kelaney. Jenkins was in the café when Al got his. We never found that document we wanted."

The Kid half turned, surveyed the plainclothes detective with half-curling lip.

"Well, Sherlocko, go on."

"But I doped it out later," went on Clancey. "The thing was simple. Kelaney was chewing gum when he was croaked. He had a second or two in the dark after he knew he was gone, but before he got unconscious. He stuck the paper to the bottom of the café table with chewing gum."

The Kid was stiff now, erect, poised, snarling.

"And this is a hell of a place to spill *that*!"

Bull Clancey shook his head.

"Nope. I looked there this afternoon. Know what I found? The table with a part of a wad of dried gum there, and some little shreds of paper clinging to it. The paper was gone. Maybe that's how Ed Jenkins got himself horning in on this deal."

The Kid moistened his lips with his tongue, swallowed once, audibly.

"He'll kick through if I have to rip his skin off with pincers," he said, and meant it.

Lena caught my gaze for the merest fraction of a second. The men were not holding her so tightly now. Her hand slipped back of her breast under her left arm, came out, flashed.

Something went through the air that looked like a glass globe. It struck the floor, crashed.

Men turned, looked at each other, at the floor. They seemed motionless with surprise. It had happened, just like that. There was nothing they could do. And their minds refused to adjust themselves to the changed situation.

The girl with the gray eyes was on her feet.

Something choking, an invisible hand, clutched at my throat, shut off the wind, seared the membranes, and that was just a first whiff.

The main body of the gas was rising as a white fume, a milky fog of gray death.

The Kid tried to yell something, but his throat had constricted and no sound came. He made for a window.

The stampede started.

One of the men fell over, gasping. The gray-eyed girl went through the door into the back corridor. Lena went for the stairs. I was after her. Pistols crashed.

A man came up the stairs, stood with gawking mouth and wide eyes. "What the hell . . ."

And then his hand streaked for his hip.

Someone was running behind us, coming closer. The man on the stairs yanked out a weapon, raised his hand. Lena swung to the side, jostled against me.

I remembered the open door at the head of the stairs. It was closed now, but I flung myself on the knob. It turned. The door opened and we fell into the room.

"Look out!" yelled Lena.

A revolver blazed. A bullet zipped past my head, shattered a pane of glass in the window.

I grabbed up a submachine gun.

The man in the door ducked, sidestepped, cursed, fired through the partition. The bullet tore off plaster, missed me by a foot.

I whirled the machine gun, started it into action.

Coughing spurts of flame belched from the end of the weapon. I could feel the purr of the explosions. The door leapt into a mass of splinters, dissolved into kindling wood. Lena picked up a hand grenade, slipped the catch, rolled it through the door.

I heard it give three or four bumps on the stairs, heard a man scream, and then a blast of red fire shot through the door. The floor of the house rocked. A rush of air almost burst my eardrums.

Plaster went off the walls, left the bare laths. The ceiling rained to the floor. A hole showed in the roof. The corridor yawned through a great jagged hole where the door had once been.

I knew from the feel of the weapon that I was still working the machine gun, but no sound of it came to my deafened ears.

I quit pressing the trigger, turned to Lena.

Every light in the house had gone out with that explosion, but there was a licking tongue of red flame which curled up from the stairs, growing constantly in volume. By its light I could see her face.

The thin upper lip was curled back from her fangs. Her bruised countenance shone with unholy joy. But the eyes were the things that arrested my attention. In them was the cold light of Norse rage, the love of battle that asks only to fight, thinks nothing of consequences.

I saw her hand flash again.

This time the grenade went out the window, over toward the remodeled stable. I looked out after it.

There was a great mushroom of white flame that turned to red on the edges. The corner of the building melted in the fierce blast. One of the trucks buckled, listed over on its side. Again the house rocked with the force of the explosion.

The tongue of flame had now become a whirling spiral of red menace. It showed Lena's face plainly.

She was laughing.

A man's hulking figure showed in the corridor, silhouetted against flame. He fired at us. I pressed the trigger of the machine gun. Lena rolled out three more bombs, one right after the other.

The house rocked, seemed to rain down upon us. A heavy scantling, one end torn to a veritable splinter brush, came hurtling between us. I could feel the wind of it on my cheek. It must have grazed Lena.

She continued to laugh, reached for the grenades, started for the place where the door had been. The hall was now a twisting inferno of flame. Dust was everywhere, a white plaster dust that filled the air like a fog.

I looked out the shattered window.

The garage was on fire. Flames had spread over one of the trucks, were licking at the gasoline tank. Even as I looked, there was a bubbling mass of foaming flame that boiled out into the night. Then a reserve supply of gasoline caught fire.

Someone cut loose with a machine gun on the lower floor. I could not see what they were firing at. I looked for Lena. She had gone. Her arms filled with grenades, clutching them to her exposed breasts, she had disappeared into the crackling flame.

I looked back into the corridor and deemed it best to escape from the window, when it should be possible to escape. But the machine gun was still stuttering from the lower floor.

Men ran toward the garage. The machine gun stopped, sputtered, coughed, hesitated and then tattooed into full-throated rhythm.

The figures sprawled upon the ground, motionless.

A man ran with flat-footed awkwardness, seeking to cut around the blazing end of the garage.

The figure was that of Bull Clancey, the detective.

He ran heavily, lumbering toward the outer circle of darkness, and, as he ran, he glanced back over his shoulder.

The machine gun from the lower floor stuttered out an ominous message. I could see little spurts of dust made by the spattering bullets. Those dust spurts came slowly nearer to the running figure, sweeping up on it from behind.

It was as though someone had turned a garden hose slowly along a path of dust.

Bull Clancey saw those dust spurts, too.

His face distorted. His mouth twisted, his eyeballs rolled back, and he gave a terrific spurt of awkward speed. But it was of no use. Those little dust spurts approached closer, moving with remorseless certainty. They were at his heels, clipping the ground almost under his running feet.

He screamed.

The bullets raised. His right leg crumpled in midstride. He fell forward, tried to crawl on hands and knees. A bullet cut his shoulder. He sprawled. Bullets whipped little spirals of dust from his coat. He twitched and lay still.

A form ran out into the yard, a lean form with skirt flapping, waist torn to ribbons, flat breasts exposed to the ruddy glow of the firelight.

Lena was laughing no longer. Her clothes had been burnt in places. Her face was grimed.

She drew back an arm. I saw a dark streak come toward the side of the house. I ducked back from the window. I was knocked from my feet. Timbers ground and ripped. One corner of the house sagged, toppled, crashed.

I staggered to the window, lowered myself. There had been a porch beneath, but that porch was now only a mass of splintered supports.

I dropped.

My feet missed a timber. Splinters caught my hands. I felt a rip of cloth, and then there was another explosion, fragments of metal and wood hurtled through the air, and I was on the ground.

One last glimpse of Lena I had, as she stood before the flaming garage with its gasoline sending great tongues of fire up into the swirling mass of spiraling smoke.

She threw a grenade squarely into the center of the flame vortex.

I cried out a choked alarm, ran for the darkness.

Someone shot at me. I could feel the cold air of bullets fanning my cheek.

Then the ground rocked. The flame from the burning gasoline fanned out in the heavens and came down in a rain of fire, a crackling shower of blazing fluid.

Someone screamed, a scream of agony, shrill and long drawn, and that scream was followed by a rasping staccato of mirthless merriment—the laugh of Lena.

The fire had attracted attention. I could see the lights of automobiles upon the side road that led to the blazing inferno. As contrasted with the red rage of the fire, those lights seemed white, cold, pitifully pale, inadequate. They jostled and jolted over the inequalities in the road.

The stock of booze in the house flamed into action. A store of explosives followed. Blazing debris flung far into the air, rained down upon the countryside.

I ran to the road. A cab took me to the center of town. Two cabs in shifts took me back to the place where I was Doctor Chew, the Chinese herb doctor and psychic.

And it was well I had a stock of soothing herbs. I was more than an hour doctoring my superficial burns and cuts.

Then the telephone rang.

It was a blind telephone as far as I was concerned, listed under the name of the prior occupant, but I was not greatly surprised when it rang. I had come to have a strong respect for Lena.

"Hello," I said.

It was her voice all right.

"Listen, you may be a fake or you may know your onions, but you sure gave me one straight steer today. I gotta see you again. I want to find out something about the future."

I was grave, dignified.

"It is late. You come tomorrow two o'clock," I said, and hung up. I wanted no further conversation until I knew more about what had happened, who had been working that lower machine gun, how it happened Bull Clancey had attracted such a murderous rain of lead.

The telephone rang again. I did not answer it.

Nor did I sleep in the flat of Doctor Chew. Instead, I ascended the stairs and slept in the character of Colonel Grayson.

And it was as that mustached, spectacled, dignified gentleman that I strolled to the corner in the morning and purchased the papers.

I read the account of the fire. The police had pieced together some things reasonably well. The newspaper boys had gone farther.

One account closed with a paragraph I liked. I knew that paragraph would be read by the district attorney, and, reading between the lines, I knew that it would make a good message for him.

"On the surface," said the article, "the destruction of the isolated dwelling house was but another step in the gang war which was expected when Harry the Hun and Slick Williams were tricked to their death. But there are those 'in the know' in the underworld who are shaking their heads in doubt. According to these people, the absorption of the two gangs headed by the murdered leaders had been arranged even before the death of the captains. In last night's terrific struggle, culminating in the death of some seven gangsters and one sergeant of detectives, these people see some mysterious influence at work in the underworld. It is even hinted that some dark horse has pitted his strength against one of the most notorious and powerful of the underworld leaders—and has, in this first round, come off the victor. If such is the case, and the terrific toll of last night was but a fiery first round, the finish of this struggle may assume such proportions as to rock the underworld to its very foundations."

I smiled as I folded the newspaper.

Round one. Let the district attorney read that and think. If I could only keep

Lean Lena alive and direct her activities, the prophecy of the paper bid fair to be realized.

Gangdom would not organize in its war upon society, not until after Lean Lena and Ed Jenkins had been accounted for; and there remained that mysterious Lady of Death with the gray eyes and the calm manner, who kissed dying men as she searched their pockets.

It was Hell's Kettle all right, and it was bubbling into a stew of death.

Gardner in *Black Mask*

1923–1943

Series characters: Bob Larkin (BL)
Ed Jenkins (EJ)
Black Barr (BB)
Ken Corning (KC)
Pete Wennick (PW)

•—included in *The* Black Mask *Boys*

"The Shrieking Skeleton" (as "Charles M. Green") 15 December 1923
"The Serpent's Coils" (as "Green") 1 January 1924
"The Verdict" (as "Green") 1 February 1924
"A Fair Trial" (no byline) June 1924
"Accommodatin' a Lady" (BL) September 1924
"Without No Reindeer" (BL) December 1924
"Beyond the Law" (EJ) January 1925
"Hard as Nails" (EJ) March 1925
"Painless Extraction" (BL) May 1925
"Not So Darn Bad" (EJ) June 1925
"Three O'Clock in the Morning" (EJ) July 1925
"Ham, Eggs an' Coffee" (BL) August 1925
"The Girl Goes With Me" (BB) November 1925
"The Triple Cross" (EJ) December 1925
"According to Law" (EJ) January 1926
"Goin' Into Action" (BL) February 1926
"Register Rage" (EJ) April 1926
"Thisissosudden!" (EJ) May 1926
"Forget 'Em All" (EJ) June 1926
"Laugh That Off" (EJ) September 1926
"Buzzard Bait" (BB) October 1926
"Money, Marbles and Chalk" (EJ) November 1926

"Dead Men's Letters" (EJ)   December 1926
"Whispering Sand" (BB)   January 1927
"The Cat-Woman" (EJ)   February 1927
"This Way Out" (EJ)   March 1927
"Come and Get It" (EJ)   April 1927
"In Full of Account" (EJ)   May 1927
"Where the Buzzards Circle" (BB)   September 1927
"The Wax Dragon" (EJ)   November 1927
"Grinning Gods" (EJ)   December 1927
"Yellow Shadows" (EJ)   February 1928
"Whispering Feet" (EJ)   March 1928
"Snow Bird" (EJ)   April 1928
"Out of the Shadows" (EJ)   May 1928
"Fangs of Fate" (BB)   August 1928
"The Devil's Deputy" (BB)   September 1928
"Curse of the Killers" (BB)   November 1928
"The Next Stiff" (EJ)   December 1928
"One Crook to Another" (EJ)   January 1929
"Bracelets for Two" (EJ)   February 1929
"Hooking the Crooks" (EJ)   March 1929
"No Questions Asked" (EJ)   April 1929
"Scum of the Border" (BL)   June 1929
"All the Way" (BL)   July 1929
"Spawn of the Night" (BL)   August 1929
"Hanging Friday" (BL)   September 1929
"Straight From the Shoulder" (EJ)   October 1929
"Brass Tacks" (EJ)   November 1929
"Triple Treachery" (EJ)   December 1929
"Double or Quits" (EJ)   January 1930
"The Crime Crusher" (EJ)   May 1930
•"Hell's Kettle" (EJ)   June 1930
"Big Shot" (EJ)   July 1930
"Tommy Talk" (EJ)   July 1931
"Hairy Hands" (EJ)   August 1931
"Promise to Pay" (EJ)   September 1931
"The Hot Squat" (EJ)   October 1931
"Strictly Personal" (EJ)   December 1931
"Face Up" (EJ)   January 1932
"Feet First" (EJ)   March 1932
"Straight Crooks" (EJ)   April 1932
"Under the Guns" (EJ)   May 1932
"Crooking Crooks" (EJ)   June 1932
"Rough Stuff" (EJ)   July 1932

"Black and White" (EJ)   September 1932
"On Two Feet" (BL)   October 1932
"Honest Money" (KC)   November 1932
"The Top Comes Off" (KC)   December 1932
"Close Call" (KC)   January 1933
"The Hour of the Rat" (EJ)   February 1933
"Red Jade" (EJ)   March 1933
"Chinatown Murder" (EJ)   April 1933
"The Weapons of a Crook" (EJ)   May 1933
"Making the Breaks" (KC)   June 1933
"Devil's Fire" (KC)   July 1933
"Blackmail With Lead" (KC)   August 1933
"Whispering Justice" (EJ)   September 1933
"The Murder Push" (EJ)   October 1933
"Dead Men's Shoes" (EJ)   December 1933
"A Guest of the House" (EJ)   January 1934
"Cop Killers" (EJ)   March 1934
"New Twenties" (EJ)   April 1934
"Burnt Fingers" (EJ)   June 1934
"The Heavenly Rat" (EJ)   September 1934
"Hot Cash" (EJ)   November 1934
"Winged Lead" (BB)   January 1935
"A Chance to Cheat" (EJ)   May 1935
"Crash and Carry" (EJ)   October 1935
"Above the Law" (EJ)   December 1935
"Beating the Bulls" (EJ)   May 1936
"This Way Out" (EJ)   March 1937
"Among Thieves" (PW)   September 1937
"Leg Man" (PW)   February 1938
"Muscle Out" (EJ)   April 1938
"Take It or Leave It" (PW)   March 1939
"Dark Alleys" (EJ)   September 1939
"Tong Trouble" (EJ)   June 1940
"Jade Sanctuary" (EJ)   December 1940
"The Chinese People" [translation] (EJ)   May 1941
"Rain Check" (EJ)   December 1941
"Two Dead Hands" (EJ)   April 1942
"The Incredible Mister Smith" (EJ)   March 1943
"The Gong of Vengeance" (EJ)   September 1943

Behind the Mask:
Raoul Whitfield

•

His full name was impressive: Raoul Fauconnier Whitfield. As was his social standing; the *Cleveland Press* identified him as "Andrew Carnegie's nephew." Certainly, heading into the new century, he was part of a financially strong family, and he had the added advantage of being an only child.

Born in New York, on November 22, 1898, he received his basic education in that city. But Whitfield was destined for world travel, and he was still a boy when he accompanied his father to the Philippines. William F. Whitfield had accepted a position with the Territorial Government in Manila. Raoul spent most of his teenage years there, making side trips into China and Japan, soaking up the colorful atmosphere of the Far East which would later serve him well as a writer.

Young Whitfield became ill in 1916 and was sent back to the States in order to regain his health. He was soon well enough to set out for California, where his dapper good looks helped him break into films as a Hollywood silent-screen actor. (The "talkies" were still more than a decade away.)

Indeed, Whitfield *was* a handsome fellow, inclined to be photographed with a rakish scarf at his neck. A tall six-footer, he sported a fashionable cane and custom-leather gloves, parted his dark, slicked-back hair in the middle, had a cleft chin (à la Cary Grant) and a neatly trimmed mustache.

Bored by film acting, he enlisted in the ambulance corps, desperate to be part of what he called "the Big Show"—World War I. Seeing a chance for overseas action, he quickly transferred to the air service and received flight training at Kelly Field in San Antonio, Texas. By the summer of 1918 Whitfield was in France, having won his wings as a second lieutenant.

Spoiling for combat, he was frustrated at being assigned the job of "ferry pilot," flying unarmed De Havillands to the front lines. Next, he was given the equally frustrating job of towing targets for aerial gun practice at St. Jean de Monts.

Before the war ended, however, young Whitfield got his chance to pilot a fighter plane in the skies of France. His brief combat record was not exceptional, but it provided the basis for dozens of wildly melodramatic air-adventure tales he would write for the pulps.

After the armistice, Whitfield began to prepare for a career in Pittsburgh, where his family wanted him to work his way up in the steel business, beginning as a laborer in the mills. This didn't last long. "The truth is, I was born to be a writer," he later stated. "So I began my *real* career on the staff of a newspaper in 1919."

Whitfield had joined the *Pittsburgh Post* as a cub reporter. He stayed with "the news" long enough to develop the professional writing skills that eventually carried him into the pulps.

During this period Whitfield met his first wife, Prudence Van Tine, who also worked for the *Post.* They were married in the mid-1920s. By then, he'd sold a few pieces of fiction and felt that he could make a career of writing. Prudence encouraged him. The pulps were flourishing and needed the kind of adventure tales Whitfield could provide.

He quit his job and moved, with Prudence, to the west coast of Florida, where he settled into full-time writing.

Raoul Whitfield's first *Black Mask* story was printed in the March 1926 issue; he was twenty-seven and ready "to set the world on fire."

As Joe Shaw said about him, "Whitfield was a hard, patient, determined worker. His style [at first] was hard and brittle and over-inclined to staccato."

This was true. The young author was a great admirer of Hammett's work and attempted to pattern his own fiction in the same lean style.

Eight Whitfield stories were printed in *Black Mask* during 1926, and by the following year he'd broken into *Everybody's, War Stories,* and *Boy's Life* with his rousing air-adventure fiction. In September of 1927 he began to appear regularly in *Battle Stories;* where his output was so prolific he was forced to use a pen name, "Temple Field," in addition to his own byline.

Editor Fred Dannay (in *Ellery Queen's Mystery Magazine*) described Whitfield in action: "[He] always wrote easily and quickly, with a minimum of correction. He had a particular talent for starting with a title and writing [a story] around it . . . He would place neat stacks of chocolate bars to the right of his typewriter, and a picket fence of cigarettes to his left. He wrote and chain-smoked and ate, all in one unified operation."

Having now moved to Los Angeles, Whitfield continued his assault on the pulp markets, notching new sales to *Adventure, Air Trails,* and *Triple-X,* while continuing to supply Joe Shaw with a steady flow of material. During 1929, in *Black Mask,* Shaw printed a series of linked stories featuring Gary Greer, an ex-World War I flier who operated a private airfield and flew planes of his own design.

Whitfield's work was rapidly improving, and by the end of that year *Black Mask* began running his new "Crime Breeders" series, the bullet-splattered saga of an ex-con named Mal Ourney caught square in the middle of a murderous search for a cache of stolen emeralds. The narrative was centered in Pittsburgh, Whitfield's old stomping ground, and a paper called the *Post-Dispatch* figured prominently in the action.

Green Ice (its final title) was brittle, mannered, swift, and oddly compelling, containing over a dozen murders, most of them personally witnessed by Ourney —whose dialogue was *Black Mask*-tough:

"They think I've got five hunks of green ice worth fifty thousand a hunk. I said no—and Christenson blackjacked me out. Then he made a duck. When I came out of it the girl held a gun on me and tried to vamp me into telling her about the emeralds I haven't got. I played up and got her by the throat. She talked . . . and some of her story sounded fair enough . . . She said they were going to give Steiner a funeral . . ."

And the action was lean and Hammett-hard:

He straightened . . . shrilled out something that sounded like "Christ!" His right hand dropped.

I shoved the door out of the way—and hit him just as he was tugging at the rod. We both went down, only he was underneath. I gave him a knee in the stomach and a left that was meant for the jaw and landed over the right eye. The knee did the trick.

After an exchange of letters, Whitfield met Dash Hammett in San Francisco, and the two tough-guy writers struck up a lasting friendship. Hammett read the Ourney series and suggested that tearsheets be sent to his editor, Blanche Knopf, for possible book publication.

It was a good suggestion. *Green Ice* was released by Knopf in 1930, launching Raoul Whitfield's career as a novelist.

By its publication, Whitfield was living in New York, and Hammett was working there as a mystery reviewer for the *New York Evening Post*. He praised *Green Ice* in his "Crime Wave" column: "Here are 280 pages of naked action pounded into tough compactness by staccato, hammerlike writing."

The critic at *Judge*, however, felt that Whitfield was no more than a shameless Hammett imitator: "Mr. Whitfield has evidently doused himself thoroughly in the best detective writer of the times . . . and has helped himself to the master's style, tricks, and ideas . . ."

Yet Will Cuppy, in the *Herald Tribune*, disagreed totally, declaring that Whitfield's first novel was actually *superior* to Hammett's latest in the genre.

Mystery novelist S. S. Van Dine also lauded *Green Ice* as "a first-rate crook story —swift and exciting and colorful."

Whitfield and Hammett attended plays and got drunk together in Manhattan bars. As one friend put it, "They'd get soused and clown around a lot." Hammett would amuse Whitfield by slipping his friend's name into various stories. The first draft of *The Thin Man* was set in "Whitfield County"—and he had named a racehorse "Ruthless Raoul" in an earlier pulp tale.

As the two became "soused," they would argue about writing. Prudence Whitfield later recalled that "they talked shop endlessly . . . debating whether a story should have seven murders or twenty-seven!"

Joe Shaw elaborated on this: "Long and fascinating were the discussions between Whitfield and Dash. Whit maintained that given character and a general plot, it was a cinch to write a detective story. When you got into a spot, all you had to do was use well-known props."

Unfortunately, much of Whitfield's work reflected this mechanical approach. His fiction was often thinly conceived and hastily written to meet pulp deadlines. He was able to grind out stories at an astonishing rate. In *Black Mask* alone, during 1930, he had fifteen stories printed. That was the year he began his "Jo Gar" series for *Mask* under the byline of "Ramon Decolta."

Called "the Island detective," Gar was based in the Philippines, with an office in Manila. He was a tough, taciturn little man who carried a .45 army Colt automatic in his hip pocket and chain-smoked brown-paper cigarettes. Spanish-Filipino, his enemies called him "the half-breed."

Whitfield wrote two dozen stories about Gar for *Black Mask* (into 1933), drawing upon his own early experiences when he had lived with his father in the Philippines. He kept the little detective moving. As pulp historian E. R. Hagemann observed: "He sails to Nagasaki (Kyushu) on one venture, ends up in San Francisco on another, solves one up-country slaying, and [another] in Baguio, the summer capital of the Philippines, 150 miles north of Manila, high in the mountains of western Luzon."

Whitfield's main output, however, centered around the sky-fighting tales he churned out for such pulps as *Battle Stories* and *Triple-X*. Readers thrilled to his "Avengers of the Air," "Flaming Coffins," "Lyons of the Cloud Patrol," "Vultures of the Sky," and "Wings of Death." The editor of *Battle Stories* proudly proclaimed Whitfield to be "America's foremost writer of aviation fight stories."

Knopf published a book of his sky tales, *Silver Wings*, in 1930 as a "collection of thrilling aviation stories for boys . . . based on personal experience." Eleven of the twelve stories in the collection had been printed in *Boy's Life*.

The *Boston Globe* praised the book: "[Here are] stories that pulsate with the vitality and the glamour of the flying service." A second collection of sky tales, also aimed at young readers, *Wings of Gold*, was published that same year by Penn.

Late in 1930, the Whitfields left New York for Europe, where they lived on the French Riviera for two years, with excursions into Italy, Sicily, and Tunisia. (He utilized this Riviera background for a superb detective story, "Mistral," sold to *Adventure* in 1931.)

Knopf also published Whitfield's *Danger Zone*, in 1931, which they called "a memorable account of actual war experiences." Indeed, the publisher's description of this book indicates that Whitfield utilized the genre of juvenile adventure fiction as a base for an autobiographical account of his wartime exploits:

> An exciting book, based on the author's own experiences, which begins in a Texas aviation field and ends with the hero's first nerve-wracking flight in France. But the story's greatest thrills concern crossing the Atlantic on a transport in war-time—the long watches from the crow's nest for enemy submarines, the torpedoing of another transport, and the wrecking of a submarine by a British destroyer.

Whitfield separated, from his wife in 1932, and their marriage was terminated the following year.

California was his next stop. Whitfield's Hollywood-based novel, *Death in a Bowl*, was optioned in 1932, and he was hired as a contract writer for Paramount Studios.

First printed in *Black Mask*, and published in book format in 1931 by Knopf, *Death in a Bowl* features private detective Ben Jardinn who solves the murder of German conductor Hans Reiner, shot during a concert at the Hollywood Bowl. The novel was well treated by critics. The *Detroit News* called Whitfield "one of the few American authors who knows what a detective is and what makes his wheels go round . . . He has . . . proved himself a master of his subject."

Hollywood historian Carolyn See traced a nihilistic, Hammett-like philosophy in her commentary on *Death in a Bowl:*

> . . . Jardinn is morose, tough, and cynical . . . He trusts neither his best girl nor his best friend, and inspires them in turn with distrust for each other . . . Hollywood is, from Jardinn's point of view, a grotesque mixture of tranquillity and shocking violence . . . His toughness . . . is only appearance, an individual's defense against an intolerably meaningless world.

Critic Curtis Patterson, in *Town & Country*, wrote an extravagant essay praising Hammett and Whitfield: "Personally, I think Mr. Hammett and Mr. Whitfield are as important in the history of picaresque fiction—of which the murder-mystery is obviously a part—as are Cézanne and Matisse in the field of art . . . One of my missions is to point out how genuinely important I consider their work."

Raoul Whitfield's labors in Hollywood resulted in just *one* recorded screen credit, *Private Detective 62*, starring William Powell, released in 1933 by Warner Bros. Richard Watts, Jr., reviewed it for the *New York Times:*

> Raoul Whitfield, one of the most expert practitioners of the school of hard-boiled detective fiction, studies the fine old American institution of the double-cross in this new film at the Radio City Music Hall . . . Mr. Whitfield contemplates the shady activities of private detectives, and presents their adventures in homicide, blackmail and perjury amid a wealth of entertaining detail.

In New York City, on July 19, 1933, Whitfield married socialite Emily Davies Vanderbilt Thayer. Their marriage was deemed "a surprise" by the *New York Times:* "The wedding . . . was extremely quiet and took place at the home of the bride. Mrs. Whitfield is the former wife of William H. Vanderbilt and Sigourney Thayer. She is one of the leaders of New York's social intelligentsia."

Playwright Lillian Hellman described the new Mrs. Whitfield as "a handsome, boyish-looking woman [seen] at every society-literary cocktail party."

The couple enjoyed an extended honeymoon trip through the Southwest, then purchased the Dead Horse Ranch near Las Vegas, New Mexico, east of Santa Fe. The ranch was large enough to accommodate its own polo field and golf course, and Whitfield settled here to live "the good life."

As a result, his production of fiction suffered a sharp decrease. In the earlier eight-year period from 1926 through 1933, he had more than 155 stories printed, including 88 in *Black Mask*. But after his second marriage Whitfield published only a bare handful of stories, including his final two for Joe Shaw, printed in early 1934.

The last of his nine books, *Danger Circus*, another juvenile, was published late in 1933. This circus-aviation mystery was dedicated: "For Emily Vanderbilt."

The dust jacket claimed that the narrative "moves with the speed of a forest fire in a high wind. Boys and girls alike will be held breathless. . . . Mr. Whitfield has hung about circuses since his childhood and has gone in for flying since his youth. He loves both and in this grand story he has written about both."

As his writing career dissolved, so did his new marriage. By February of 1935 the Whitfields had separated. He went back to work in Hollywood, while Emily remained at the ranch. Three months later, on May 24, she was found there, shot to death. Whitfield flew back to New Mexico and was told that his wife had committed suicide. A coroner's jury had determined that the bullet wound was self-inflicted, and Whitfield became the sole heir to her estate.

In the August 1937 issue of *Cosmopolitan*, Whitfield's byline appeared for the last time, on a Jo Gar story, "The Great Black."

The good life had turned dark. By 1944 every dollar of Emily's money had been spent, and Whitfield's health had failed. When Hammett learned that his old friend had been hospitalized without funds, he sent a check for $500 to cover Whitfield's medical expenses.

Raoul Whitfield failed to recover. At forty-six, in January of 1945, he died of tuberculosis in a Southern California military hospital.

Joe Shaw mourned him, pointing out that in the field of crime fiction Whitfield had stood "shoulder to shoulder with the best . . . [but] he was ambitious, and wanted to invade other fields [beyond] crime detection and criminal conflict." Whitfield never attained these goals, cut off by an early death from what (as Shaw declared) "might very well have been a brilliant future."

Shaw was being overly kind. At his best, Whitfield never approached the Hammett-Chandler level; and at his worst (as he was much of the time in the pulps), his work was hackish. His last Knopf adult mystery, *The Virgin Kills* (1932), is an outright disaster—dull and flat, totally lacking in narrative tension.

With hard-boiled fiction, toughness must be natural; it cannot be forced or self-conscious. In much of Whitfield, it is both. You don't really appreciate the tightrope act involved in the creation of genuinely tough fiction until you watch a writer fall off the rope. Raoul Whitfield took many falls.

Yet, among his novels, *Green Ice* still holds up (and has been reissued as an "Avon Crime Classic"), while the Gary Greer stories also wear well. And there were other good ones (such as "Mistral") along the way.

As a major pioneer in the genre, Raoul Fauconnier Whitfield deserves to be remembered.

Sal the Dude

This is the final story in a linked series dealing with Gary Greer's dangerous pursuit of his father's killer—a man known as Sal the Dude. Gary's good pal, Pete Ranning, has been killed, and a crooked police detective named Callahan has been revealed as the murderer of Sanford Greer. In this showdown adventure, Callahan has captured Gary and plans to kill him along with his girl, Joyce Rawlings.

The story climaxes in an exciting sky duel typical of many that Whitfield wrote for aviation pulps during the 1930s.

"Sal the Dude" has never been previously anthologized; it proves dramatically why Raoul Whitfield was a top favorite with *Black Mask* readers.

SAL THE DUDE

Series character: Gary Greer

Callahan drove the car off the main highway, and turned up a fairly steep, rough road. There were tall trees on either side of the road—rain dripped through them. The car skidded badly in the mud; Callahan swore. Gary Greer pressed his lips tightly together, gave no sign of the pain sent through his head by the jolting machine.

The car swung to the right as Callahan jerked the wheel. He swore as the rear wheels failed to slide out of the rut on the right. He stepped on the accelerator —the engine clattered. But the wheels spun through the mud without moving the car forward. He smiled grimly as the clatter of the engine died under his relaxed foot pressure.

"Like *you*, Greer!" he muttered. "Got just so far—can't go on!"

He chuckled hoarsely. Gary Greer shifted a little in the seat—his hands were cuffed to a brace behind him. "Let the girl get clear—she's out of this."

Callahan swore harshly. "She's *your* girl, Greer!" he snapped. "And nothing that belongs to you is out of this."

Gary's eyes met those of the detective. He nodded his head.

"You can handle me, Sal," he stated. "But the girl doesn't know anything."

Callahan grunted. "I ain't that dumb, Greer," he muttered. "What I'm going to do for both of you is the right thing—*for me!*"

He stepped on the accelerator again. The car jerked forward, slid back. Callahan swore steadily. Gary half closed his eyes.

It was ironical—the way the thing had worked out. He had held his gun against Callahan, in this same car, minutes ago. Callahan knew where the girl was—where his men had taken her. And Gary had known that he knew. He had forced Callahan to drive to a curb spot in front of Malletti's place, back in Center City's Italian section. Malletti was a gun—and he was after Callahan. The detective had played him a rotten trick—and Malletti was faithful to his relatives. Gary wanted truth. He had forced Callahan to park at the curb and he had pointed out that if he didn't get the truth he could pour lead into the detective's body—and get clear. Malletti would take the rap, unless he had an alibi that was airtight. The police knew Malletti was out to get Callahan—and Callahan knew the same thing. Gary had had him in a tough spot.

But Callahan had weakened. Fear had raised his voice. And Malletti had recognized it. From a window of his place he had turned loose a sub-caliber gun on the parked car. Only a miracle had saved them. Things had ripped loose—and Gary had been stunned. Callahan had gotten a break. He had finished Gary—cuffed him up. And now he was taking him to the girl, to Joyce Rawlings. It looked like the end.

Gary groaned. And Callahan jerked his head toward him—laughed.

"Getting yellow?" he snapped. "Ever hear of a male and female Mexican standoff?"

Gary felt his heart pounding. That was to be the dose for Joyce and himself. Lead pounding into their bodies as they stood with their backs to some wall!

"You'll burn for—the stuff you've pulled, Sal!" he muttered.

Callahan swore thickly. "Not if I finish off you and the girl!" he snapped.

The car jerked forward a few feet.

The rear wheels got on firmer earth—it bounced along, half off the road. Straining his eyes, Gary could see the dim shape of a house in the distance. No lights showed in the few windows he could see. The house was low and rambling, well obscured from the main road. And the main road was not much of a thoroughfare. It was less than five miles from the Italian section of Center City. But this part of the country was swampy, bad land.

The car was making some headway now; Callahan had ceased to swear. A figure suddenly stepped out into the glare from the headlights. The man wore a soft hat, pulled well down over his face. He called out.

"Wrong road, you—"

Callahan cut in on the other man's words. He spoke sharply.

"It's all right, Joe! Didn't have time to switch cars. Got a load of important stuff."

The man ahead stared toward the car, then waved his left hand. His right stayed out of sight. The car pulled up close to him. Callahan spoke again.

"Hop on the running board—I may need help. Meet Mr.—" Callahan's tone was grimly amused— "Greer!"

The man on the running board swore sharply. Gary couldn't see his face—he turned it to one side. Callahan drove toward a battered shed. He talked as he drove.

"You don't have to hide your good looks from Greer, Joe." Callahan chuckled. "What this gent sees or hears won't count worth a damn!"

The car was under the shed now. Callahan cut the engine. His eyes narrowed on the gray ones of Gary.

"You got Elbow and Liseman, Greer. You got Babe Lewis. You played Elbow so that he finished off Frenchy Lamonte. And then you had your try for me. It didn't go."

There was silence except for the drip of rain somewhere inside the shed and the heavy breathing of the man who stood beside Gary, on the running board.

Gary's voice was hard. "The federal bunch were after Liseman. They were after Babe Lewis. Both of them were murderers. I was sworn into the federal service before I went after them, Callahan. They both were armed. I tricked Frenchy into getting his dose, that's right. He was a rotten killer. As for Gorringe—we fought that out. He didn't shoot as straight as I did."

The one on the running board swore thickly.

"Give it to him here, Sal!" he muttered.

Callahan sucked in his breath. He shook his head.

"The other one gets it at the same time," he muttered. "Lean forward, *Mr.* Greer."

Gary leaned forward. A key turned in the steel cuffs. His hands were free. Callahan slid out of the car.

"Watch him, Joe!" he ordered.

Gary got down from the car. His head ached—he was stiff from his cramped position. The man beside him gave him a shove.

He moved slowly. The shed was dark. Outside, from the rear of the house, a faint light filtered through the rain.

Greer's head was clearing; he was thinking faster now. He stood beside Callahan, who was lighting a cigarette.

"Five hundred grand—" he said slowly—"that's a lot of coin!"

He saw Callahan's body stiffen a little. Then the killer laughed. It was a low, rumbling laugh.

"Where *you're* going—it ain't worth a nickel!" he replied.

Gary spoke in a low, level tone.

"It would be worth something—to you."

There was a silence. Then Callahan spoke to the one he addressed as "Joe."

"Better go back down the road. We don't want to take any chances. In about an hour everything'll be fine."

The other man moved off, muttering something about liking to be in "on the show." His figure was lost in the darkness. The muzzle of a gun was pressed against the small of Gary's back.

"Just walk toward that light—there's a door around the other side. And don't make any mistakes, Greer!"

Gary walked. The house was old, sagging. It was frame, and even in the semi-darkness he could see that most of the paint was gone from the wood. He moved toward a small door beyond the filtered light. Callahan spoke.

"Hit it twice—fast like," he ordered.

Gary obeyed orders. The door opened almost instantly. A white glare hurt his eyes. There was an oath. He heard a deep voice mutter.

"Jeez! It's—Greer!"

Behind him Callahan chuckled. "None other," he stated. "Show him into the parlor, boys!"

There were dim lights in the house. Gary went in. He failed to recognize any of the men, though they made no attempt to hide their features. Callahan stepped inside behind him.

"Here we are!" he stated cheerfully. "How's the moll, Jerry?"

The man addressed was short and thickset. He grunted.

"Damn quiet!" he stated grimly. "She ain't much on gabbing."

Callahan grinned in the yellow light.

"Take Mr. Greer down to the cellar," he stated. "I'll be down to see him later. Bring up a Thompson and fix her right. Keep the girl where she is. Somebody get me a drink—I need it."

A hand gripped Gary by the left arm. He was led toward some wooden steps. He was halfway down when he got the final shove. But he didn't fall. A laugh drifted down as the door closed. It was cold in the cellar. Water dripped in several places. Gary drew in a deep breath.

His fingers twisted as he thought of Joyce Rawlings. Had the game been worth this finish? There was just one answer—it hadn't. Pete Ranning was dead. They had the girl—the girl he loved. It was over . . . And yet—Callahan loved money. Five hundred grand—that had been bait. Big bait. Would Callahan give them a play for it? Or would he turn loose the Thompson he had ordered fixed up?

"Five hundred thousand!" he muttered. "I might—get a play—for that!"

The upper door opened. A flashlight beam stabbed downward, found Gary's figure. The man who held the light was Callahan. He descended the steps slowly, carefully. He would flash the beam on the steps—then flash it on Gary's figure. In his right hand something glistened dully. Callahan was taking no chances.

At the foot of the steps he hesitated, then snapped a switch. Dull light from an electric globe spread over the cellar.

Callahan faced him. He was smiling a little. There was a table not far from Gary —a rough table with a stool beside it. Callahan motioned toward the stool.

"Sit down, Greer."

He pulled another stool toward the small table, sat down, keeping his right hand out of sight. For several seconds they sat in silence. Callahan broke it.

"Five hundred grand is a lot of coin," he stated. "A lot of coin. But if it's not in cash—"

"It can be *turned* into cash."

Callahan chuckled. "I'm not that dumb, Greer. I'd have to let you loose to get the coin—but that five hundred gees wouldn't do me much good with you running loose."

Gary smiled. "It's a lot of coin to pass up," he repeated.

"Can't hurt to *listen*. What's your offer?"

Gary spoke slowly, quietly. His eyes bored into those of the headquarters' detective. Bored into those of the man who had been known to his gang only by the name of Sal the Dude.

"Let the girl go—she'll give you her word she'll keep her mouth shut. Let me talk to her, in your presence—get her to make a quick jump away from Center City. I'll tell her you and I've made a deal. That I've got to get you the price, and that I'll meet her out West. She'll go."

Callahan was shaking his head. His eyes held a mocking expression.

"And let you follow her? You know too much, Greer."

Gary smiled slightly. He shook his head.

"You can stick to me until you've got the coin, Callahan. I can take the dose —*after* you've turned the girl loose."

Callahan stiffened. There was an incredulous expression in his eyes now.

"You mean you'll let us rub you out, after you've handed over the coin?"

"Just that." Gary's eyes were serious, narrowed. "It's worth your getting the money to have Joyce Rawlings in the clear. I'm not bargaining for myself."

The detective stared at Gary. But there was doubt in his eyes. He shook his head.

"You'd cross me up, Greer. You're a fighter. To get that much cash I'd have to give you too much rope."

Gary spoke steadily. "I know when I'm licked. The girl's not important to you."

Callahan was tapping the knuckles of his left hand on the surface of the table. He was thinking hard. It was a tempting proposition. Big-money bait. He could go abroad, live like a prince. Five hundred thousand. And he knew that Gary Greer had it. The piece of ground that his flying field was on—that was almost worth it. Sanford Greer had been wealthy.

Gary leaned across the table, his eyes on Callahan's. "I can have the coin ready for you by noon. You can stick with me. After you get it—you can bring me back here for the finish."

The detective swore softly. "You've got guts."

Gary shrugged his shoulders.

"If you tried any tricks—I'd have you. You're wanted by the police. They don't know you're working with the federal outfit. I could fill you full of lead—claim that you were trying to make a break after I'd grabbed you. You wouldn't be able to talk—and my play would be that I didn't know you were under federal jurisdiction, had federal authority."

"You're using your head," Gary said slowly. "You could get me before I could spout a word. Some of your boys could see that the girl gets on a train. They could ride the train for a while, even. Big money, Callahan."

Callahan was staring beyond Gary. He was thinking of Paris, Vienna, Berlin. He was thinking of Goldie Lawrence. Five hundred grand would take her away from "Spots" Deane. And Goldie was worth having.

Gary's feet were pressed firmly against the concrete of the cellar floor. With sudden, irresistible force, he struck—struck for the point of the heavy chin.

Callahan never had the chance to get his gun up.

With a sharp, cracking thud Gary's right fist hit square on the button. Callahan groaned—his fingers relaxed; his body slumped forward, and Gary lifted the stool on which he had been sitting and tapped the unprotected forehead. Callahan's body slipped from the table edge to the concrete floor.

Gary listened. There was laughter up above—it reached him faintly. The door was bolted on the inside; he remembered that. In a flash he was kneeling beside Callahan. Blood was trickling from the detective's forehead—his pulse was in evidence.

Gary gagged him first. He had two weapons, both automatics. Gary took both of them. He dragged Callahan to a far corner of the cellar—used his belt on the man's legs. Playing safe, he used a second handkerchief as a gag.

There was a sudden pounding on the door at the top of the steps. He heard raised voices. A man was swearing fiercely. From somewhere in the house there was the sound of doors slamming. In the distance voices were calling out. Something was wrong. What?

Gary shouted, imitating Callahan's voice. "What in hell's the racket?"

A man answered from beyond the door. "It's the girl—she *gone!*"

Gary tensed, felt his heart leap. Joyce was free!

Callahan's men expected orders; otherwise they'd be down here.

"Get outside—all of you!" he called out thickly. "Get word to Joe—and search the grounds around the place."

Beyond the bolted door he heard the man Callahan had called Jerry shouting instructions. A door slammed—there were no more footfalls.

Gary went up the stairs. He unbolted the door—opened it. Dim lights gave the room a flickering yellow color. There seemed to be no one in the house. There was a heavy lock on the outside of the door—a key in it. Gary closed the door back of him, snapped the lock. He slipped the key in his pocket.

If he could get clear—get away from the house and find aid, federal aid, there would be a chance. If he could get back with help, before Callahan was found in the cellar—before the girl was caught again . . . He turned toward the door that led out to the side of the house, Callahan's gray cap pulled low over his eyes.

And then he saw the Tommy. The submachine gun rested on the floor, back of a chair. He reached for it. Loaded—ready for action.

He heard men's voices. Rain beat against the windowpanes.

There was no one in sight outside. But in the distance the beam from a flashlight cut the darkness.

Gary moved forward, machine gun at the ready. The Thompson was a sweet weapon to have with him.

He started toward the rear of the house, the shed into which Callahan had driven the car. A figure loomed up close to him; a light flashed on the ground. Gary snapped out words, trying to give them Callahan's tone.

"Douse that glare, damn you!" he ordered. Gary kept his head down.

"Sorry, boss . . . Benny tied her up, but she slipped loose. Went out a window —twenty feet up. Damn if I can see how she made it—no footprints around."

"Keep looking!" Gary grunted.

He moved away in the darkness, reached the shed, checked the car. No one inside. A chance now.

The key was in the ignition switch—Callahan had left it there.

The engine roared smoothly into life.

Gary backed the car out of the shed, in reverse. On the seat beside him was the Tommy.

Lights were flashing up toward the roof. He could hear shouts, but he couldn't distinguish the words. He was thinking about Joyce. It seemed rotten to leave her behind. Suppose she was still up there on the roof? They'd find her—search for him. When he didn't come in they'd become suspicious. How soon would it be before they'd batter down the cellar door, find Callahan below? Could he get back with aid in time to save the girl?

His face was twisted as he drove toward the road. And then, suddenly, he saw her. Joyce! She was staggering out from the darkness on the right—her clothes were mud-stained. She threw up her right hand, slumped downward to the mud of the road. In a flash he was out from behind the wheel—running toward her. Back of him from the direction of the house, he heard hoarse shouts. Some one was calling out, "Sal! Something's wrong—" Gary was lifting the girl in his arms. She had fainted. He carried her to the car, swung her into the seat. Then he gunned the car forward. He had trouble holding it on the rough road. Once it skidded off into deep mud—and he lost precious seconds getting back on the road.

Louder shouts behind them. But he was almost to the main road. He wheeled toward Center City, kept his foot hard down on the accelerator.

At his side, Joyce Rawlings stirred.

"Gary!" Her voice was faint, a whisper. She sat up a little in the seat. Her face was pale. "They came for me—said that the district attorney's office wanted me—"

"I know," said Greer.

"They brought me to the house. Tied my hands. But, somehow, I was able to get loose. I saw that one of the windows had not been boarded up all the way. I got out that way—worked around the roof to the rear of the house . . ."

"That was—nervy work!" Gary told her. He looked back. There were lights behind them on the road. He swore softly. "This bus hasn't much speed—they'll be on us before we hit the outskirts of town. Callahan—he's Sal the Dude. He's the one who ran things, had my father murdered."

Joyce Rawlings was tense in the seat. Her head was close to his. He was forced to speak loudly against the beat of the engine.

"They got—Pete Ranning, Joyce."

Her body stiffened; her eyes were wide on his.

"Pete was drugged—got the stuff meant for me. I got him to a hotel, near River Street. Thought he'd be all right. But someone traced us—and when I went to the apartment, worried about you, they finished Pete—"

The lights behind were brighter.

"They're gaining on us. Got to try and lose 'em."

He twisted the wheel hard right. They were off the main highway now—on the slope of a dirt road. It was in bad condition. The car slid to the left, dropped into a shallow ditch. Gary spoke sharply.

"Outside—quick!"

He lifted the Thompson machine gun—slipped through the mud, cut back into a field of low brush. The girl was right behind him. He stared toward the main road—saw the lights of the car behind swing in their direction as the machine made the turn.

"Down!" he cried sharply. "Don't move!"

They were both on their knees. He could hear the engine of the pursuing car; the headlights were pointed toward the field in which they were hiding.

Gary lifted his head. "They've spotted the car. Keep low—and follow me."

He led the way back toward the main road as three of the gang left the pursuit car to fan out along the edge of the field.

There was a wind across the low foliage of the field, and the rain was coming down hard.

They reached the main road again.

"We're going—across. Keep low—and run. Are you—up to it?"

She nodded. Her face was pale—her dark street dress was soaked.

Gary got a good grip on the Tommy. There was no traffic on the road—nothing within a half-mile. Straightening, he started forward. The girl was at his side, on the right. Suddenly he glanced toward the pursuit car.

Its driver, alone inside the vehicle, was backing onto the main road. In a second his lights would be flashing along the stretch they'd have to cross.

"Stay here." Gary's voice was grim. "I'm going to get that car."

He was gone even as the girl uttered a cry of protest. It was the best way out, and if he could get the car, get back of the wheel, there would be an end to the pursuit.

He got within fifteen feet of the car along the main road, before he stood up. The engine was running, throttled down, and the driver was still staring up the dirt road.

The Tommy swung up; he leveled it at the driver's head. Then he walked forward.

"One move—you get the load!" he snapped in a low tone.

The driver's head jerked—but not more than an inch. His eyes stared wildly toward the Thompson. Gary was at his side now. The glow from the headlights outlined his body faintly. He spoke again.

"Both hands outside the car—over the door!"

The driver's hands moved outside the car. They were empty. His face was white.

"Call to your pals—tell 'em to look farther up the road!" Gary's voice was like ice. "Tell 'em you saw something move—shout, and don't make any mistakes!"

The driver took a deep breath. He called out hoarsely. "Hey, Jerry! Go on—up the road. I seen somethin' move—"

"That's enough!" Gary swung the Tommy's muzzle a few inches. "Climb out. *Move!*"

The driver obeyed, eyes fixed on the Thompson.

"Got a rod—toss it!" Gary ordered.

A pistol struck the road; Gary kicked it into a ditch.

"How many—looking for us?"

The driver grunted. "Three."

Greer's voice was hard. "Walk ten feet along the shoulder. Keep clear of the car's lights. Then get down flat. On your belly. And stretch out your arms where I can see 'em."

The driver did this, muttering darkly.

Gary slipped behind the wheel of the car. A fast roadster. He got it under way. As he rolled past the driver, he shouted, "Keep your head down."

Then he was stopping—Joyce was climbing in beside him. They were picking up speed now—he shifted into high. The roadster *was* fast—and she handled easily.

"You did it! They *can't* follow us now!"

"Steady!" Gary was smiling a little. "We're not out of this yet."

There was no pursuit. But he knew that Callahan would not give up easily. And the man was powerful.

"We're heading for South Side Field," he stated grimly, staring at the road ahead. "I've got enough on Callahan to send him to the chair. He knows it. But I can't fight him—not this way. I'm going to get you clear. Then I'll come back—"

"I can't stop you, Gary. I'm tired—tired of it all."

Joyce Rawlings relaxed in the seat beside him. Her eyes were half closed. The lights of Center City gave a yellow glow in the distance.

Callahan was still alive. And while he lived there was danger. Danger for the girl beside him—and for himself. He stared down at his wrists. The skin was scraped, torn where the steel cuffs had rubbed. Callahan had put the cuffs on him —and had taken them off. He had been too sure. But the next time there would be no waiting. Money would not be even a temporary bait, Gary knew that.

He drove with his eyes on the wet road ahead. Already he was making plans—speed was necessary. Callahan would be desperate. And that quality would breed cunning. Joyce Rawlings must be gotten clear. After that—

The gate guard came out from the little house and stared at Gary. His eyes widened.

"Hello, Brooks—is Jensen inside?"

"He came in an hour ago—"

Gary nodded. He drove the car through the entrance, then headed down the road back of the deadline.

B Hanger was open. Greer turned inside. "Stay with the car, Joyce," he said. "I've got to see Jensen."

He moved toward his office.

Jensen was in charge of the field now. He wondered if he had learned yet of Pete Ranning's death.

Gary opened the door—stepped in. Jensen was talking to Eddie Lee, Gary's mechanic. They both looked relieved to see ｜him.

Gary asked Jensen: "Who's at the field—what pilot can I have? In a hurry."

"Teddy Dorres is here," said Jensen.

Gary nodded. "Get Teddy out to Hangar B in a hurry. I want him to fly a passenger, in a cabin ship. A National will do. Get the ship out—warmed up. And I'll want a Greer Special."

Jensen nodded. "I'll break out a crew—have the ships warmed up in twenty minutes. You flying alone?"

Gary's eyes went to those of Eddie Lee. He spoke quietly: "I'll need you, Eddie."

"Right. What do I *do*?"

"Callahan is desperate. Desperate enough to ride up into the sky to stop us. Can you handle a Thompson?"

Eddie nodded. "You bet."

Gary spoke in a hard tone. "You ride in the rear cockpit of the Special. I'll fly her. It may be a false alarm, Eddie—but I'm damn glad you're here. Come on—let's get some 'chutes!"

The two ships rested side by side on the deadline. The rain had ceased, but the night was black and the wind was blowing in gusts.

Gary snapped the last strap on the girl's 'chute pack. He spoke in a level tone. "I know you don't want to go, Joyce—"

"I'll go—if it's what you want."

She turned away from him. She was climbing into the cabin plane now. Teddy helped her, then faced Gary.

Greer spoke in a low, intense tone.

"You've got a load of gas—stay up until dawn. Try to make Connie Webster's field at Courtneyville. If you can't do that—get down at the Rice Airport. I'll fly along with you for a couple of hours. Get plenty of altitude. Seven thousand, at least. If I turn back at any time—you keep going. Your job is to get Miss Rawlings out of this. Never mind about me."

Dorres narrowed his eyes. He adjusted his 'chute pack. "I read you. And I'll get her clear, all right."

The cabin plane rolled out, headed into the wind. The floodlights were on. She got off smoothly on the number-one runway. Gary opened up the throttle of the Greer Special. The ship was an open cockpit plane of his own design.

He rolled her along the number-two runway, lifted her from the surface easily. Her engine had power—and she climbed up through the gusty night air at a steeper angle than that of the cabin ship.

Teddy Dorres was getting his altitude over the airport. He climbed the cabin ship in wide circles, keeping a mild bank. The ship was showing her running lights —but Gary banked the Greer Special wide and snapped his own plane's running lights out. Less than two feet of fuselage separated the two cockpits; Gary twisted his head, shouted at Eddie Lee.

"Like old times, Eddie!"

Lee nodded his head. In the dull glow from the cockpit lights, Gary could see that the mechanic was smiling.

Teddy Dorres was heading his plane westward, gaining altitude now in a straight climb in that direction. Gary banked around—pulled back on the stick, nosed the ship up. She was a quarter-mile from the cabin plane.

"Lift that Tommy and brace it against the prop wash!" he shouted to Lee. "See if you can hold it!"

When he turned his head again Eddie was leaning the gun across the curve of the cockpit fabric, on the right side. He was sighting the weapon. He nodded his head.

"I can—hold her—all right!" he shouted above the roar of the air-cooled engine.

The cabin plane was flying on a level keel now; Teddy Dorres had eight thousand feet of altitude. Gary went a bit higher, but the wind was bad. He dropped lower.

Center City lay back of them now, to the eastward—a blur of yellow light in the sky. His eyes searched the darkness for any sign of a third ship's exhaust trail. He saw none. The night was so black that it was difficult to get a horizon. The level gauge and instinct—these were the guiding factors.

Dorres was a good pilot. He would get the girl through.

Gary narrowed his eyes. The reddish glow of a ship's exhaust, low in the sky, to the south! A plane had gotten off from one of the level stretches beyond the city and was climbing rapidly upward.

Gary opened the throttle of the Greer Special wide. He watched the climbing plane. He could see the faint outline of her now. Her pilot could pick up the exhaust color from the cabin ship. And from Gary's plane.

"Callahan!" he muttered grimly. "Never started—after us. Played safe—had a plane out near his headquarters. Someone got word to him that we'd got clear. That's it—ten to one!"

He banked in close to the cabin plane.

Gary jerked his head, shouted at Eddie Lee.

"Swing that Tommy up!"

He heard Eddie shout something. Then he was diving the Greer Special toward the climbing ship.

He pulled the stick back, banked vertically over the other ship. She was five hundred feet below now—and her pilot had leveled her off. Gary reached toward the flare rack. He dropped one flare—then a second. He banked wide.

The first flare burst—and the plane below banked to the northward. Gary stared down at her.

She was bathed in white light from the drifting flare. And on her fuselage side was a serial number, and the letters—U.S.A.M.

Eddie Lee called out sharply. "She's all right, Gary! Air mail!"

The second flare burst. The plane was banking almost directly beneath it.

She was an open-cockpit job, a De Havilland type. Two men were aboard.

Gary slipped the Greer Special, and she shrilled downward. He kicked her out of the slip, got her on level keel, banked around. The mail ship was winging a hundred yards on the Greer Special's port side. Her exhaust trail cut through the darkness. Gary waved his left hand, toward the other plane. The ship had probably been forced down and had just taken off again. It was a bad night for flying.

He glanced westward—far in the distance there was the faint trail from the exhaust of the cabin ship.

Then, suddenly, the De Havilland was heading straight for Gary's plane.

Eddie shouted a hoarse warning, seconds later, as Gary was pulling back on the stick, trying to take evasive action. Too late. Gary had seen the other plane bank, but his stick movement was too late.

Red fire streaked from the nose of the air-mail ship. Fabric ripped.

The Special shuddered. Behind him Gary heard the sharper snap of Eddie Lee's Thompson. The Greer Special went over on a wing as Gary jerked back on the throttle. Callahan had tricked them at the finish—had his plane painted with the insignia of the local air-mail ships—and he had turned loose a machine gun mounted on the front cockpit cowling. And had scored a hit. The Greer Special was out of control.

Gary jerked his head. "Eddie—jump!" he shouted.

He saw Eddie rise in the cockpit. His body seemed to float away from the slipping, crippled plane.

A shape plunged down from the starboard side. Once more machine gun lead battered into the Greer Special. The propeller was shattered—Gary ducked his head beneath the cockpit as bits of metal from the engine pounded back.

Callahan was making sure this time. The crippled plane was in the first turn of a spin now. She was down around two thousand feet. Gary reached for his safety-belt buckle, snapped it loose. Waves of dizziness were sweeping over him. He pulled himself up from the cockpit seat. And then the killer plane dived again.

Red fire streaked toward Greer's ship. There was a stinging pain in Gary's left arm. Glass shattered on the instrument board.

The killer plane was in very close. Her nose dropped—her pilot was going to make sure, then dive beneath the plunging special.

It happened in the space of two flashing seconds. The Greer Special had been dropping in a spin. She slipped out of it suddenly—and the attack plane's propeller struck her in mid-fuselage.

The force of the crash almost hurled Gary from the cockpit, but he gripped a strut, hung on.

Now both ships, tangled in the sky, were plunging downward. The attack plane's pilot had timed his dive too finely.

Instantly, the other plane was afire. The shattered propeller had smashed back against the engine. A feed line had been severed.

Gary Greer, clinging desperately to the strut, stared toward the mail plane's front cockpit. In the light of the flames he saw Callahan. The gangster-detective was trying to fight clear.

For a split second Callahan's face turned toward Greer. It was twisted with fear—lighted by the flames that were shooting back. Callahan was trapped. The left wing-tip of his ship had buckled inward.

Gary laughed, a soundless laughter—as Callahan slumped down into the cockpit.

Gary swung his body around the strut, shoved himself upward.

And then he was free—somersaulting. He counted three, then jerked the rip-cord ring of his 'chute pack.

The silk crackled free. Harness tightened about his body. He was drifting now. A dull booming sound reached his ears.

A line of trees drifted past his swaying body. He struck.

He was down in the mud now.

He didn't lose consciousness. The 'chute silk collapsed slowly. Greer struggled to his knees. His whole body was battered, aching. Heat from the flames had seared his face. His left arm was numb, bleeding. He got clear of the harness, walked a few feet, sat down. He fumbled for a cigarette.

Somewhere beyond the field into which he had dropped there was a dull, red glare.

Howard Alling spoke very quietly. His eyes went from those of Joyce Rawlings to the gray ones of Gary Greer.

"Jerry Contis was riding that ship with Callahan. He lived for three hours—and he talked plenty. . . . With the information we have, we can smash the present political outfit in Center City. And a lot of them will face federal charges."

Gary Greer smiled. "Good," he said. "Good going."

Alling sighed. "Well, guess I'll leave you two. I've got work to do."

And he left the hotel room.

Gary shifted position on the couch. Joyce smiled at him.

"Three broken ribs—and my left arm out of commission," he said. "Could be worse. At least the job's done."

Joyce was silent for a moment. She couldn't talk about her feelings, two nights ago, in the air beyond Center City. She had seen the third plane climb into the sky—she had seen Gary dive his ship. And Teddy Dorres had winged her away. It had been a terrible moment.

"I won't ask you if it was worth it, Gary," she said simply. "I know the answer —it wasn't. But you *had* to do it."

"Callahan killed my father," he said slowly, coldly. "Yes . . . I *had* to get him." Joyce nodded.

Gary smiled at her. It didn't hurt him much to move his right arm. So he moved it.

Whitfield in *Black Mask*
1926–1934

Series characters: Bill Scott   (BS)
Chuck Reddington   (CR)
Mac   (M)
Gary Greer   (GG)
Mal Ourney   (MO)
Jo Gar   (JG)
Ben Jardinn   (BJ)
Alan Van Cleve   (AC)
Don Free   (DF)
Dion Davies   (DD)

*—indicates use as basis for published novel
•—included in *The* Black Mask *Boys*

"Scotty Troubles Trouble" (BS)   March 1926
"Scotty Scouts Around" (BS)   April 1926
"Jenny Meets the Boys"   June 1926
"Black Air"   July 1926
"Roaring Death"   August 1926
"Flying Gold"   September 1926
"Delivered Goods"   November 1926
"Ten Hours" (CR)   December 1926
"Uneasy Money"   January 1927
"White Murder" (CR)   February 1927
"Sky-High Odds" (CR)   March 1927
"South of Savannah" (CR)   May 1927

"Bottled Death" (CR)   June 1927
"Live Men's Gold" (CR)   August 1927
"Sixty Minutes"   October 1927
"Red Pearls"   November 1927
"The Sky's the Limit" (CR)   January 1928
"Soft Goods"   February 1928
"Little Guns"   April 1928
"Black Murder"   May 1928
"First Blood" (M)   June 1928
"Blue Murder" (M)   July 1928
"High Death" (M)   August 1928
"Red Wings" (M)   September 1928
"Ghost Guns" (M)   October 1928
"The Sky Trap" (M)   November 1928
*"On the Spot" (GG)   February 1929
*"Out of the Sky" (GG)   March 1929
*"The Pay-Off" (GG)   April 1929
*"High Odds" (GG)   May 1929
*"Within the Circle" (GG)   June 1929
*"The Carnival Kill" (GG)   July 1929
*"River Street Death" (GG)   August 1929
*"The Squeeze" (GG)   September 1929
•*"Sal the Dude" (GG)   October 1929
*"Outside" (MO)   December 1929
*"Red Smoke" (MO)   January 1930
*"Green Ice" (MO)   February 1930
"West of Guam" (as "Roman Decolta") (JG)   February 1930
*"Oval Face" (MO)   March 1930
"Death in the Pasig" (as "Decolta") (JG)   March 1930
*"Killers' Show" (MO)   April 1930
"Red Hemp" (as "Decolta") (JG)   April 1930
"Signals of Storm" (as "Decolta") (JG)   June 1930
"Enough Rope" (as "Decolta") (JG)   July 1930
"Murder by Mistake"   August 1930
*"Death in a Bowl" (BJ)   three-parter   September, October, November 1930
"Nagasaki Bound" (as "Decolta") (JG)   September 1930
"Nagasaki Knives" (as "Decolta") (JG)   October 1930
"The Caleso Murders" (as "Decolta") (JG)   December 1930
"Murder in the Ring"   December 1930
"Silence House" (as "Decolta") (JG)   January 1931
"About Kid Deth"   February 1931
"Diamonds of Dread" (as "Decolta") (JG)   February 1931
"The Man in White" (as "Decolta") (JG)   March 1931
"Face Powder"   April 1931

"The Blind Chinese" (as "Decolta") (JG)   April 1931
"Soft City"   May 1931
"Red Dawn" (as "Decolta") (JG)   May 1931
"For Sale—Murder"   June 1931
"Blue Glass" (as "Decolta") (JG)   July 1931
"Diamonds of Death" (as "Decolta") (JG)   August 1931
*"The Sky Club Affair" (AC)   August 1931
*"Red Terrace" (AC)   September 1931
*"Steel Arena" (AC)   October 1931
"Shooting Gallery" (as "Decolta") (JG)   October 1931
*"Van Cleve Calling" (AC)   November 1931
*"Unfair Exchange" (AC)   December 1931
"The Javanese Mask" (as "Decolta") (JG)   December 1931
"The Black Sampan" (as "Decolta") (JG)   January 1932
*"Skyline Death" (AC)   January 1932
"Inside Job"   February 1932
"China Man" (as "Decolta") (JG)   March 1932
"Man Killer" (DF)   April 1932
"The Siamese Cat" (as "Decolta") (JG)   April 1932
"Walking Dynamite" (DF)   May 1932
"Climbing Death" (as "Decolta") (JG)   July 1932
"Blue Murder" (DF)   September 1932
"Dead Men Tell Tales"   November 1932
"The Magician Murder" (as "Decolta") (JG)   November 1932
"Murder by Request" (BJ)   January 1933
"The Man From Shanghai" (as "Decolta") (JG)   May 1933
"The Amber Fan" (as "Decolta") (JG)   July 1933
"Dark Death" (BJ)   August 1933
"A Woman Can Kill" (DD)   September 1933
"Money Talk" (DD)   October 1933
"Not Tomorrow"   November 1933
"Murder Again"   December 1933
"High Murder"   January 1934
"Death on Fifth Avenue"   February 1934

Published Whitfield Novels Derived
from *Black Mask*

Green Ice—New York: Knopf, 1930
    (Derived from "Outside," "Red Smoke," "Green Ice," "Oval Face,"
    "Killer's Show")

Five—(as "Temple Field") New York: Farrar & Rinehart, 1931
  (Derived from "On the Spot," "Out of the Sky," "The Pay-Off," "High
  Odds," "Within the Circle," "The Carnival Kill," "River Street Death,"
  "The Squeeze," "Sal the Dude")
Death in a Bowl—New York: Knopf, 1931
  (Derived from the three-part serial)
Killer's Carnival—(as "Temple Field") New York: Farrar & Rinehart, 1932
  (Derived from "The Sky Club Affair," "Red Terrace," "Steel Arena," "Van
  Cleve Calling," "Unfair Exchange," "Skyline Death")

Behind the Mask:
Frederick Nebel

•

He was reading Schopenhauer at fifteen, yet spent just *one day* in high school. He didn't believe in formal schooling, he believed in self-education. He felt that he had "a natural gift for storytelling," and proved it by selling more than 300 pieces of fiction to the widest possible range of magazines, from pulps to slicks. Sometimes he used pen names. One of them was "Grimes Hill." An editor asked Nebel about this pseudonym. "I was born at the foot of Grimes Hill on Staten Island, New York, in November of 1903," he explained. "So it seemed a logical choice."

Although he finished grade school, Frederick Nebel determined he would not "waste good years" in high school. By 1918 he was employed as a car checker on the New York wharf. At the age of seventeen, in 1920, he was living in the Canadian north woods, working his great-uncle's homestead as a farmhand. He loved this wild country, absorbing its lore and legends, becoming a self-taught expert in Canadian history.

Out of his teens, Nebel returned to New York and obtained a job with the railroad, where he functioned as a brakeman on passenger trains. When he wasn't working, he was writing.

The byline of Frederick Lewis Nebel began to appear regularly in the pulp pages of *Northwest Stories* during 1925. These "true tales of the North country" were accompanied by an ink sketch of the twenty-one-year-old author, a pipe between his teeth, looking resolute in a wide-collared fur parka with tall, snow-covered pine trees in the background. Nebel's specialized knowledge of the Canadian wilderness had helped launch his career as a professional storyteller.

As "Lewis Nebel," he sold his first *Black Mask* story to editor Phil Cody early in 1926. His second tale for the *Mask* was printed under Joe Shaw's editorship late that year, and Nebel became one of Cap's "boys," beginning a close ten-year relationship.

During the winter of 1926, obeying a restless urge for travel and adventure, Nebel shipped out for the Caribbean aboard a Scandinavian tramp steamer.

Europe was next, and after a sojourn in London, he headed for Paris, where (in 1928) he met a young lady named Dorothy Blank. She was the daughter of a well-to-do merchandising manager, and her conservative upbringing had not prepared her for this encounter with a globe-trotting young adventurer. Nebel fascinated her; they arranged to meet back in the States—and were married in May of 1930 in St. Louis, Missouri.

By this stage of his career, Nebel was selling to a large number of pulp markets, including *Action Stories, Danger Trail, Sea Stories,* and, steadily, to *Black Mask.* Shaw encouraged his authors to create series characters that could be featured year after year, and Nebel came up with a two-man series team, Captain Steve Mac-Bride, of the Richmond City police, and a news reporter with the *Free Press* named Kennedy.

Dave Lewis, a leading Nebel authority, described the physical differences between them: "MacBride is chisel-jawed with a beak nose, ruddy brown skin and windy blue eyes; Kennedy has tired eyes, pale hair and a washed-out face. MacBride has a hard, bony frame and stands ramrod straight; Kennedy is fragile and stoop-shouldered."

Influenced by Hammett's "Poisonville" series, Nebel created his fictional town in the same corrupt vein. The crimes in Richmond City keep MacBride very busy, and Lewis expands on the series' law-and-order theme:

> To MacBride, it is "treason" for a cop to betray the force. He demands the law be respected and strives to carve out a system of two-fisted justice in Richmond City. "You go right on, year after year, banging your head against a stone wall," Kennedy tells him, "and damn me if sometimes you don't actually bust the wall down."

Although he's an ace news reporter, who often gets MacBride out of trouble, Kennedy drinks constantly and claims that his career interferes with his drinking. "Work," he tells MacBride, "is the curse of the drinking class."

In 1930, after the phenomenal success of *The Maltese Falcon,* Shaw wanted more Sam Spade stories, but Hammett refused to provide them. He was earning big money in Hollywood and had quit the pulps.

Shaw asked Nebel to come up with a new private eye directly in the Spade mold, a series character he could feature in *Mask.*

Nebel obliged with ultratough "Donny" Donahue, of the Inter-State Detective Agency in New York, an ex-cop discharged from the force because he wouldn't bend to local corruption. His agency boss is "pontifical" Asa Hinkle, who sends the big Irishman out to do battle with the forces of crime.

The Donahue stories are crude and rough-carved, lacking the polished depth of Hammett's Spade. However, Nebel's tall, hard-knuckled detective proved to be a winner with *Black Mask* readers, and the author kept him in action for the next five years, turning out fifteen Donahue stories into March of 1935.

Nebel was gratified by Joe Shaw's "encouragement and enthusiasm," and felt that the *Mask* was a full cut above the level of most pulps. In an early letter to Shaw he expressed "a keen interest in the progress of *Black Mask*. I like the punch in it, the true-to-life characters, the logical situations."

Capable of turning out five thousand words a day, Nebel blazed through the pulps like a prairie fire, creating one successful series character after another: Corporal Chet Tyson, a Canadian "Mountie," for *Northwest Stories;* The Driftin' Kid for *Lariat;* flying adventurers Bill Gales and Mike McGill for *Air Stories;* Brinkhaus, a middle-aged police sergeant, for *Detective Fiction Weekly*—and, for *Dime Detective,* another tough private eye, Cardigan, from the Cosmos Agency in St. Louis. In addition to all these, Nebel kept the MacBride-Kennedy series going strong for Joe Shaw, writing three dozen stories about the pair over an eight-year span.

To ease the pressure of turning out so much pulp wordage, Nebel and his wife spent their summers vacationing in the Maine woods.

Golf was one of Nebel's favorite pastimes, and he told Joe Shaw that he used these summers in Maine "for the express purpose of straightening out the old hook . . ." He was never more than a fair golfer but maintained an abiding interest in the sport.

In 1932 Nebel tackled a novel, slowing his output to "only three novelettes a month" while he worked on the longer manuscript. It took him eight months to finish *Sleepers East,* published in 1933 by Little, Brown. His early experiences on passenger trains had provided the background he needed for this suspense thriller.

As one critic described the novel's plot:

> Its entire action takes place within less than ten hours on a train traveling from the Midwest to New York. The story gives a cross section of the lives of twelve characters, whose skeins of existence tangle and are briefly interwoven during the course of the train ride.

Pulp historian Philip Durham examined the author's theme:

> In *Sleepers East* Nebel wrote a novel of murder and intrigue . . . in which the action is governed by the toughness and weakness in men. The theme, not infrequently appropriated by hard-boiled writers, concerns man's inability to control the incidents of life; man cannot really make the grade, but if he gives it a good try he may get some of what is coming to him . . . To live as much and as violently as one can—even for a single night—may be the only way.

When *Sleepers East* became an immediate best seller, and screen rights were sold to Fox Studios for $5,000, Nebel realized that he needed a sharp agent to guide his burgeoning career. Shaw introduced him to Carl Brandt (of the influential Brandt & Brandt Agency in New York), and a lasting relationship was formed.

Another major change in Nebel's life involved a permanent move East in 1934.

As a friend of the period recalled: "Fred and Dorothy found this two-hundred-year-old farmhouse in Ridgefield, Connecticut . . . Needed a lot of work, so they totally renovated the old place. Really fixed it up nice."

Nebel grew to love the Connecticut woods country, which reminded him of Maine. His new life here inspired him to look toward an expansion of his career.

Under Brandt's guidance, he published two more hardcover novels, *But Not the End* and *Fifty Roads to Town,* and began selling regularly to the higher-paying slick markets beginning with the *Saturday Evening Post.* Nebel found that he was particularly adept in writing short-shorts and sold many of these to *Collier's.*

He had ceased writing for *Black Mask* by the end of 1936, when Joe Shaw had been fired. Shaw lived in Scarsdale, New York, and the Nebels visited him there. Nebel considered Shaw's dismissal from *Mask* to be "a damned outrage." It had helped strengthen his decision to leave the pulps.

By the spring of 1937, with his final Cardigan tale in *Dime Detective* that May, Nebel was finished with the wood-pulp markets. In all, over a twelve-year period, he had contributed more than 230 stories, most of novelette length. (Ironically, the death of his pulp writing marked the birth of his son, Christopher Nebel, that same year.)

Crime writing no longer held Nebel's interest, and by 1940, when he failed to sell a 50,000-word short mystery novel, *Regret the Night,* he decided to concentrate on stories of "contemporary romance."

Financially, this was a wise decision. The slick magazines thrived on romantic fiction, and Carl Brandt was able to sell almost everything Nebel wrote to such top markets as *Cosmopolitan, McCall's, Redbook, Liberty, Good Housekeeping,* and *Woman's Home Companion.*

On a number of occasions, Nebel received offers to write for Hollywood, but he refused all studio bids. His pal Hammett had returned to New York with bitter stories about working in films; Nebel wanted nothing to do with screenwriting.

Several of his stories were purchased for motion pictures, but he had no hand in the adaptations. Nebel sold rights to his MacBride-Kennedy characters to Warner Bros. in the 1930s, and the studio subsequently produced a series of nine pictures. In these, newsman Kennedy underwent an amazing book-to-film transformation, becoming a wisecracking news *woman,* "Torchy" Blaine. Warners wanted to provide some love interest for the big cop, and Torchy gamely pursued Mac-Bride through all nine films!

When a new film version of his first novel, *Sleepers East,* was released, it had become *Sleepers West,* and his third novel, a drama, was transformed into a lighthearted screen musical.

Nebel was pragmatic about such alterations: "Hell, they always change the stuff around. But I don't mind—just so *I* don't have to make the changes."

On television, his work was adapted for such shows as *General Electric Theater* and *Studio One.* Again, Nebel stayed well clear of the scripting. But he happily cashed the checks these TV shows generated.

In the early 1940s, during the years of World War II, Nebel served on the

Ridgefield rationing board. During the same period, Joe Shaw was preparing a collection of *Black Mask* tales for Simon & Schuster, featuring the writers who had been influential in molding the magazine's hard-boiled style. He cleared rights to work by Hammett, Chandler, Whitfield, Cain, and other "stars of the *Mask,*" but Nebel declined Shaw's offer to reprint a MacBride-Kennedy story, "Winter Kill."

Shaw was stunned. "Dammit, Fred," he protested in a letter, "you can't be left out, any more than Dash or Ray Chandler."

But Nebel felt that his early detective fiction was "dated"; he would not grant his permission. *The Hard-Boiled Omnibus* went to press in 1946 without Frederick Nebel.

Three years later he changed his mind about reprinting his *Black Mask* work and accepted a $1,000 offer from Avon Books for a Donahue collection of novelettes they wanted to call *The Black Mask Murders*. After due consideration, the editors decided to use a gaudier sales title, *Six Deadly Dames*—and the book was published as an original paperback in the fall of 1950.

Nebel planned several more collections from *Mask,* but when a selection of the MacBride-Kennedy novelettes failed to find a publisher, he lost interest. (In 1980, Gregg Press issued *Six Deadly Dames* in hardcover; it remains Nebel's sole collection.)

In 1956, at the urging of editor Fred Dannay, Nebel agreed to "return to the fold" and write some new stories for *Ellery Queen's Mystery Magazine*. The six he completed marked his final work in the genre.

Plagued with high blood pressure, Nebel sold his home in Connecticut and moved to California in 1958, settling with Dorothy in Laguna Beach the following year. He was frustrated when his failing health would no longer permit him to play golf.

At age fifty-eight, in 1962, Nebel's last short story was printed; he had sold more than seventy pieces of fiction to the slick-paper markets, emerging as one of the pulps' stellar graduates. He would live another five years.

"As sick as he was, Fred didn't quit writing during those last years," a friend revealed. "He was working on a novel, but just didn't have the strength to finish it."

Robert Randisi, who wrote the introduction to the 1980 Gregg Press edition of *Six Deadly Dames,* commented on Nebel's final novel: "The outline was done, the characters created, but . . . he was unable to concentrate for very long and [could write] only two or three pages. . . . [Nebel had] a heart condition . . . an enlarged aorta, and had been on Digitalis for years."

On May 3, 1967, three days after suffering a cerebral hemorrhage, Frederick Nebel died in Laguna Beach at the age of sixty-three. His widow spoke of "Fred's wonderful sense of humor" which had helped sustain both of them through the long decade of his illness. In photos, this element of humor is absent; he is inevitably grim, an intense, long-faced man with dark, penetrating eyes. He inscribed one of these glowering photos: "For Joseph T. Shaw, with true regard."

And, surely, Nebel had done his most vigorous and characteristic work for Shaw, in the days when Donahue and Steve MacBride fisted and shot their way through the pages of *Black Mask*.

Critic Will Murray rates Nebel as "one of the few writers to portray the tough detective realistically." He adds:

> His characters are genuinely hard-boiled . . . [existing] in the grim world of Depression America in which survival is the guiding imperative, a world of greed, political corruption and . . . violence. His detectives . . . are insular, pragmatic men . . . survivors who pride themselves on their toughness and their ability to "take it." . . . [They are] never motivated by sentiment, but rather by pride . . .

Rough Justice

Will Murray called the hero of this story "Nebel's quintessential hard-boiled character."

He's a tall, raw-boned Irish detective from New York. Tough-talking. Tough-acting. His sense of basic morality keeps him on the legal side of the law, but he doesn't hesitate to bend some rules (and some heads) in order to get a job done. "I hate like hell to lose," he says. "I'm the world's sorest loser."

He's Bogart in a straw hat; he's John Wayne without the horse. He's Donahue.

In this, his first case, the tough Irishman is thrust into the sweltering heat of a St. Louis summer. (Nebel makes the weather so real you can feel the sweat under your collar.) Donahue faces wily lawyers, publicity-hungry cops, crooked cons "on the lam"—and then there's the deadly dame. . . .

"Rough Justice" is not included in Nebel's published collection *Six Deadly Dames* and has never been reprinted in any form since its original appearance in *Black Mask*.

Donahue.
Very tough.
Very terse.
Very Nebel.
Don't ever try to play him for a sucker.

ROUGH JUSTICE

Series character: Donahue

Donahue came in through the door from the outer office and stood with his hat in one hand. He was a big lanky man with black hair, deep-set dark eyes, a long jaw, and a long straight nose. He wore a lightweight dark gray suit, no vest, a white oxford shirt with soft collar attached, and a blue crepe tie. He looked hot and uncomfortable, and there were two lines attesting to that between his rather wiry eyebrows.

"You Stein?" he asked.

The small dapper bald man behind the shiny oak desk nodded, and the motion of his head made the daylight flash on his horn-rimmed spectacles in a way that for a moment hid his eyes.

"I'm Donahue."

Stein said, "Oh, yes. I had a wire from Hinkle."

"Here's a letter," said Donahue as he crossed to the desk.

He sat down in an armchair facing Stein while Stein tore open the letter and read a few lines.

Stein nodded and said, "Oh, yes." He folded the letter, laid it on the desk, and crossing his hands on the desk said, in a gentler tone, "Yes—yes, indeed."

Donahue was fanning himself with his straw hat. He saw a water-cooler in a corner beyond Stein's right shoulder. He said, "It's hot," and got up and went to the water-cooler. He drew out a glass of water, tasted it, carried the glass back to the chair and sat down again. He looked squarely at Stein, took a long draft, and put the glass down on the desk. He smacked his lips and said, "That's good. St. Louis is not a burg for a cold-weather guy."

He smiled, showing long hard teeth.

Stein smiled back at him. Stein's smile was not spontaneous, not particularly friendly.

Donahue leaned forward. "Hinkle said you'd be a lot of help. We've got something hot, and of course you'll be on hand if I get in trouble. But aside from that, he said you'd see I met the right guys."

"Of course," said Stein. "But just what sort of right guys do you want to meet?"

"A cop that knows this burg up, down, and across—and"—he lowered his hard blunt voice—"a cop that'll keep his jaw shut and stay out of the way. No harness bull. A bigger guy."

Stein said, "Anybody with you?"

"No. This is a lone tail and no small fry."

"Did Hinkle say how much you're to spend?"

Donahue shook his head. "No. He said you'd reason that out. All I want is a cop in the know, and he's not going to know *too* much about what I'm after."

Stein picked up a paper cutter and probed beneath a thumbnail. "What *are* you after?"

"Let that slide for now," said Donahue.

Stein shrugged. He scaled the paper cutter back on the desk, picked up the telephone, and called a number. When he had the connection he said, "Luke? I've got a friend here from New York. I want you to treat him right . . . Sure, he's okay. Where can you meet him? . . . Huh? Oh, yeah. That's okay. When? . . . In an hour . . . Okay, then. In an hour."

He hung up and said, "Luke Cross. Plainclothes. He'll meet you in Constantine's. A Greek joint in Sixth Street."

"That's jake. I'm staying at the Braddock. I'll be seeing you."

Donahue got up, put on his straw hat, and went out through an office where a stenographer punished a typewriter. He descended in an elevator, passed through a lobby into the broiling street, and turned to the right. He crossed and turned south into Sixth. He stopped at Market against traffic, took off his hat, wiped the sweaty band, wiped his forehead. Opposite a parking lot he saw a green board sign with the word *Constantine's* on it.

He crossed the cobbled street, pushed open a glass door with green curtains, and entered a long, narrow room with a lot of porcelain-topped tables. At the right was a counter with a cash register and a cigar case. A fat man stood behind the counter smoking a cigar.

Donahue said, "I'll be waiting for Luke Cross," and went to a table in a corner farthest from the counter.

The Greek followed him, grinned, and said, "He your friend?"

"Yeah."

The Greek wiped the table with a soiled napkin and said, "Warm, ain't it?"

"Hot as hell."

"You like a beer?"

"Sure."

Donahue put his hat, crown down, on the table, stood up and took his coat off and hung it on the back of the chair. His shirt was dark with sweat. He sat down again.

The Greek brought a bottle of beer, poured a glassful, grinned, and Donahue raised the glass, said, "How," and emptied half of it.

He was finishing up when the door opened and a man came in. The man was short and fat, dressed in a shiny alpaca suit that was open, revealing a round paunch and a blue-striped shirt. A narrow-brimmed hat of soft brown straw was tilted over his forehead. His face was chubby with red cheeks, a bulbous nose, and little blue eyes that looked across the room at Donahue.

"Hello, Cross."

The man said nothing but thumped slowly across the room, pulled up a chair, and sat down opposite Donahue. He took a toothpick from a glass on the table, put it between his fat lips, and said: "Donahue?"

"Yeah."

"Well, how do you like St. Louis?"

Donahue said, "How about a bottle?"

"Sure."

"Flag the Greek."

But the Greek was on the way over, and Donahue ordered two bottles. He lit a cigarette, exhaled sharply, eyed Cross with blunt eyes, hard like round brown marbles.

"Stein says you're okay, Cross, so let's talk business."

Cross picked his teeth. "I'm listening." He did not look at Donahue. His small blue eyes wandered back and forth across the table absently. When the Greek brought the bottles and poured out two glasses, Cross picked up his with a fat reddish hand, grunted, and drank noisily. He set the glass down but kept his hand around it, looking at the glass with his small blue vacant eyes.

"Like this," said Donahue, placing both elbows on the table. His voice was low, throaty, earnest. "I'm looking for a guy named Micky Shane. I tailed him from New York to Cleveland and Indianapolis. Shane's an alias he's been using, and he may be laying up in this burg under the name of Shannon. Shannon's his real name, but he cuts it up into Shane, or Hannon, or O'Shane. It's been Shane on the way west."

"What's your racket?"

"Used to be with the cops. For two years. New York. I got canned. Raided the wrong gambling joint one night and shot a guy that tried to kick me in the belly. I'm a private dick now. With Inter-State."

Cross continued to stare at his glass.

"Well, what do you say? I've got a hunch this guy Shane is laying up here. He bought a ticket to St. Louis with stopover privileges, and he's been stopping over. You know the joints, and you ought to have an idea where a gun would lay up if he came here."

Donahue reached back into the inside pocket of his coat, took out a soiled large envelope, and laid a photograph on the table. "That's the guy."

Cross's face, for all its red chubbiness, was about as animated as dough. His small blank eyes passed over the picture.

Donahue hammered home his argument— "Stein will fix you up, Cross. Our outfit retains him. Just get me a line on this guy—you've got stoolies of your own —and give me a ring at the Braddock Hotel. You'll be clean, Cross."

"Well," Cross picked up the photograph, stared at it, then threw it back on the table. Then he drained his glass of beer, wiped his fat lips with a fat hand. He said, "Well," again and shoved back from the table. Then he cleared his throat and rose, saying, "I got to get back on the job."

He shifted his straw hat to the back of his head, took a handful of toothpicks, said, "Braddock Hotel."

"Yeah," said Donahue.

Cross turned and moved toward the door, his fat body rolling from side to side on short fat legs. The Greek called, "S' long, Luke." Cross muttered, "Um," and went out through the door.

Donahue was chuckling to himself.

The room had two windows overlooking Locust Street. The windows were open and there were screens of fine mesh, more a bulwark against coal dust than insects. An electric fan on the wall swung slowly in something less than a half-circle and droned monotonously. The room was green; bed, desk, carpet, chairs were green.

The drapes in which the windows were framed hung motionless. A bar of hot sunlight slanted obliquely through both windows. The corridor door was open, but there was another door with horizontal blinds, fastened by a hook, intended to stimulate circulation. It was August in St. Louis. It was eighty-eight Fahrenheit in the room—worse in the street.

Donahue lay on the bed, stripped but for a pair of blue trunks. Around him were spread the *Post-Dispatch, Judge, The New Yorker, Time,* and the *New York Sun.* On the desk which he had drawn up beside the bed were two bottles of Perrier, three-fourths of a bottle of Bourbon, a couple of glasses, and a bowl of cracked ice. Donahue lay motionless on propped-up pillows, hands behind his head. It was his third day in St. Louis, the third day of an insufferable heat wave in a city whose summers are never clement. His black hair was rumpled, and beads of sweat glistened on his forehead. He stared meditatively at the blank green field of the ceiling. Even the motor horns in the street below sounded hot and muffled.

The phone rang.

"Hello."

"Donahue?"

"Yup."

"Stein. I'm coming up."

Donahue frowned, then said, "Come on." He hung up, a little puzzled. He rose and walked over to unhook the door with the horizontal blinds. He went back to the bed, sat down on the edge of it, picked up a rumpled packet of cigarettes from the desk, took one out and put it between his lips. He tore a paper match from a book of matches, struck it, lit the cigarette, and lay sidewise on one elbow.

When Stein knocked he said, "Come in."

Stein came in, small and thin and neat in a suit of Palm Beach cloth and a broad-brimmed panama hat. He let the door close behind him and stood looking at Donahue. His thin face with the shiny horn-rimmed glasses looked grave and portentous.

"Well," he said, "what do you think happened?"

"Sit down," said Donahue.

"Cross got bumped off."

Donahue finished taking a drag on his cigarette and let the smoke drift lazily from his nostrils.

"Did he?"

"Yes. They found him about two hours ago in an alley down by the river. Must have been bumped off last night."

"That's tough."

Stein took off his hat, walked to a chair and sat down. He stared levelly at Donahue. "Now what the hell are you after?"

"What's that got to do with Cross?"

Stein's glasses flashed. "Listen to me, Donahue. That cheap outfit you work for has retained me in this city to help out any of its operatives who might need help here. I've a right to know what you're after. Play ball."

"I told Cross to get a line on a guy named Micky Shane, alias Shannon, alias Hannon, alias O'Shane."

"Why?"

"I'm looking for Shane."

"That's no answer."

Donahue got up, poured some Bourbon into a glass, threw in some cracked ice, made the glass half-full with Perrier.

"Want a drink?"

"No!" Stein looked worried.

"The gumshoes will poke around to all the joints, and the Greek might remember that you and Cross had a talk the other day. If I'm going to be your lawyer, I want facts, or you and the whole damned Inter-State can go to hell."

Donahue grinned at him. "If you think Hinkle will tell you more, there's the phone."

Stein stood up, slapped on his panama. He pulled a silk handkerchief from his breast pocket and mopped his face. He regarded Donahue with sharp eyes.

"Just a bullheaded mick, eh?"

"Don't get sore, Stein. Have a drink."

Stein said, "Go to hell," and strode out.

At police headquarters on Clark Avenue, Detective Hocheimer sat at a battered desk and gnawed at the stem of a corncob pipe. He sat in shirt-sleeves, bald head splotched with red heat spots and high blood pressure, white hair above the ears damp, thick jowls hanging over a soiled stiff collar.

A head poked in the door. "Guy wants to see you."

"Who is he?"

"Dunno. Want to see him?"

"Send him in."

The head disappeared. Donahue came in, fanning himself with his straw hat. He pulled a chair around, sat down, laid his hat on the table.

The detective's voice was rough. "Well, who are you and what do you want?"

Donahue took out his wallet, removed a white card, handed it to Hocheimer. The detective glanced at it. "Yeah, so?"

"So I knew Cross. Had a drink with him the other day in a Greek joint on Sixth. At the time I thought he could help me out."

"Help how?"

"I'm looking for a guy. I thought Cross could give me a steer."

"What guy? What do you want him for?"

Donahue pulled his chair six inches closer to Hocheimer. He tapped Hocheimer's knee. "Not so fast. I may be able to give you a break if you give me one. I'm not going to go into detail, so get that straight."

"You might be in a tough spot, buddy."

"I haven't done anything except ask Cross to give me a steer on a guy I was tailing. There's nothing to show that he got bumped off because of that, and even if he did, it's no fault of mine. Have you had a lineup yet?"

"No. We're picking up a lot of guys and we'll go over them in the morning."

"Good," said Donahue. "Now if the guy I'm after is in that lineup, I'll tip you off, provided—*provided*—you give me an hour alone with him before you get your hooks in him."

Hocheimer sat farther back in his chair. His thick mouth twisted. "You trying to bargain with me, Donahue?"

"What's it sound like?"

Hocheimer sat up straight, put his elbows on the arms of the chair, thrust his face forward.

"Suppose," said Hocheimer with a gentleness that did not fit his voice or bulk, "I lock you up on general principles."

Donahue's eyes darkened, but he shrugged. "You wouldn't be such a fool."

"Wouldn't I?" croaked Hocheimer thickly.

"Try it. The Inter-State has lots of money behind it. You haven't got a leg to stand on except suspicion, and I'd be out inside of eight hours, and just for spite I'd let you try finding this guy yourself."

"Yeah?"

Donahue made an impatient gesture. "You hick cops are the berries. Well, are you going to pinch me? If you are, go to it. Or if you want to get a break, play ball."

"Who is the guy?"

"If he's in the lineup you'll find out."

"And if he ain't?"

"Then we'll *both* be out of luck."

Summer rain . . .

Donahue stood by the window watching the sheets of rain thrash against the glass. Clark Avenue was barely visible through the smeared panes.

The door opened. Hocheimer, grinning loosely, barged in. He jerked a thick thumb over his shoulder. "Okay, he's your cookie. Have a go at him."

Donahue nodded. "Lead on, brother."

Hocheimer chuckled and they went out of the room, through a corridor, into another room that was small, gloomy. There was a dusty desk, two straight-backed chairs. A young man sat on one of the chairs. He had yellow hair and a thin white face, and his mouth was thick and red-lipped, loose, weak. His eyes were insolent. His hands were manacled together. A policeman leaned against the desk.

Hocheimer said, "All right, Schwartz."

Schwartz twirled his stick and strolled out of the room. Hocheimer looked at the pale-faced youth on the chair, looked at Donahue, winked one of his fat watery eyes, said, "Okay," and went out.

Donahue turned slowly to stare at the door. He stared at the door for fully a minute. Then he crossed to it, put his hand around the knob, turned the knob and opened the door. Hocheimer was standing there. He coughed behind his hand, waved the hand, said, "Okay, Donahue." Donahue grinned at him. Hocheimer chuckled hollowly, coughed again, then walked away whistling.

Donahue closed the door, turned and leaned against it. His dark deep-set eyes settled on the pale-faced youth and studied him keenly. The youth's eyes were mutinous and he was trying to make his mouth hard. Thunder rumbled roughshod over the roof. Lightning blazed in the room. The pale-faced youth blinked his eyes and appeared to cringe momentarily. The thunder tumbled away, diminishing.

Donahue left the door, picked up a chair, put it down in front of the youth, straddled it. Donahue's face was shadowed, his back to the window.

"Hard guy, eh?" he said.

The youth spat out a word.

"Don't get tough with me, kid. I know all about you. About that shooting on Ninth when they almost got you. And about the other shooting in Harlem when they almost nailed you again. You bear a charmed life, kid."

The youth said nothing.

"I know you blew the big town to come out here—but there's one thing I *don't* know. Where the ring is." He leaned forward, eyes hard. "Tell me about that seventy-grand diamond engagement ring."

"Jeez!"

"You've got it. That's why your boyfriends tried to get you. You were holding out on them."

"I was like hell!"

"Kid, the insurance company hired us to watch you as soon as you came out of stir, and we've been doing just that. When you pulled that job in Westchester two years ago, I'll admit you got a tough break. You did the inside job, blew the safe, and your buddies on the outside breezed when the cops showed. You got away by the skin of your teeth, but the cops got you a week later. They got all the jewelry except the seventy-thousand-dollar hunk of ice. I'll say you had guts to plant that and take the beatings they gave you. I don't blame you for holding out on the guys that left you in a tough spot. You needed the jack when you came out, and that hunk of ice was big enough to bring you fifty thousand from a fence. But I'm on a salary to get that ring or find out where it is. And I'm going to get it."

Micky snarled, "You're all wet. I haven't got it. I never had it."

"Let's tune out the bedtime story, kid. The guys who stuck up the house with you were after you when you came out. I tailed you here and got Cross to help me get a line on you. Hocheimer's got you for that job, with a good motive. You found out that Cross was looking for you, and you let him have it."

"That's a lousy lie. I never saw Cross, and I didn't know he was looking for me. I left New York because those guys were after me. They thought just like you— that I'd planted the ring before I went up and got it when I came out. But I didn't. Do you think I'd come out here if I had a hunk of ice worth seventy thousand?"

"You'd go anywhere to save your hide. You're in bad now. You come across to me and I'll do everything I can to get you a break. My job is to get the ring, and not the killer of a cop that didn't watch his tricks."

Thunder banged against the roof. Lightning crackled, spat, flashed in the dim room. Micky jerked on his chair.

"Jeeze, I tell you, I'm broke—flat, on my uppers! I never saw the damn ring! So help me God, I never saw it!" He suddenly began to sob.

His head fell down to his chest.

Donahue stepped in front of Micky, grabbed a handful of hair, jerked his head up and held it back, peering down into the pale, tear-and-sweat smeared face. His voice came low, husky: "Get this, kid. You're in a pinch. Come across about that ice and I'll do anything I can for you. You play dumb on me, and Hocheimer and his boys will take you over the coals. And then you'll hang, sure as hell! You better *listen* to me, kid!"

Thunder exploded. The window rattled, and sheet lightning blazed through the glass.

The kid was shaking. "I don't have the damn ring! Dunno where it's at. I swear I don't *know.*"

Donahue said, "Oh, hell," softly, and let the head drop.

His teeth shone between curled lips. He leveled an arm at Micky. "Just before they hang you, baby, I'll come around, and maybe you'll tell me for the good of your soul."

Stein sat behind his shiny flat-topped desk and probed abstractedly beneath a thumbnail with a long, slender paper knife. The thunderstorm of three days before had in some measure broken up the heat wave. It was still hot, but not unbearably so. Stein looked very neat in his light tan summer suit, with a henna-colored tie trimly meeting a tan silk collar. Below in Olive Street a trolley car bell clanged petulantly.

Donahue came in strolling, hands in jacket pockets. He was smoking a long, thin panatela.

The electric fan in the office droned with the hot monotony of a bee. The typewriter in the outer office began clicking spasmodically.

Stein shifted his horn-rimmed spectacles, took them off, took the silk handkerchief from his breast pocket, polished the glasses, held them up and looked at them —and beyond them, at Donahue.

"Little cooler, Donahue?"

"I didn't come here to talk about the weather."

Donahue took three hard steps that brought him to the desk. His wiry brows almost met above his nose, and dark fury burned in his eyes, his lips thinned against his teeth.

"I know I'm in a rotten game, Stein. I'm not defending it. I don't know why I'm in—but I'm in it. It keeps me in butts and I see the country and I don't have to slave over a desk. I get places. It's not a pretty game, and no guy ever wrote a poem about it. But it's the only hole I fit in. My boss sent me out here with your address. So I came here. Told you what I wanted. It was none of your damn business what I was after and you knew it. But you got sore because you couldn't buffalo me. So you pulled a little double-cross."

"Donahue, I tell you—"

"Shut up! For two cents I'd break a chair over your head!"

Stein's spectacles flashed. "Take it easy, Donahue! I'm not standing for any loose talk from a cheap gumshoe, and you and your agency can go to hell. Get out of my office!"

"You went to Micky Shane because you knew I wouldn't tell what I was after. You're *his* lawyer now, and I know damned well you wouldn't work for charity. There's money in this job. You know what I'm after. You know what Shane has, or you know that he's got money that represents what he did have. And you're figuring to get that money by taking his case and saving him from the gallows."

Stein smiled his thin, artificial smile. "Yes, I'm Shane's attorney. No law against that. But the rest of what you're saying is nonsense. Now, will you get out of my office?"

Donahue laughed harshly. "Don't spend too much time on Shane. You'll lose money on him."

Stein sat with his fingertips lightly touching, his face expressionless, daylight shining on his spectacles and hiding his eyes.

Donahue said, "Shane claims he's innocent, doesn't he?"

"Read the papers, didn't you?"

"Yeah. Wouldn't it be funny if he is?"

Donahue pulled open the door and went out chuckling.

Donahue was talking with the Greek.

"Luke Cross was a nice guy."

"Sure," said Constantine.

Donahue sipped his beer. "Luke used to meet people here?"

"Some," said the Greek.

"Like who?"

"Um . . . was Charley Hart, from the newspaper. Um . . . was Johnny Murphy, from over the station house. And . . . um . . . was Tony Nesella."

"What's Nesella do?"

"Waiter. Down at the Show Boat Club."

"Where's that?"

"On Second Street. Near river. Likker ain't no damn good in dat place. But maybe when you see Tony you tell him my name, he give you some good."

"I'll keep that in mind," said Donahue.

That night Donahue went down to the Show Boat.

It was located in a slanting cobbled alley two blocks from the river. A damp, warm mist had come up from the Mississippi. It hung motionless in the alley. Brick houses, dark-windowed, loomed above the cobbles, and a blue glow outlined a doorway. The glow revealed a square board sign with the words *Show Boat Club* painted in large letters. There were a half-dozen cars parked in the alley, and a man in a wrinkled white duck suit stood leaning outside the doorway.

Donahue had no trouble getting in. A man inside took his hat and gave him a check. Another led him down a musty hallway where blue lights glowed, into a large room on the walls of which were painted a hazy idea of a show boat and some plantation scenes. The tables were rough board, without covers, and lined three walls. Against the fourth wall was a raised platform that was supposed to look like the stern of a show boat. Negro musicians sat there and mopped shiny black faces. Four wooden propellers thrashed beneath the ceiling.

Donahue sat down at a table, and a waiter said, "Help you?"

Donahue looked at him. "Tony Nesella around?"

"No."

"Off?"

"He don't work here."

"He did."

The waiter looked at the table. "What you want to drink?"

"What you've got. It's probably bathtub gin, but I'll take a Brody. And some Canada Dry."

The waiter walked away.

The jazz band cut loose. Couples got up, began to dance.

A dark-haired girl was sitting at a table near the band. Her hair fitted her head like a helmet, showing the lower half of each ear and running around her forehead in severe bangs. Her cheeks were a bad paint job.

Donahue went over and asked her to dance. She had nice teeth and used them. They stepped around.

When the dance was over, Donahue steered her to his table.

"You step pretty good, kid," he said.

"Oh, you think so." She smiled. "You're not bad yourself."

The waiter brought her drink, and she looked at Donahue and said, "Here's how."

He drank with her and set down the glass, scowled at it. "Mouthwash! When Tony Nesella was here, a guy could get a drink."

She shrugged, said nothing.

Donahue said, "Where *is* Tony?" and threw a packet of cigarettes on the table.

She took one, and Donahue struck a match for her. She said with a puff of smoke, "Tony? I guess he left."

"That's too bad, I'd like to see him."

Out of the side of his eye Donahue saw a big rangy man standing in the doorway with the waiter who had brought the drinks. The big rangy man had fuzzy red hair. Donahue thought he saw him raise a hand and move a finger.

Donahue looked down at his drink. After a minute the girl said, "Excuse me, big boy. Gotta go powder my nose." She left the table.

Donahue leaned on his elbows and moved his glass back and forth over a wet smear on the table. The jazz band exploded again.

The girl with the black tight hair and the bad paint job came back to Donahue's table and sat down, showing her teeth in an intimate grin. Donahue ordered more drinks.

Donahue said, "I think I'll get tight. Want to get tight?"

"Do you want to get tight?"

"Yeah. I'm on a spree. I feel like making hey-hey, and I've got the jack to make it on."

She rubbed her palm over the knuckles of his hand. "You're nice, big boy— you're sure nice."

They danced again. The man with the fuzzy hair came to look in through the door. He had pale glassy eyes beneath beetling brows. He wore a white silk shirt with purple arm garters, white flannels, black-and-white shoes.

Donahue and the girl went back to the table after the dance and ordered more drinks. She said her name was Eva. Donahue drank in big gulps. He ran his hand through his hair until it became disheveled. His dark face became shiny with sweat. When, at the end of an hour, they danced again he staggered, and they returned to the table before the end of the number.

He lounged back in his chair. His eyelids drooped and he gazed around the room blearily. The big man with the fuzzy hair appeared in the doorway again and looked at him. The girl Eva looked at the man in the doorway and raised her eyebrows. The man in the doorway nodded.

Donahue groaned and put his head down on the table. The girl put a hand on his wet hair and said: "Maybe the heat's getting you in here, honey. There's a cooler room upstairs, on top. Want to rest up?"

Donahue mumbled, "Yeah . . . You're a good kid, Eva."

"Well, come on, hon."

Donahue got up, looking very drunk, very wilted. The girl took his arm and steered him through the door into the blue-lit hallway. Donahue walked with his head hanging.

"Watch the stairs, hon."

"Yeah."

He climbed the stairs in fits and starts, hanging to the banister. He reached the top and stood swaying in the hall there.

"This way," said the girl.

He stumbled after her to the rear of the hall. He stopped and waited while she opened a door.

The girl found the switch and turned on the light. The room contained a single bed, a washstand, a small table, and two chairs. Donahue lurched across the room and stopped with arms braced against the sill of the window. He put his head out and looked down. They were on the second story.

The girl was tugging at his arm. "Come on, hon, lay down on the bed and rest. Take your coat off."

He turned around and blinked sleepily at her. He grinned. He put his arms around her and hugged her. She smiled up into his sweaty brown face.

"You're some dame, Eva."

"Glad you think so, big boy. . . . Come on, lay down."

She urged him toward the bed.

When his knees touched the edge of it he half twisted and sank down. But he dragged the girl with him. She protested.

"Please, honey—"

He swung her down on the bed with sudden violence and a low curse. One big hand smacked across her mouth and stifled a cry, and he heaved up to bend his left leg and plant the lower part of it across her legs. Her eyes sprang open with sudden terror.

He laughed bluntly. "Well, you little bimbo. I didn't think they were as dumb as this even in the sticks."

With his free hand he drew a folded handkerchief from his breast pocket, bent over her, forced it into her mouth. She heaved and writhed and gagged, but he got all of the handkerchief into her mouth. He rolled her over, yanked her hands behind her, took a pair of manacles from a hip pocket, and snapped them on her wrists. Then he stood up.

"So you think that a pint of bathtub gin can get a good man tight? Well, sister!"

He laughed softly, lifted her from the bed, and laid her on the floor. Her face worked as she tried to yell, but not a sound came from her gagged mouth. He pulled a counterpane and two sheets from the bed and tied them together. The end of one sheet he tied to the bed. The end of the counterpane he lashed around the girl's waist. He moved quickly.

He carried the girl to the window, shoved her out, and gradually lowered her to a dark yard below. When the tension on the improvised line lessened, he stood up. He went back to the door and locked it.

As he was moving toward the window a fist rapped loudly on the door. He looked back once but kept on toward the window. He swung a leg out, then another, then grabbed the line and lowered himself to the yard, where the girl lay.

Bending down, he untied her and hauled her to her feet. He unlocked the manacles and put them in his pocket. He dragged her over a fence and five minutes later came into a dark, mist-ridden street. Here he paused to shove the muzzle of his automatic against her stomach. "Sister, you're going places with me, and if you try to run, I'll let you have it."

He yanked her through the dark street.

The electric fan in the room at the Hotel Braddock had a subdued drone.

The girl lay on the bed sobbing, an arm across her face. Donahue stood at the foot of the bed, holding a tall glass of ice water, looking darkly at her. He had taken off his coat and tie and rolled up his shirt-sleeves.

He growled, "Cut the bawling!"

Eva sniffled., Her face was red, and strands of black hair were pasted wetly to her forehead.

"What—what do you want with me?"

"I want Tony Nesella."

"I don't know where he is."

"You're a damned liar! Why did you want to get me in that room?"

She broke out crying again.

Donahue cursed, slammed his glass down on the desk, sat on the edge of the bed, leaned over her, spreading her arms until her hands were at either side of the bed. He glared down into Eva's wide, terrified eyes.

"You listen to me, sister! I saw that byplay of yours with the mutt in the doorway. When you first came over to my table, I saw the big mutt give you the high sign and you went out. Nesella's name spelled trouble there, and getting me in that room was a frame. Now get this: You come across to me and you'll walk out of this room. You tighten up and I'll call in the cops."

"You—you're hurting my wrists!"

"I'll hurt more than your wrists. Who was Tony Nesella?"

"Please . . . let me go!"

"You'll go, baby, as soon as you give me a line on what's behind all this damned monkey business. Why did my mentioning Nesella's name start things?"

She looked haggard, miserable. She shook her head slowly. "I don't know what you're talking about. Honest!"

He got up from the bed, walked over and stood beneath the fan.

"Will you come across?"

"I don't know—anything—anything!"

He went to the telephone. The girl on the bed turned and looked at him. She bit her lip.

"Hello," he said into the mouthpiece. "Hocheimer there? . . . Yeah, put him on."

He leaned toward the girl. "How about it, sister?"

She was still biting her lip.

"Hello, Hocheimer. This is Donahue . . ."

He told the detective what had happened. Then he leaned back in the chair, nodded, said, "Um . . . yes," and finally, "all right, I'll bring her over."

He slipped the receiver quietly into the hook, put his hands on his knees, and grinned broadly at the girl.

"You might have gotten out of this by telling me that Nesella was a stoolie of Luke Cross's. Hocheimer is going down to see Brennan, that big bum of a friend of yours."

Eva's lower lip was drawn in between her teeth. A pallor was creeping through the flush on her face, and her hands were fists, white-knuckled. Suddenly, she swept the heavy glass water pitcher from the table beside the bed and hurled it at

Donahue. He caught it neatly in both hands, set it down on the dresser. He grinned.

Then he steered her from the room.

Eva sat disconsolately in an armchair at police headquarters. Donahue sat on a desk, dangling his legs. From time to time he looked at his strap-watch.

The hot dark night hung outside the open window, and a greasy, corroded electric fan hummed on the desk.

A scuffle of feet and a rumble of voices sounded outside the door.

It banged open, and a knot of men came in. Blood and bruises were visible.

Hocheimer's straw hat had a broken crown. He slammed Brennan, the frowzy-haired man, into a chair. A couple of policemen roughhoused two other men into chairs. Hocheimer took off his broken hat, looked at it, threw the hat on the desk, and looked at Donahue.

"Well, there y'are, Donahue—there y'are."

Donahue smiled. "You had a hot time."

Brennan was glaring at Eva and cursing silently.

Hocheimer said, "When we got down there the joint was closed, so we went around back and crashed through a window. One of my men found the lights, and when the lights went on some bum pulled a gun. We had to kill two of them, and one of my boys ended up in the hospital."

He mopped his face.

Brennan snarled at Eva, "What a cheap broad you turned out to be!"

"I didn't—"

"You didn't—like hell! You double-crossing tramp!" He looked up at Hocheimer. "Take it from me, fat boy, this frail is going to get hers!"

He glared at Eva.

"You would double-cross me, eh? You would pull a fade-out with this dick and send headquarters down on me? Ah, I should have broken your neck long ago!"

She stared at him, shaking her head.

"I didn't say a word—but *now* I will, by God! And you'll hang!"

She turned to Hocheimer.

"This man killed Cross. The gun he used is buried in his cellar beneath an old icebox. He *meant* to kill Tony Nesella because he thought Tony was stooling to Cross about the liquor they were running on the river. It was a dark night and pretty misty. Brennan followed Tony to that corner in Commercial Alley, and he fired and missed. Cross had been waiting for Tony. And Cross got the bullet. Tony ran. Brennan ran after him and finally nailed him down by the river. He crushed his skull, tied a rock around his neck, and pitched him in."

Donahue chuckled and said, "Hell, it's been some merry-go-round!"

Hocheimer swallowed hard. "I never expected this."

Donahue said, "Look" and counted on his fingers. "You get credit for nabbing the killer of Luke Cross, *and* the killer of Tony Nesella. Shouldn't be surprised if they made you a sergeant or whatever they make smart detectives in this burg."

Hocheimer actually grinned then, said to the policeman: "Lock these birds up." He looked at Eva. "And give her a drink."

When he and Donahue were alone, Hocheimer sighed into a chair and opened his shirt. Donahue, sitting on the desk, said: "So far you've got everything out of this show. I haven't got a thing except a lot of trouble."

"Well, you were wrong about Shane. He didn't even know this gang."

"Sure, I was wrong. How was Shane picked up?"

"Kelly picked him up on a hunch, that's all. And he was packing a gun."

"He can get a bondsman easily enough for that."

"Sure. He'll be out tomorrow."

Donahue stood up. "I'll be around here. I want to know just when he goes out."

"Listen, Donahue," complained Hocheimer. "For God sake, don't start any more trouble!"

"Cross my heart," grinned Donahue.

But Hocheimer looked worried.

At noon, Micky Shane walked out of headquarters into bright sunlight. He started east on Clark. A moment later Donahue came out, crossed the street, following in the same direction.

Micky turned south into Tenth, then east onto Spruce, passed Ninth and Eighth and turned south into Seventh. He was delayed by a string of truck traffic. Then he crossed Chouteau, walked west on the other side of the street.

Donahue saw him enter a three-story dirty red-brick apartment house. Two minutes later Donahue drifted past, then crossed the street and entered a cigar store.

Inside the store he bought a paper. He pretended to read it, able to see the red-brick building through the window. A yellow taxi stopped at the place. Stein got out, very dapper in a tan suit and panama hat. Stein went inside the apartment building.

Donahue crossed the street and entered the apartment. He walked into a dark hall that was cool and damp.

He stopped and blinked, trying to accustom his eyes to the darkness. Then he walked softly toward the rear of the musty hall and stopped before a door. There were voices beyond the door, and he recognized Stein's voice, but not the words. Then he heard Micky Shane's. This kept up for ten minutes while Donahue waited outside the door.

Presently a key turned in the lock. Donahue stepped back, into the deeper shadow. He took out his gun, holding it loosely.

The door opened.

Stein came out, putting on his hat. Shane was behind him.

Donahue stepped forward. "In," he said. "Back inside."

They hesitated, staring at him.

"Get *in*!"

He straight-armed Stein into the room so fast that Stein almost lost his balance. He jammed his gun into Micky Shane's stomach and backed him step by step into the room. He closed the door quietly, leaned back against it, a faint smile on his lips.

Stein was a cool bird. Having regained his balance, he drew out a silk handkerchief, patted his lips, coughed gently into the handkerchief, then tucked it carefully back into his pocket.

Micky Shane was rattled. He kept licking his red soft lips. His eyes burned feverishly.

"Donahue," said Stein. "I *demand* that you clear the door and permit me to go about my business."

"I don't give a damn if you go or stay—once I get what I came for."

"I don't know what you're talking about."

"Sure, you don't." His grin was icy. "I want it, Stein! By God, I *want* it!"

Micky Shane said, "Don't, Stein."

Donahue took one quick step. His gun rose, came down hard against Micky's head, and Micky hit the floor with glazed eyes. Stein made a leap for the door. Donahue jumped after him, caught him by the collar, yanked him back and sent him spinning across the room. Stein hit a chair, tumbled over it, banged his head against the windowsill. He lay panting and gibbering, holding his head.

"Get up," said Donahue. "Get up and give me what I came here for."

Stein drew his knees up to his chest, crouched on the floor. Donahue went over, grabbed a handful of Stein's shirt and hauled him to his feet. He shook him violently.

Micky Shane was crawling on hands and knees. Donahue heard him and twisted about. Stein drove a fist to Donahue's ear. Donahue shook his head, swung back on Stein. Micky flung himself at Donahue's legs. Donahue went down.

In falling, he grabbed one of Stein's legs and Stein went down too. Stein was kicking Donahue in the face, and Donahue reached back, caught one of Micky's arms and forced him off his back. He muscled around, dragging Stein with him, his gun beneath his stomach. He recovered his gun, suddenly heaved toward Stein, and rapped the barrel against Stein's head as Micky was scrambling to his feet. Stein grunted and lay flat on his back, and Donahue was on one knee when Micky kicked him in the jaw. The blow drove him tumbling back, but he rose, blood dripping from his face, and with his left hand caught Micky by the throat. With his right he clubbed Micky's head, held him for a moment with his left hand, then let him drop limply to the floor.

He stood for a brief moment breathing heavily, while drops of blood from his face stained the front of his sweat-soaked shirt.

He put his gun in his pocket and got down slowly to his knees beside Stein. He went through Stein's coat pockets, drew out a leather wallet.

He opened it, pulled out several bills. A ring fell out with the bills. Donahue snatched it from the floor, stood looking at it. He smiled, shoved the ring into his pocket. He lit a cigarette and sat down on a chair.

Ten minutes later Micky Shane sat up, looking like a man in the throes of a hangover. He held his head between his hands and grimaced and said, "Oh, hell."

Donahue stood up. He drew the ring from his pocket and held it between thumb and forefinger. "See, Micky?"

Micky Shane stared bleakly at the ring. "Oh, hell," he said again.

"You should have got rid of it in New York."

"I couldn't. The only fence I knew was a friend of them palookas that was my buddies. I was looking for a fence here I knew about, but he's been in stir for three months."

"And Stein said he'd find one for you, eh?"

Micky groaned and held his head.

Donahue walked to the door, opened it. "When he comes around, tell Stein I enjoyed my little visit to Saint Louis."

Donahue took a cab to his hotel and sent a wire that said, "Got it. Leaving tonight."

Then he spent half an hour in a cold tub reading all about how Detective Rudolph Hocheimer had tracked down and apprehended the murderer of Detective Lucas Cross and Antonio Nesella. Hocheimer got his picture on the front page.

Donahue got a big laugh.

Nebel in *Black Mask*

1926–1936

Series characters: Buck Jason (BJ)
MacBride and Kennedy (MK)
Donahue (D)

•—included in *The* Black Mask *Boys*

"The Breaks of the Game" March 1926
"Grain to Grain" November 1926
"Dumb Luck" January 1927
"China Silk" (BJ) March 1927
"Hounds of Darkness" (BJ) April 1927
"A Man With Sand" July 1927
"Emeralds of Shade (BJ) August 1927
"A Grudge is a Grudge" September 1927
"With Benefit of Law" November 1927

"The Penalty of the Code"   January 1928
"A Gun in the Dark"   June 1928
"Hell to Pay"   August 1928
"Raw Law" (MK)   September 1928
"Dog Eat Dog" (MK)   October 1928
"The Law Laughs Last" (MK)   November 1928
"Law Without Law" (MK)   April 1929
"Graft" (MK)   May 1929
"New Guns for Old" (MK)   September 1929
"Hell-Smoke" (MK)   November 1929
"Tough Treatment" (MK)   January 1930
"Alley Rat" (MK)   February 1930
"Wise Guy" (MK)   April 1930
"Street Wolf"   May 1930
"Ten Men From Chicago" (MK)   August 1930
"Shake-Down" (MK)   September 1930
•"Rough Justice" (D)   November 1930
"The Red-Hots" (D)   December 1930
"Gun Thunder" (D)   January 1931
"Get a Load of This" (D)   February 1931
"Junk" (MK)   March 1931
"The Kill" (as "Grimes Hill")   March 1931
"Beat the Rap" (MK)   May 1931
"The Spot and the Lady" (as "Hill")   May 1931
"Death for a Dago" (MK)   July 1931
"Spare the Rod" (D)   August 1931
"Pearls Are Tears" (D)   September 1931
"Death's Not Enough" (D)   October 1931
"It's the Live Ones That Talk"   November 1931
"Some Die Young" (MK)   December 1931
"The Quick or the Dead" (MK)   March 1932
"Backwash" (MK)   May 1932
"Shake-Up" (D)   August 1932
"He Could Take It" (D)   September 1932
"The Red Web" (D)   October 1932
"Red Pavement" (D)   December 1932
"Doors in the Dark" (MK)   February 1933
"Rough Reform" (MK)   March 1933
"Farewell to Crime" (MK)   April 1933
"Save Your Tears" (D)   June 1933
"Song and Dance" (D)   July 1933
"Champions Also Die" (D)   August 1933
"Guns Down" (MK)   September 1933

"Lay Down the Law" (MK)   November 1933
"Too Young to Die" (MK)   February 1934
"Bad News" (MK)   March 1934
"Take It and Like It" (MK)   June 1934
"Be Your Age" (MK)   August 1934
"He Was a Swell Guy" (MK)   January 1935
"It's a Gag" (MK)   February 1935
"Ghost of a Chance" (D)   March 1935
"That's Kennedy" (MK)   May 1935
"Die-Hard" (MK)   August 1935
"Winter Kill" (MK)   November 1935
"Fan Dance" (MK)   January 1936
"No Hard Feelings" (MK)   February 1936
"Crack Down" (MK)   April 1936
"Hard to Take" (MK)   June 1936
"Deep Red" (MK)   August 1936

Note: A Nebel story from *Detective Fiction Weekly*, 11 February 1933, was
reprinted in *Mask* as:
"The Green Widow" January 1951

Behind the Mask:
Horace McCoy

●

Of all the *Black Mask* boys, Horace Stanley McCoy most wanted to achieve genuine fame and fortune. At one point in his career, he actually *was* famous (in Europe)—and he certainly earned a small fortune from Hollywood, where he worked on nearly one hundred screenplays. Yet he died broke, and his overseas fame was never matched on American shores.

And although one of his novels, *They Shoot Horses, Don't They?*, is a minor American classic, McCoy remains an obscure name with modern readers.

McCoy's epic rags-to-riches saga began in the small township of Pegram, in the hill country of Tennessee, twenty miles west of Nashville. One of four children, he was born here, in a cabin, on April 14, 1897, to Nannie Holt and James Harris McCoy. His parents were "book-rich and money-poor." Horace McCoy's father taught in a country school, and his attractive Irish mother had been a scholarship student who retained a lifelong passion for literature.

McCoy spent the early years of his childhood in Nashville, growing up (as he later recalled) "in a house filled with books." Always aggressive, at six McCoy was selling papers to earn his own spending money and, at sixteen, had quit school to work as an auto mechanic and traveling salesman. He also drove cabs in Dallas and New Orleans.

After his family moved to Dallas, McCoy joined the Texas National Guard in the spring of 1917. He was twenty and anxious to see combat in the First World War. Early in 1918 he arranged a transfer to a motor-mechanics regiment in Georgia, where he received instruction as an aerial observer. By July of 1918 he was overseas as a member of the American air service, stationed near Romorantin on the Normandy plain of central France. During that same month young McCoy saw action over German lines as bombardier and aerial photographer in a bomb-laden De Havilland.

These big, relatively slow-moving aircraft proved to be easy targets for enemy fighters—and, on August 5, McCoy's observation plane was attacked by four swift German Fokkers. The pilot was killed, and McCoy had to take over the dual controls. Although twice wounded by machine-gun fire, he shot down one of the enemy planes and managed to fly the bullet-riddled D.H.4 back to its home base. For this heroic exploit, McCoy was awarded the Croix de Guerre.

A young Red Cross nurse from California was attracted to the wounded hero, and they had a brief, passionate affair. Out of the hospital, McCoy dreamed of further glory as a fighter pilot—and told his parents, in a letter from the front: "I love a battle, and am willing to go anywhere to get into one."

By November of 1918 he had qualified as a pilot and eagerly awaited his chance to become a lieutenant, commanding his own plane in a pursuit squadron. But the war ended, and McCoy never got his assignment. It was a blow to his fighting spirit, and he bragged (in another letter) that had he been allowed to fly against the enemy he would have "outshone Rickenbacker." (Eddie Rickenbacker was the top American ace in World War I.)

Years later, in *Black Mask*, he would write: "The air was the last outpost of chivalry [and] romance."

Even as it stood, however, McCoy's war record was outstanding. He had survived four months of combat, logging a total of four hundred hours over enemy lines, had been wounded again, and had won another medal.

As McCoy's early love of flying found expression here in France, so did his early love of theatre. Before he returned to the United States, he functioned as publicity director (or "flack") for a small theatrical service troupe. McCoy toured Europe with their song-and-dance review, *The Romo Follies of 1919.*

Discharged as a corporal, he was back in Dallas by late August of that year, at twenty-two, with plans "to become a writer."

That fall he talked himself into a job as a sports-and-crime reporter with the *Dallas Dispatch,* where he spent eight months "learning the newspaper game." Brash and confident, when he couldn't find enough sensational stories to cover, McCoy made them up.

His bold, dramatic reporting caught the eye of an editor at the more prestigious *Dallas Journal.* McCoy was hired there as sports editor in the spring of 1920 (a position he would hold for more than nine years).

Although his starting salary was only thirty-five dollars a week, this job provided McCoy with the base he needed to "run with the rich." A dedicated social climber, he aspired to an upper-class life and used his editorial clout to involve himself with the town's wealthy sportsmen. A friend of the period declared that "Mack was consumed with ambition. He always had big ideas."

An extraordinary athletic talent paid off for him; McCoy was a competitive swimmer and played expert tennis. He also won local championships in golf and handball.

In July of 1921 he married Loline Scherer, and, three years later, they had a son, Stanley. But McCoy found that fatherhood and family life did not appeal to him; he was restless, nervous, and impulsive, constantly driven to explore new areas.

A stalwart six-footer, having inherited his mother's dark Irish good looks, he cut a ruggedly handsome figure in Dallas society circles and was noted for his flamboyant taste in clothes. He owned a dozen suits and thirty-five dress shirts, and considered himself a "dandy."

McCoy's flamboyance led him into joining The Dallas Little Theatre in 1925. A natural actor, he quickly mastered this new craft and won national attention for his stage performances over the next few seasons. An actress he worked with in Dallas summed up the McCoy of this period: "He was alert, romantic, and sure of himself."

McCoy loved big, flashy automobiles but could not really afford to drive them. In fact, his steadily mounting debts forced him to look for "some other way to bring in the bucks." In 1927, in order to supplement his modest newspaper income, McCoy turned to pulp fiction.

His earliest market was *Black Mask*.

"Cap" Shaw was looking for writers who "knew how to turn out swift, hard-boiled stories." In McCoy, he found such a writer—and Shaw purchased a gaudy South Seas adventure tale, "The Devil Man," for his December 1927 issue.

At thirty, Horace McCoy had joined the *Black Mask* boys—and over the following seven years he would sell Joe Shaw sixteen more stories. Fourteen of these involved the adventures of Captain Jerry Frost, a tough Texas Ranger who leads a group of Air Border Patrol daredevils known as "Hell's Stepsons." Unhappily, these stories fall victim to McCoy's penchant for overt melodrama and arch, self-conscious characterization. Frost was given to awkward, stream-of-consciousness declarations about the meaning of Good and Evil, Life and Death. . . .

> He had no illusions about death . . . When fighting men go, they go with tight lips and keen eyes. There is little beauty in death for them. They leave that to the poet. No angelic symphony, no fluttering of spirit, no singing heart—just plain, unvarnished death.

Although Shaw sent back most of McCoy's hastily written manuscripts for revision and polish, he failed to blue-pencil these literary side trips. (McCoy remained guilty of such stylistic excesses throughout his writing career.)

By September of 1929, McCoy had been forced to leave his newspaper job. Whether he quit under pressure or was actually fired is not clear, but McCoy *did* admit that many of his unpaid creditors were "hounding" the publisher of the *Journal,* trying to extract some of the money McCoy owed them.

His marriage had also ended, and he was, as he put it, "at loose ends." In January of 1930, McCoy found a fresh outlet for his energies, as editor of a local literary magazine *The Dallasite* (described by one of its founders as "a Texas version of *The New Yorker*").

McCoy tackled this new job with verve and determination, quickly becoming a "crusader," exposing graft and corruption in the Dallas police department and attacking the local papers as "gutless." In addition to his firebrand editorials, he wrote sports columns, gossip, memoirs, reviews, and short stories for the publication, but *The Dallasite* failed to attract advertisers, expiring after the April 1930 issue.

Two months later, in keeping with his courtship of the rich, McCoy eloped with a young debutante from a wealthy Dallas family—but this reckless marriage was quickly annulled when the young lady's parents learned about it.

McCoy was now living in a run-down three-story stucco house he called "the Pearl Dive" (because it was located on Pearl Street) with five other "bohemians" —two architects, a musician, and two painters. Here he labored at pulp fiction for *Black Mask*, *Battle Aces*, *Action Stories*, *Detective-Dragnet*, *Man Stories*, *Western Trails*, and *Detective Action Stories*. His air-adventure stories were particularly popular, and McCoy did indeed shoot down more enemy planes than Rickenbacker. What he'd missed in the skies of France he made up for in the pages of *Battle Aces*.

These gaudy tales were slammed out carelessly, for eating money, and McCoy never revised his manuscripts unless an editor forced him to do so. But despite long hours at the typewriter and steady sales, he knew he could not continue to survive on low-paying pulp rates.

Flying was still a passion, and to divert himself during this period he often borrowed planes from rich Dallas friends. He reportedly smashed up a "Jenny" biplane trying for a local altitude record in 1930.

By the spring of 1931 he had decided to leave Dallas. Impressed by one of his stage performances, an MGM talent scout offered to set up a Hollywood screen test. McCoy eagerly agreed, driving out to Los Angeles in May "for a go at the movies."

But the screen test failed to generate work—and during that first year in California, as the Great Depression ravaged the country, McCoy became, by his own admission, "a road bum." He slept in wrecked cars in junkyards, or on park benches, picked fruit and vegetables in the Imperial and San Joaquin valleys, worked as a drugstore soda jerk, and as a bodyguard and strike picket—and later claimed to have been hired as bouncer for a marathon dance contest in Santa Monica. This experience provided the basis for an original screen story he submitted to the studios, called "Marathon Dancers."

Based in Hollywood, working as an extra, McCoy began to get some bit parts in films such as *The Last Mile* (1931) and *Hold the Press* (1932)—in which he played "a tough newsman."

However, he found the life of a Hollywood extra to be degrading and hopeless —and by the close of 1932 had abandoned the idea of screen acting. McCoy signed on as a contract writer with RKO, beginning what he later termed "my notable career as a studio hack."

He was married (for the third and last time) in November of 1933 to Helen Vinmont, the daughter of a wealthy oil magnate. Helen's father, however, did not approve of the marriage, and the newlyweds were forced to live on McCoy's salary as a screenwriter.

In addition to fulfilling his script assignments, he managed to finish a draft of his first novel based on the "Marathon Dancers" screen idea.

He was excited about the project and told his wife that it was "the best damn thing I've done yet." Indeed it was. In fact, Horace McCoy would never write anything as fine again. *They Shoot Horses, Don't They?* became his masterwork, a hard, cynical, lyrical portrait of a failed actress, Gloria, who from the depths of despair talks her dance partner into killing her during a nightmarish marathon dance contest in California.

McCoy had visions of earning "big money" from the novel and wrote to a Texas friend: "Here's one baby who's had his fill . . . The minute I get my hands on fifty grand I'm thumbing my nose at these bastards here."

This was the sum of money McCoy felt he needed in order to say "the hell with Hollywood" (a title he used for one of his California short stories).

Published in 1935, *They Shoot Horses, Don't They?* sold just 3,000 copies that year, actually a very respectable showing for a first novel in the Depression, but far below the figure McCoy had hoped for. Hollywood scripting would remain his primary source of income.

The last Frost adventure tale for *Black Mask* was printed in the October 1934 issue, and although Shaw kept asking for new work, McCoy was finished with pulp writing. Captain Jerry Frost had become a popular character with *Black Mask* readers, and Shaw hated to lose one of his "boys."

Despite the fact that Joe Shaw credited him with being "one of the writers who helped establish the *Black Mask* standard," McCoy's Frost stories were far below Dashiell Hammett's trailblazing fiction. McCoy was never the painstaking craftsman that Shaw justly proclaimed Hammett to be, and he had steadfastly refused to take his pulp writing seriously. With *They Shoot Horses, Don't They?* he proved that he was capable of truly superior fiction.

Having "graduated" from the pulps, McCoy was now claiming kinship to John O'Hara and Hemingway. In Hollywood, after the publication of his first novel, his friends began calling him "Horses" McCoy. In 1936, he was the best-known "B" picture writer at Republic, which did *not* please him. "Dammit, these bastards never give me a shot at the 'A' pics," he complained. "They always hand me the second-string jobs."

McCoy's complaint was justified. The films he worked on in the 1930s were strictly low-budget "bread-and-butter" productions, bearing titles such as *Island of Lost Men, King of the Newsboys, Undercover Doctor,* and *Parole Fixer.*

During 1936, between these hack screen jobs, McCoy completed his second novel, *No Pockets in a Shroud,* featuring a tough Irish crusading news reporter, Mike Dolan. This character was an idealized version of himself—and the novel was based directly on McCoy's life in Dallas (including his little-theatre experiences). He later referred to it as "my autobiography." Hopelessly melodramatic, totally lacking the control and objective power of *Horses,* this new novel was a misfire with U.S. publishers, and McCoy was forced to sell the manuscript to a British firm in order to get it printed.

His third novel, *I Should Have Stayed Home,* was almost as bad—an overwrought, blackly cynical attempt to dramatize his bitter experiences as a Hollywood extra. Although Knopf published it in the U.S., the book failed to generate much critical enthusiasm. *The Saturday Review* rendered a caustic appraisal: "Horace McCoy hates Hollywood, not enough to stay away from it, but enough to get all the bile out of his system in a . . . bitter, name-calling novel."

Frustrated and angry, McCoy resigned himself to his "dark fate" at the studios and signed with Paramount in 1937. In less than three years he turned out sixteen original scripts. By 1942 he was at Warner Bros. where he scripted *Gentleman Jim,* a major boxing film for Errol Flynn.

However, once this job was completed, McCoy sank quickly back into what he called "the bottomless muck" of "B" films.

In 1945 a son, Peter, was born to the McCoys; a daughter, Amanda, had been born five years earlier.

The burdens of fatherhood weighed on McCoy, particularly since his career as a screenwriter was faltering. Late in 1946, he confessed to a friend that he was "out of work and absolutely dead broke."

Adding a further burden was his growing fear that he'd lost the ability to write good prose. In near panic, he tackled an ambitious new novel set in the 1930s and featuring a ruthless criminal protagonist.

But the pages came slowly—and McCoy was bogged down with the manuscript in February of 1947 when he received some startling news from France. In Paris, he had been discovered by Sartre, Malraux, Gide, and de Beauvoir, who declared that *They Shoot Horses, Don't They?* was "the first existentialist novel to have appeared in America." Based on new translations of his three novels, McCoy's reputation soared, and European critics were ranking him alongside Steinbeck, Hemingway, and Faulkner.

This sudden wave of critical acclaim from overseas gave McCoy the ego boost he desperately needed. In a letter, he admitted that he had allowed himself to get "fat, from too much food and booze." He wanted, more than ever, to get away from screen work ("I want to forget this whoring"), and he expressed a strong desire to move to Connecticut and live "a quiet, rural life" working on novels.

By Christmas of that year he had completed his new book. "I feel like Lazarus up from the grave!" he told his agent.

His editors at Random House were enthusiastic about *Kiss Tomorrow Good-bye,* which they published in May of 1948. This novel was, for the most part, the author's best since *Horses,* and reflected the talent and hard work that had gone into it.

In his best moments, McCoy achieves a superb blend of toughness and tension, far beyond his *Black Mask* level:

> He took a step backward, uncradling his Winchester in a vague, instinctive sort of way, and I shot him in the stomach. He had the Winchester and I wasn't taking any chances with him. You can shoot a man in the head or in the heart and he may live long enough to kill you, it is possible; but if you hit him in the stomach, just above the belt buckle, you paralyze him instantaneously. He may be conscious of what is happening, but there is not a goddamn thing he can do about it. I saw the bullet go into the little island of white shirt that showed between his vest and his trousers. The Winchester spilled out of his arms and he went down . . . sprawled in a heavy heap like a melted snow-man.

Three months after the publication of his new book, McCoy was stricken with a severe flu attack which damaged his heart. He lost thirty-two pounds and was bedridden for over a month.

Prior to this illness, he'd been working very hard, having delivered a revised version of his earlier novel, *No Pockets in a Shroud,* to the editors at New American Library; they had agreed to issue the first American edition as an NAL paperback.

Although McCoy considered *Kiss Tomorrow Good-bye* a symbol of his "rebirth" as a serious writer, several critics disagreed. *Time* called him "a literary caveman," describing *Good-bye* as "one of the nastiest novels ever published in this country."

Ironically, this review may have inspired Warner Bros. to purchase screen rights, as a vehicle for tough guy James Cagney, who was looking for another "really nasty" role. The film was released in 1950 and boosted McCoy's reputation in Hollywood.

"I have been making some very solid movie money," he told an eastern friend who inquired about his proposed move to Connecticut. "I just can't afford to leave now."

Early in 1951, McCoy hit a $100,000 jackpot with the sale of an original story, "Scalpel," to Hal Wallis Productions. He immediately took his wife and children on a trip to France, where he was hailed in Paris as an American genius. ("I've met all the French intellectuals [and] I'm their darling boy.") By the fall of that year, back in the States, McCoy was working on a major "A" film production, *The Lusty Men,* dealing with the lives of professional rodeo riders. Always a meticulous researcher, he traveled the nation's rodeo circuits for five months to guarantee the authenticity of his script.

He was also working on *Scalpel* as a novel. The rodeo film was released at the same time that *Scalpel* was published, and 1952 proved to be one of McCoy's most successful years; his novel became a best seller and his film proved itself a box-office winner.

The protagonist of *Scalpel,* Dr. Thomas Owen, was McCoy's fantasy portrait of what *he* had dreamed of becoming as a young man in Dallas. In *Saturday Review,* W. R. Burnett described Owen as: "big, strong, handsome, virile . . . a university graduate . . . a fraternity man and a great athlete . . . well versed in literature . . . an expert on expensive automobiles . . . [and] a personal friend of Picasso. He was awarded the Distinguished Service Cross for extraordinary bravery in World War II . . . is a gourmet, knowledgeable about women's clothes . . . a connoisseur of wine . . a great surgeon [and] a genius with a scalpel . . ."

However, the amazing Dr. Owen also thinks of himself as a "phony"—and this, too, fitted McCoy. More than once, to interviewers, he admitted to "over-dramatizing myself."

The success of McCoy's first hardcover best seller prompted his publishers to arrange an advance of $7,500 (on a hardcover-paperback deal) against a novel to be called *The Hard Rock Man.* (Although McCoy never revealed the origin of his idea, it was probably inspired by the cover story, "Hard Rock" by Victor Shaw, featured in the issue containing McCoy's first *Black Mask* tale.)

McCoy was just getting under way with this manuscript when he suffered a serious heart attack. But he rallied to complete the book's first section by the fall of 1955.

His editors were enthusiastic about its potential as a best seller. Concerning a legendary, ultratough dam builder, known as "the greatest construction boss in the business," *The Hard Rock Man* marked a return to McCoy's two-fisted *Black Mask* style.

The book was never completed.

On December 15, 1955, McCoy was struck down by a final heart attack, dying in his Beverly Hills home at the age of fifty-eight. Perhaps he had been pushing himself too hard; at the time of his death, beyond his work on the novel, he'd been planning to direct (as well as script) a film called *Night Cry,* on pro wrestling, and he was also actively engaged in his new hobbies of photography and oil painting.

Typically, he died broke, having spent his money as fast as he'd earned it. His widow was forced to sell his books and his prized collection of jazz recordings in order to pay outstanding debts.

McCoy once observed that his protagonists were always "guys who get pushed around by destiny." He felt that way about himself.

As Thomas Sturak has observed: "Throughout his life, McCoy struggled . . . to fulfill a heightened conception of himself as an artist. The clash of this romantic illusion and the inexorable realities of time and existence resulted in deep feelings of guilt, self-doubt and self-division."

Yet, despite an inability to meet his own high standards, he *was* an original.

Critic John Whitley best sums up McCoy's special talent: "At his best he had a vigorous style, a keen ear for dialogue and a robust sense of the dark underside of the American dream [exemplified by] . . . the marathon dance contest of his first novel, captured with a brilliant intensity never repeated in his later work . . . His characters were individualistic, tough, and doomed."

As, indeed, was Horace Stanley McCoy.

Frost Flies Alone

In the pages of *Black Mask,* Captain Jerry Frost was usually accompanied on his adventures by a group of fellow Texas Rangers known as Hell's Stepsons. As a team, Frost and his quick-shooting crew ranged the Mexican border country, dealing out hard justice to wrongdoers.

But in this story, Jerry Frost tackles a shipload of crooks single-handed. In "Frost Flies Alone," he wins out against high odds in the best pulp tradition.

Horace McCoy's Frost stories have never been collected or anthologized. This one is the first to appear in book format. It reflects the author's love of flying and is filled with the kind of action Joe Shaw relished.

The prop is spinning. The sky is wide and waiting. For Frost of the Rangers— trouble ahead!

FROST FLIES ALONE

Series character: Jerry Frost

Frost felt that he and the woman were being followed, had been followed since they crossed the border. They emerged from the Plaza Madero and turned down the crooked street toward the Café Estrellita.

To satisfy himself that he was not the victim of his own imagination, so often the case when he invaded old Mexico after nightfall, he halted briefly before a shop window. He'd been right. The footsteps behind him stopped when he did.

Fully alive now, his nerves on edge, Frost spoke to his companion, and they walked on. In the distance he could see the lights of the café and the shadowy forms of customers at the sidewalk tables. Frost walked slowly, did not look around.

The woman took Frost's arm nervously. He leaned over and whispered: "I'd like to know if you can use a gun."

"Yes, I've got one." She patted her handbag. "I haven't been a newspaper woman ten years without learning a few things."

Frost nodded, steered her into the café without looking back.

La Estrellita was a little square room overcrowded with tables at which, outside and inside, sat perhaps half a hundred persons. The ceiling was almost obscured by cigarette smoke. It was the hour when Algadon blazed with the specific intent of luring tourists.

At one end of the room was a bar. Two Mexicans were mixing drinks; behind them was the traditional frosted mirror and long rows of bottles.

On a raised platform sat a quintet of native musicians languidly strumming guitars. They simulated indifference, ennui, hoping to chisel a round of drinks from a sympathetic tourist.

Frost led his companion inside, and halfway to their table he recognized Ranger captain George Stuart.

As Frost slowly passed Stuart, he said under his breath: "Don't look up, George. Just get set for some action."

Frost and the woman sat down at a table near the end of the bar, facing the door.

Frost glanced at George Stuart.

Stuart crossed his legs and as he did so slid his six-gun inside his thigh. At that moment three men came through the doorway. Young Mexicans, with sharp faces and narrow eyes.

Frost ordered two bottles of beer from a waiter and looked at his companion as the three men sat down at a nearby table. "You're liable to get a good story before this party ends. There's a window directly behind you. If—*if* anything happens, get out and keep going."

"As bad as that?" She was smiling and the smile annoyed Frost. He didn't answer. He thought her question was stupid. Hell, of course it was bad. She had no business here. But that was the way with the newspaper tribe—all of them. They thought that their profession was protection.

Few spots on the border are safe for a woman after dark; Algadon was no spot for a woman at *any* time. But Helen Stevens had insisted, and as the final persuasive force she had brought a letter from the adjutant-general. So here she was.

The waiter returned with the beer and two glasses. He poured the drinks, placed the empty bottles on a tray, and started away.

"Deja las botellas!" Frost said sharply.

The waiter lifted his eyes and put the empty bottles back on the table. He moved off.

There was nothing comparable to the efficiency of a beer bottle at close quarters, and Frost had a hunch he'd be at close quarters soon.

"I guess you wish we hadn't come," Frost said.

"Why?" she demanded. She seemed positively to be enjoying it. "I'm glad that I can see you against your proper background." She inclined her head. "Captain, I'm afraid you dramatize yourself fearfully."

Frost smiled. She could think what she damn well pleased. He glanced at the table where the three men were sitting.

One of the three got up. The impression he meant to convey was drunkenness. Frost caught the eye of George Stuart and nodded.

The Mexican started off between the tables.

He purposely stepped out of the way to trip against Frost's foot, almost falling to the floor. He righted himself and poured out a volume of Spanish; swept the glasses from the table.

Here it was. The big blow-off.

Frost didn't hesitate. He leaped from his chair and put all his power into a short uppercut that landed flush on the Mexican's chin and sent him reeling against a table. Then he turned abruptly to find himself looking down the blue barrels of pistols held in the hands of the other two Mexicans.

The career of Jerry Frost might have ended on the spot had it not been for George Stuart. He had come from behind softly, but fast, and brought the butt of his gun down upon the head of one of the Mexicans.

The man groaned and fell to the floor. Stuart quickly tackled the third man.

Helen Stevens was missing, but Frost had no time to speculate on where she was or how she got away.

He swung the beer bottle with all the force he could muster, and it crashed against the head of the man with whom Stuart was wrestling. The Mexican's cheekbone ripped through the skin, and blood poured down his face. Stuart let him slide to the floor.

An unseen hand pressed a switch and La Estrellita was swept into darkness.

A pistol cracked, light blue and scarlet, and the bullet whistled by Frost's head. Pandemonium.

Frost lashed out in the dark, heard a grunt, and lashed out again.

La Estrellita was an inferno. Tables and chairs rattled, glasses crashed.

Someone was calling for lights, and it struck Frost that the sensible thing to do was retreat before the lights went up. He shouted for Stuart to follow him, ducked quickly, and moved toward the window.

Outside, he could hear the shrill police whistles of the Mexican constabulary.

Frost set his teeth and dived forward, and some of the mob went down before the force of his body. He fought his way slowly to the window.

He could see it as a rectangle of outside light a few feet ahead, and he pushed and struggled and continued to swing. His fist crashed against the blurred vision that was a head; there was a smothered exclamation, and the man went down.

Frost reached the window, climbed up, and literally fell into the night. With the first intake of air he thought of the woman and Stuart.

Where were they?

Frost began to shout: "George! George!"

George Stuart tumbled through the window.

"Thank God!" Frost panted. "You hurt?"

"Nope. I'm okay."

Frost scowled. "George, we've got to find the woman!"

They moved quickly across the street.

Stuart said, "Who the hell *is* this dame?"

"A newspaper woman the Old Man sent down."

"Where do you suppose she went?"

"I tried to tell her what was coming," Frost said. "If she was smart she went back across the border."

At the international boundary they questioned the customs officials.

Sorry, but no woman had passed into the States.

"A mess," Frost exploded—"a first-class mess. God," he breathed, "if anything's happened . . . Well," resolutely, "I can't return without her."

Stuart lighted a cigarette and said, "Wanna go back to La Estrellita?"

"It's not a question of *wanting* to, George. But the Old Man sent her—"

"Sure."

The café had quieted considerably when they returned, but many of the tables were overturned and everywhere there were unmistakable signs of the fight. The five-man Mexican orchestra was back on the platform playing in the same listless fashion. A brawl, a pistol fight, a knife duel—nothing to them. Just another night.

They summoned the proprietor.

"I know this guy Rasaplo," Stuart said.

Rasaplo waddled up solicitously, portly after the vogue of Mexican café owners, with long mustachios and sagging jowls.

Stuart's voice was steely. "The *captain* here brought a woman with him—*la mujer Americana. Ella desvaneca*—disappeared. *Sabe* what that means?"

Rasaplo's eyes widened in surprise.

"*Impossible!*" he managed. "Never in La Estrellita. Never!"

"Now get this," snapped Frost, "the woman disappeared in here tonight—and she's got to be found. Tell me something before I—"

Rasaplo shrugged. "I know nothing—but *this*—it is for you!"

He handed over a letter addressed to Jerry Frost.

Frost ripped it open: "*Thanks, Capitan, for the woman.*"

"Who gave you this?" Frost held up the letter.

Rasaplo shrugged his shoulders once again.

"Who *gave* you this?" Frost repeated.

"I no remember," he said. "A man—" His voice trailed off.

Stuart gestured disgustedly to Frost.

They could do no more, and they were risking further trouble by remaining in La Estrellita.

Fifteen minutes later the telegraph wires of the border country were humming:

Kidnaped in Algadon, Mexico, on the night of February eleventh: Helen Stevens, representative of Manhattan Newspaper Syndicate of New York City. Light brown hair, blue eyes, wearing brown coat and skirt. Notify Texas Air Rangers, Captain Jerry Frost, Gentry, Texas.

Within seventy-two hours the Manhattan Syndicate, Inc., of New York City, had taken official cognizance of the disappearance of one of its representatives by bringing the matter to the attention of the ranking officer of the sovereign state of Texas. Powerfully allied, as are all important syndicates, it lost no time in applying all the pressure at its command.

Messages were exchanged and the austere Mexican government moved, as a gesture of courtesy, a detachment of *rurales* into Algadon. Nobody, of course, expected them to achieve results.

Helen Stevens had disappeared as completely as if the earth had swallowed her.

On the fourth day after her disappearance there was a conference within the great, gilt-domed state capitol at Austin, in the inner office of the governor's suite. Three men were there: the Great Man himself, the adjutant-general, and Jerry Frost.

"It is unfortunate," the governor was saying, "most unfortunate." He was tapping his glasses against his chin: a dignified patriarch, product of the expansive state he represented.

"Yes," the adjutant-general agreed. He was commander of the Texas Rangers, big and gaunt, the sort of an official who would, if needs be, climb into the saddle himself and take the trail. "I feel somewhat responsible in a personal sense. I insisted Captain Frost take her across."

"No," Frost said quickly, "the fault was mine."

"Well," the governor declared, "whose fault it was is beside the point. We've got to *do* something."

The immense, carved door to the inner office swung open, and the governor's secretary entered.

"Sorry to interrupt, sir—but I have an urgent message for Captain Frost."

The governor said: "Come in, Leavell."

The secretary walked to Frost and handed him the message.

He scanned it, then passed it over the desk to the governor—who put on his glasses and read aloud:

Coast Guard Cutter Forty-Nine sighted Rum-Runner *Catherine B* longitude ninety-seven east latitude twenty-seven near Brownsville with woman aboard answering description Stevens stop cutter outdistanced stop rum boat one of former Al Thomas fleet.

O'Neill

The governor removed his glasses and tapped them against his chin.

"Who is Al Thomas?" he asked.

"A gunman killed in a plane crash a couple of months ago after a dogfight with Hell's Stepsons," Frost replied. "His men seem to be carrying on."

"'Cutter outdistanced,'" the governor went on. "I wonder how—"

"Please, sir." Frost was on his feet now. Hours of inactivity, of recrimination, of criticism rushed to a climax. "I'd like to play this single-handed. It started as mine and—" his voice was grim—"I'd like it to finish the same way. I don't want any help."

"But, Captain—" the governor protested. "You can't just go flying off alone!"

Frost raised a hand. "Please," he said again, firmly. He looked at the adjutant-general, and the adjutant-general understood. "I've *got* to go it alone."

Coast Guard cutter forty-nine's base was at Corpus Christi, and it was there that Frost headed when he hopped off from Austin. He was at Cuero in fifty minutes, stopping only long enough to wire Jimmy O'Neill that he was on his way.

Two hours and fifty minutes after he had circled the dome of the state capitol, he dipped into the airport at Corpus Christi and taxied his battle plane into a hangar. He got O'Neill on the phone at the government docks.

"Coming right over, Jimmy."

"Great," said O'Neill.

When he arrived, O'Neill filled him in on the situation. "That rum-runner is damned fast," he told Frost. "The way that baby slipped away from forty-nine was nobody's business. We took a couple of shots—but . . ."

"What about the woman?"

"Oh, she was aboard, all right. We spotted her on deck—brown suit, brown hair."

"Right!" said Frost. "Now, tell me about the boat."

"Used to belong to the Singleton outfit. Name's the *Catherine B.* Lately taken over by Thomas. His gang got it when you fellows rubbed him out. She's the prize of the Gulf, can store about three thousand cases of rum and make close to forty knots. We know they load on the stuff at Tampico, Vera Cruz, and God knows where else—and about a hundred miles out they transfer it to the launches."

"I see," Frost said. "The launches don't dare get out farther than that?"

"Exactly. They work close to the Mexican side. There must be five hundred coves between here and the Laguna de la Madre. If we could grab the *Catherine B*, we'd stop a lot of the smuggling. What's your idea about this, Jerry?"

"Well, I'm going to have a look for her," Frost said quietly. "I'll get pontoons and try to take her."

"Alone, it's suicide!" said O'Neill, shaking his head.

Frost asked: "How am I going to know her?"

"Easy," said O'Neill. "Brass taffrails. She's ebony black all over but for her taffrails. You can see 'em rain or shine. She carries one funnel, has a heavy stern, and her cutwater and bow lines are as pretty as I ever saw."

Frost nodded. "Don't guess I can miss her."

"You can't," O'Neill said.

"Would it be possible for me to requisition silencers?"

O'Neill swung open a drawer and took out two pistols fitted with longish muzzles. He handed them to Frost. "I'll let you use mine."

"Are they apt to jam?"

"The first shots will be all right. After that you gamble."

"Phone Roland at the field that I'm on my way."

Major Oliver Roland, commander of the flying field at Corpus Christi, was a stout admirer of Jerry Frost personally and professionally, being a veteran airman himself. Yet he thought Frost's plan to take the air alone in an effort to locate the kidnapped woman was a wild idea.

"Just because you've had a lot of success along the border you think you're invulnerable." He sighed. "Well . . . you want a flying boat?"

"Nope, pontoons. Just pontoons. Will you fit me?"

Roland nodded.

It required two hours to fit the pontoons and service the ship; and then the silver-winged bird cascaded through the Gulf of Mexico, left the water in a stream of fume, and turned southward.

Frost climbed to fifteen thousand feet to deaden the roar of his motor and swung down the jagged coastline. The Gulf lay beneath, a somber expanse as far as his eyes could see, its surface rippling with whitecaps in long, thin, broken lines.

The coast was dotted with innumerable coves, sanctuaries which afforded natural shelter for the lawless. No cartographer could have marked them all.

Frost rocketed down the coast for a hundred miles, then veered over the Gulf in a wider flight. Already he had come to realize that finding the *Catherine B* out there was going to be rough.

She had been seen in longitude 97 east and latitude 27. He consulted the map on his board. That would be, as near as he could estimate, fifty miles out of the Laguna de la Madre in a line with Rockport and Vera Cruz. Of course, she wouldn't be there now. But she had started—and there was a reason why.

She was on her way to keep a rendezvous.

He rolled back closer to the coast and maintained his vigil.

Then he looked down and was surprised to see a boat directly below. Bang, like that. He had been looking away for only a moment and when he gazed down again the boat was there. Speeding southwest, occasionally outlined against wide swells.

She looked capacious and businesslike. Worth investigating.

He turned the nose of his ship. Over to the left was a perfect cirro-cumulus formation which invited him with its natural protection, and he went for it. At a gap in the fleece his eyes caught a reflection.

Brass!

The *Catherine B*!

Frost knew it would be fatal to attempt a landing now. Too much light. He must wait. Hang back and wait for the dark.

Dusk was eighty minutes away, and they were the longest eighty minutes Frost ever spent. Occasionally he stole through a rift in the bank to check his quarry to make sure it was within range. The *Catherine B* had now reduced speed and was drifting idly: quite plainly at its trysting place.

The sun reached the end of the world, slid off the rim.

Five minutes later it was dark.

Frost took off his gauntlet and slipped the silencer-equipped .38 into the seat beside him. Its touch comforted him, reassured him. "Well, here we go!"

He fell into a glide and kicked his switch off. It was his farewell to the air. Dropping fifteen thousand feet, his motor would get cold, too cold to start again in an emergency. But, he told himself, there must *be* no emergency.

A quarter of a mile back he nosed up into a drift, timing the distance with that sense all good flyers possess. And his landing was perfect.

The *Catherine B* rode in a wide circle as the little battle plane slowly moved by its stern.

Frost kicked his rudder bar around and turned in toward the boat. He flattened out against its sides when he saw a spurt of flame and heard the crash of the report. The man shot from the rail amidships. Frost leveled his gun and fired.

There had been no far-carrying report from his gun, but the man had dropped. Frost was out on the wing in a moment, over the rail in another.

A husky fellow shoved through the wheelhouse door, and Frost saw him level a rifle. The ranger fired again, and the big man fell to the deck.

Frost ran forward.

There was a scuffling sound aft, and another man's head and shoulders appeared. He seemed to rise out of nowhere.

Frost tensed, gripping his pistol. He pressed himself close to the skylights as the man stepped out gingerly and came toward the wheelhouse.

The man stopped suddenly and sucked in his breath in a swift intake. He had seen the plane.

Frost was beside him. He rammed the gun into his ribs. "Get down flat!"

Silently, the man obeyed.

"How many people on this tub?"

"Eight."

"One of them a woman?"

"Two women."

"Two!"

Frost thought that over.

"What's this boat doing out here?"

"Meeting the *Mermaid* at midnight."

"Liquor?"

"Yep."

"I'm a Texas Ranger."

"I know. You're Frost. We been expecting you."

"Expecting me?"

"Sure. Catherine said you'd come."

"Who's Catherine?"

"Flash's girl."

Frost rolled his tongue against his cheek. "Singleton?"

"Yep."

Frost hesitated.

"Go over and call the others up here. And remember that I've killed twice. You'll be next if you make a false move."

The man moved to the ladder, Frost a step behind.

"Hey—Hans!" he yelled. "Joey!"

There was a mumble from below.

"Come up here! Hurry!"

Two men climbed out on deck.

Frost stepped out and leveled his gun. "Unless you do exactly as I say, I'll kill you!"

He looked at Hans.

"Toss your gun over!"

The man groaned and threw his gun overboard. Frost backed them toward the hatch. "Unbatten it!" he commanded.

They did.

"Pile in!"

"But, we'll—"

"In there!"

They disappeared below, and Frost wrestled the hatch and battened it down.

Then he moved to the wheelhouse, entered. The wheel had been chained by the helmsman to keep the boat steady.

Frost checked the helmsman's body. Bullet through the mouth. Frost put him over the rail. Then he went to the foredeck where he had glimpsed the first sailor.

He had fallen forward on his face, his gun at his feet. Frost kicked the gun across the deck into the water. Then he pitched the man over.

The night now had come on in full. The stars were gleaming and a pale moon glowed off the starboard.

Frost went down the steps slowly.

Eight on board. He'd killed two, locked three others in the hold. That left the two women and the boat's engineer. No need to worry about him as yet.

Frost walked along the passage and heard music. He paused at a cabin door and listened. An electric gramophone. Someone evidently was unworried. He forced the door open, thrust his foot inside, entered, his gun drawn.

He faced a woman—and gasped.

His companion of La Estrellita!

Frost had just been told there were two women on board. One he expected to find a prisoner—Helen Stevens. But she was no prisoner—

She was Singleton's woman!

"Ah, Captain Frost!"

She moved with a swagger.

"Here at last."

"So you're really Catherine, eh? You tried to trap me, at the café, get me killed?" She glared at him.

"Why not? *You* killed the only man I ever loved, and for that—you're going to die!"

She lunged at him, a knife flashing in her hand. Frost slapped her hard across the face, knocked her across a couch, disarmed her. "Where's the *real* Helen Stevens?"

She got up sullenly and unlocked a narrow door. Through it another woman stumbled, her hair disheveled, clothes wrinkled.

Frost observed that both women were about the same height and build, and that the genuine Helen Stevens wore a brown ensemble similar to the one worn by his companion that night in La Estrellita.

"I'm with the Rangers," Frost said. "What happened?"

"I was kidnapped in Jamestown, drugged, and brought here. I don't know why."

"There's no puzzle," Frost said. "This jane here is the ex-sweetheart of a racketeer who was allied with the Black Ship gang and bumped off by Hell's Stepsons. She wanted revenge on me; the way to get that was remove you and assume your identity." He smiled appreciatively. "That right, sister?"

"You go to hell!"

Helen Stevens was surveying the broad figure of Jerry Frost, remembering tales of his prowess in the skies of France and in the jungles of Latin America—*El Beneficio*, they called him then—surveying him in frank admiration.

Frost said, "We'd better get moving. But first we tie up this hellcat."

His eyes fell on the silk cord knotted around porthole draperies, and he said to Helen Stevens, "Get that cord."

She untied it and brought it to him. Frost slipped it around the woman's wrists and tied her hands behind her. Then he took off his belt and strapped it tightly around her ankles.

"I'll need a gag."

Helen Stevens did not hesitate. She lifted her dress, revealed a silk petticoat. She jerked off a strip and handed it to Frost.

Frost smiled. "I'm beginning to think you'll do!"

"Damned right I'll do!" she said.

Frost tied the gag and then stepped back.

The woman grunted and her eyes flashed. Frost picked her up and deposited her, none too carefully, on a lounge.

Helen Stevens handed him his pistol and said: "Don't you think we should use the radio and let somebody know where we are?"

"Right," said Frost. "Let's do that."

They came out on deck, entered the deserted wheelhouse. It was dark and quiet; a light glowed from the compass box.

On one side was the wireless, and Frost seated himself and cut on the switch. The motor hummed; tiny sparks glowed. He adjusted the headset, tapped out a message. Presently there was a light cracking sound in the headphone.

"They're on their way," he said.

He took a look at the binnacle and moved to the chart table. "Now to figure out which way to go," he remarked. "I'd hate to wind up in Cuba." He studied the chart for a few silent minutes. Then Frost moved to the wheel and unchained it.

"Think you can hold this wheel on one-eighteen when I get her on course?"

"Sure," she said.

Frost spun the wheel and held her circling until she was on the course he had determined upon as most likely to intercept the cutter he'd summoned. Frost reached into his shoulder holster and took out his other pistol. He laid it on the table beside her. "That's a thirty-eight," he said, "fitted with a silencer. Keep it handy."

She nodded.

"I have to pay a little visit to the engineer."

He went out.

Helen Stevens gripped the wheel, teeth clenched, and stared into that disk of white light that held the magic number, 118, wavering across a red line.

She heard a muffled thudding from below decks.

Some time later Frost emerged from the shadows of the deckhouse and came forward into the wheelhouse wearing a wide smile. "I'll take charge of that."

He took the wheel, and she stood beside him and shivered.

"Are you okay?" he asked.

"I'm all right," she said. *"Now!"*

And she smiled up at him.

Two hours later a siren sounded off the port side. Frost watched a cutter pull up. Half a dozen men vaulted the rails. The leader came forward. Frost could see in the half-light he was an officer.

"Frost?"

"Right!"

"I'm Al Bennett. Coast Guard." They shook hands. "We picked up your message. I radioed Corpus that I'd located you."

"Thanks," said Frost.

Bennett nodded his head toward Helen Stevens. "So you're the little girl who's been leading us such a merry chase?"

"Afraid so," she said.

Frost gestured. "The crew's locked in the hold. Engineer's below—with a cracked skull. Two others dead. And Singleton's woman is tied up in her cabin."

Bennett looked at him, his eyes wide. "Is it possible you took this baby all alone?"

"It was a cinch."

"Yeah? Well, I don't mind telling you the whole Coast Guard has been trying to land this one for weeks."

"Miss Stevens is exhausted," Frost said. "I'd better take her below."

"Sure."

Frost and the woman walked out—close together.

Bennett turned to the man at the wheel and said: "Ever hear of anything like it?"

"Beats me."

"They must be right about this guy, Frost. I've heard about one-man cyclones, but I never met one before."

The *Catherine B*, in the firm hands of the Coast Guard, slipped on toward Corpus Christi.

In four hours they would be in port.

McCoy in *Black Mask*
1927–1934

Series character: Jerry Frost   (JF)

•—included in *The* Black Mask *Boys*

"The Devil Man"   December 1927
"Dirty Work" (JF)   September 1929
"Hell's Stepsons" (JF)   October 1929
"Renegades of the Rio" (JF)   December 1929
"The Little Black Book" (JF)   January 1930
•"Frost Rides Alone" (in *BMB* as "Frost Flies Alone") (JF)   March 1930
"Somewhere in Mexico" (JF)   July 1930
"The Gun-Runners" (JF)   August 1930
"The Mailed Fist" (JF)   December 1930
"Headfirst Into Hell" (JF)   May 1931
"The Mopper-Up"   November 1931
"The Trail to the Tropics" (JF)   March 1932
"The Golden Rule" (JF)   June 1932
"Murder in Error"   August 1932
"Wings Over Texas" (JF)   October 1932
"Flight at Sunrise" (JF)   May 1934
"Somebody Must Die" (JF)   October 1934

Behind the Mask:
Paul Cain

●

He was described as "slender, blond, bearded." In 1933 he lived at 6650 Franklin Avenue, at the posh new Montecito Hotel apartments in Hollywood. He was then thirty-one years of age and had already written the coldest, swiftest, hardest novel of them all—printed as five linked novelettes in *Black Mask* the previous year and published by Doubleday (in late October of 1933) as *Fast One*.

The novel was bylined "Paul Cain," but that was not his real name. He was writing films as "Peter Ruric," but that was also a pseudonym. He had been born George Sims in Iowa on May 30, 1902. Biographical details on his childhood are not available, beyond the fact that he grew up in a grim neighborhood in Chicago where, as Joe Shaw later observed, "he saw . . . life in its toughest phases."

In 1918 he moved to Los Angeles. Five years later, he entered the film industry as a twenty-one-year-old screenwriter. By then he had assumed the Ruric name and, in 1925, was working with director Josef von Sternberg on *The Salvation Hunters*.

The years between the mid–1920s and the early 1930s (when he began to write for *Black Mask* as Paul Cain) are also biographically obscure.

Apparently he spent some of these years roaming the world. In a brief sketch of his life (written in 1946), Cain claimed that he had "traveled extensively in Central and South America, the West Indies, Europe, Northern Africa and the Near East, been a bosun's-mate on tramps, a . . . Dada painter, [and] a professional gambler . . ." (Certainly his gambling scenes in *Fast One* carry an authentic bite.)

He was twenty-nine when he made his first pulp sale to Joe Shaw (the initial story in the *Fast One* series). He continued to write for *Black Mask* until Shaw left the magazine late in 1936. When Joe Shaw exited, so did Cain. In fact, there is no record of any Paul Cain story beyond 1936. (He *did* make one sale each to *Detective Fiction Weekly* and *Star Detective Magazine*, but these stories were printed during the 1935–1936 period.) Cain's pulp career, therefore, began and ended in *Black Mask*, although he continued to write for films and television into 1960.

Again, facts on his personal life are sparse indeed. It was reported that he married "a starlet" during his Hollywood career, and that this marriage failed to last.

We know that he felt emotionally close to actress Gertrude Michael, who once played a jewel thief in a "B" movie of the 1930s. Cain dedicated *Fast One* to her, and she may have been the prototype of Granquist, the book's tough, attractive, amoral lady.

Tongue in cheek, Cain once listed his likes and dislikes for an original paperback edition of his best stories (*Seven Slayers,* from Saint Enterprises, 1946):

Likes: Mercedes motor cars, peanut butter . . . Scotch whiskey, some of the paintings of Chirico, gardenias, vegetables and sour cream, Garbo, Richebourg 1904 . . .

Dislikes: parsnips, the color pink, sopranos . . . white nylon sox, backgammon, cigars, and a great many men, women, and children.

The publisher claimed that Cain wrote as he had lived, "at high speed, and with violence."

Shaw called him "an aesthete in taste and ambition. Allied with his aesthetic moods is a grim sense of realism in its hardest texture."

Indeed, Cain's fiction was lean and diamond-hard in the Hemingway tradition.

As critic Irvin Faust has observed: "He picks up his literary scalpel and [cuts] away conjunctions as if they were bad merchandise . . . He digs into the page with a hard sentence: simple, declarative, exact . . . He also knows . . . big-city politics . . . snooping reporters and cops on the take . . . He was a man who had obviously been around [and] L.A., Hollywood and environs [were his] turf every bit as much as Chandler's . . ."

E. R. Hagemann, who has done extensive research on Cain, also commented on the author's unique portrait of Los Angeles:

I like to imagine Paul Cain in his elegant Montecito apartment on Franklin Avenue writing episodes of *Fast One* for Shaw . . . evoking Los Angeles of a long-gone time as no other writer ever has. Maybe, through his windows, he saw the Lido apartments (6500 Yucca, at Wilcox), the Musso and Frank Grill (6669 Hollywood Boulevard), the Brown Derby on Vine . . . the Hollywood Knickerbocker Hotel (at 1714 Ivar) . . . and the Hollywood Division Police Station . . . They all figure in the novel.

What else do we know about Sims/Cain/Ruric? Not much. We know that he was an enthusiastic cook who published several articles in the slick pages of *Gourmet* in 1951. Mainly, we know that he wrote many films for various Hollywood studios.

As Ruric, he scripted *Gambling Ship* for Paramount in 1933 (said to be "derived" from *Fast One*). In 1934 he wrote *The Black Cat* for the famed fright team of Boris Karloff and Bela Lugosi, and was credited, that same year, with the co-screenplay on *Affairs of a Gentleman*, for Universal.

Other Ruric films include: *Dark Sands* (1938), *Twelve Crowded Hours* (1939), *The Night of January 16* (1941), and *Grand Central Murder* (1942). Of this latter film from MGM, screen historian Don Miller reported: "Sue MacVeigh's novel was one of a series, written in a combination of the 'Thin Man' and 'had-I-but-known' breathless school. Assigned to the screenplay was Peter Ruric . . . He toughened it up, disposed of the husband-and-wife sleuthing team from the novel, and re-wrote the [central] role for Van Heflin as a private investigator . . . Ruric's script was on target."

In 1943, he signed a sixth-month contract with MGM, where he worked on a total of seven scripts, then moved over to RKO in 1944 for one of his most ambitious films, *Mademoiselle Fifi*, directed by Robert Wise and produced by Val Lewton. This one was praised by no less a critic than Pulitzer Prize winner James Agee. Writing in the *Nation*, Agee was impressed with Ruric's "well-edged script," and praised the "gallant, fervid quality about the picture . . . which signifies that there is one group of men working in Hollywood who have neither lost nor taken care to conceal the purity of their hope and intention."

Certainly Ruric was in good company with Wise and Lewton, both of whom have deservedly become Hollywood legends.

Illness forced Cain/Ruric to retire from film writing in the late 1940s—and his last recorded big-screen credit was on the MGM film *Alias A Gentleman*, released in 1948.

Apparently he preferred to be known as Ruric and kept his real name well hidden. In the mid–1940s, when he was putting together *Seven Slayers*, his collection of *Black Mask* stories, he crossed out the Paul Cain byline and substituted Peter Ruric. However, the publisher insisted on retaining the original pseudonym.

Cain did some undistinguished writing for television in 1960 (*The Lady in Yellow* for Screen Gems), and died of cancer at his Los Angeles home on June 23, 1966. He was sixty-four, and had published no novels after *Fast One* in 1933.

Yet this single novel has maintained Cain's reputation as "the hardest of the hard-boilers" for five decades. For sheer toughness, slam-bang violence, and narrative drive, it has never been surpassed. *Fast One* stands at the top of its class, a book Raymond Chandler rated as a "high point in the ultra hard-boiled manner."

Philip Durham, an authority on the hard-boiled genre, summed up the plot line: "Having acquired in the East two thousand dollars and a reputation for knowing how to play 'rough,' Gerry Kells arrived in Southern California. His reputation made it possible for him to begin taking over the Los Angeles rackets, which he proceeded to do by playing off one racketeer against another and by eliminating a few himself. Double-crossing, smashing, shooting and ice-picking were all in the act . . ."

With Kells, the gambling, quick-shooting killer, Cain created the quintessential tough guy. Kells spoke clipped, cynical dialogue and was capable of standing up to incredible punishment. As scholar Carolyn See commented: "Literally riddled with bullets, and with an ice pick between his ribs, [Kells] survives for an extra chapter to work out his destiny."

His destiny is fulfilled on the rain-slick coast highway south of Malibu when (after a road shoot-out) his car skids off a high curve into a ravine. Kells's woman, Granquist, has been killed in the crash, and he's dying too, lying there in the chilled rain. . . .

> He kissed Grandquist's cold mouth and turned and crawled through the mud away from the light, away from the voices.
>
> He wanted to be alone in the darkness; he wanted the light to please go away . . .
>
> In the partial shelter of a steep sloping rock he . . . sank forward, down.
>
> There, after a little while, life went away from him.

And the novel ends.

Chandler called this last episode "as murderous and at the same time poignant as anything in that manner that has ever been written."

Press reaction to *Fast One* was generally positive, with the *Los Angeles Times* critic commenting on the novel's "short, staccato sentences [that] jet from the pages like black sparks." The *Philadelphia Ledger* called it "a nervous novel full of fire and fever," and the *Cincinnati Times* claimed that the book contained "all the sinister silence of Faulkner, the cryptic dialogue of Hemingway."

The *New York Times Book Review,* however, thoroughly disliked it, describing *Fast One* as "a ceaseless welter of bloodshed and frenzy, a sustained bedlam of killing and fiendishness . . ."

Certainly, the novel *is* violent. But the violence is so terse and stylized that it becomes surreal, dreamlike. . . .

> The little man came into the room quickly and kicked the side of Kells' head and face several times. [The little man] was dark and composed and he was breathing hard. He kicked Kells very carefully, drawing his foot back and aiming, and then kicking very accurately and hard.
>
> The kitten jumped off the desk and went to Kells' bloody head and sniffed delicately. Kells could feel the kitten's warm breath. Then everything got dark and he couldn't feel anything anymore.

Irvin Faust, writing about the novel in 1978 for a new edition, was impressed with "the leanness, the authentically colloquial dialogue . . . and evocative strength of character, time and place . . ."

For the mysterious, reclusive Sims/Cain/Ruric, *Fast One* still holds its own, as tough and effective in the 1980s as it was in the 1930s. One can almost hear him telling us, "Okay, so I wrote just *one* novel. But people still read it, remember it, respect it. And that's *something*."

Sure. It's something, all right. One *hell* of a something.

Gundown

Ex-stuntman Johnny Doolin, the protagonist of "Gundown," is a married man whose wife worries about him (with *good* reason). He isn't a series character, although Joe Shaw would undoubtedly have welcomed more Doolin tales in *Mask* had Cain chosen to write them. Surely, in narrative toughness and intensity, this story ranks on an equally high level with *Fast One*. It's loaded with the same cold-hearted dialogue, surprise plot twists, and rich sense of character.

Never anthologized or reprinted since its inclusion in the long-unavailable paperback collection *Seven Slayers* (1946), this is prime Cain.

Enough said.

GUNDOWN

Character: Johnny Doolin

Coleman said: "Eight ball in the corner."

There was a soft click of ball against ball and then a sharper click as the black ball dropped into the pocket Coleman had called.

Coleman put his cue in the rack. He rolled down the sleeves of his vividly striped silk shirt and put on his coat and a pearl gray velour hat. He went to the pale fat man who slouched against a neighboring table and took two crisp hundred-dollar notes from the fat man's outstretched hand, glanced at the slim, pimpled youth who had been his opponent, smiled thinly, said: "So long," went to the door, out into the street.

There was a sudden roar from a black, curtained roadster on the other side of the street; the sudden ragged roar of four or five shots close together, a white pulsing finger of flame in the dusk, and Coleman sank to his knees. He swayed backward once, fell forward onto his face hard; his gray hat rolled slowly across the sidewalk. The roadster was moving, had disappeared before Coleman was entirely still. It became very quiet in the street.

* * *

Mazie Decker curved her orange mouth to its best "Customer" smile. She took the little green ticket that the dark-haired boy held out to her and tore off one corner and dropped the rest into the slot. He took her tightly in his arms, and as the violins melted to sound and the lights dimmed they swung out across the crowded floor.

Her head was tilted back, her bright mouth near the blue smoothness of his jaw. She whispered: "Gee—I didn't think you was coming."

He twisted his head down a little, smiled at her.

She spoke again without looking at him: "I waited till one o'clock for you last night." She hesitated a moment, then went on rapidly: "I act like I'd known you for years, an' it's only two days. What a sap I turned out to be!" She giggled mirthlessly.

He didn't answer.

The music swelled to a brassy crescendo, stopped. They stood with a hundred other couples and applauded mechanically.

She said: "I love a waltz! Don't you?"

He nodded briefly, and as the orchestra bellowed to a moaning foxtrot he took her again in his arms and they circled towards the far end of the floor.

"Let's get out of here, kid." He smiled down at her, his lips a thin line against the whiteness of his skin, his large eyes half closed.

She said: "All right—only let's try to get out without the manager seeing me. I'm supposed to work till eleven."

They parted at one of the little turnstiles; he got his hat and coat from the checkroom, went downstairs and got his car from a parking station across the street.

When she came down he had double-parked near the entrance. He honked his horn and held the door open for her as she trotted breathlessly out and climbed in beside him. Her eyes were very bright and she laughed a little hysterically.

"The manager saw me," she said. "But I said I was sick—an' it worked." She snuggled up close to him as he swung the car into Sixth Street. "Gee—what a swell car!"

He grunted affirmatively, and they went out Sixth a block or so in silence.

As they turned north on Figueroa she said: "What've you got the side curtains on for? It's such a beautiful night."

He offered her a cigarette and lighted one for himself and leaned back comfortably in the seat.

He said: "I think it's going to rain."

It was very dark at the side of the road. A great pepper tree screened the roadster from whatever light there was in the sky.

Mazie Decker spoke softly: "Angelo. That's a beautiful name. It sounds like angel."

The dark youth's face was hard in the narrow glow of the dashlight. He had taken off his hat and his shiny black hair looked like a metal skullcap. He stroked the heel of his hand back over one ear, over the oily blackness, and then he took his hand down and wriggled it under his coat. His other arm was around the girl.

He took his hand out of the darkness of his coat and there was a brief flash of bright metal; the girl said: "My God!" slowly and put her hands up to her breast. . . .

He leaned in front of her and pressed the door open and as her body sank into itself he pushed her gently and her body slanted, toppled through the door, fell softly on the leaves beside the road. Her sharp breath and a far, quavering "Ah!" were blotted out as he pressed the starter and the motor roared; he swung the door closed and put on his hat carefully, shifted gears and let the clutch in slowly.

As he came out of the darkness of the dirt road on to the highway he thrust one hand through a slit in the side curtain, took it in and leaned forward over the wheel.

It was raining, a little.

R. E. Winfield stretched one long leg out and planted his foot on a nearby leather chair. The blond woman got up and walked unsteadily to the phonograph.

The blond woman snapped the little tin brake; she lifted the record, stared empty-eyed at the other side.

She said: "'s 'Minnie th' Moocher.' Wanna hear it?"

Mr. Winfield said: "Uh-huh." He tilted an ice- and amber-filled glass to his mouth, drained it. He stood up and gathered his blue dressing gown about his lean shanks. He lifted his head and walked through a short corridor to the bathroom, opened the door, entered.

Water splashed noisily in the big blue porcelain tub. He braced himself with one hand on the shower tap, turned off the water, slipped out of the dressing gown and into the tub.

The blond woman's voice clanged like cold metal through the partially open door.

"Took 'er down to Chinatown; showed 'er how to kick the gong aroun'."

Mr. Winfield reached up into the pocket of the dressing gown, fished out a cigarette, matches. He lighted the cigarette, leaned back in the water, sighed. His face was a long tan oblong of contentment. He flexed his jaw, then mechanically put up one hand and removed an upper plate, put the little semicircle of shining teeth on the basin beside the tub, ran his tongue over thick, sharply etched lips, sighed again. The warm water was soft, caressing; he was very comfortable.

He heard the buzzer and he heard the blond woman stagger along the corridor past the bathroom to the outer door of the apartment. He listened but could hear no word of anything said there; only the sound of the door opening and closing, and silence broken faintly by the phonograph's "Hi de ho-oh, Minnie."

Then the bathroom door swung slowly open and a man stood outlined against the darkness of the corridor. He was bareheaded and the electric light was reflected in a thin line across his hair, shone dully on the moist pallor of his skin. He wore a tightly belted raincoat and his hands were thrust deep into his pockets.

Winfield sat up straight in the tub, spoke tentatively: "Hello!" He said "hello" with an incredulous rising inflection, blinked incredulously upward. The cigarette dangled loosely from one corner of his mouth.

The man leaned against the frame of the door and took a short thick automatic out of his coat pocket and held it steady, waist high.

Winfield put his hands on the sides of the tub and started to get up.

The automatic barked twice.

Winfield half stood, with one hand and one leg braced against the side of the tub for perhaps five seconds. His eyes were wide, blank. Then he sank down slowly; his head fell back against the smooth blue porcelain, slid slowly under the water. The cigarette still hung in the corner of his clenched mouth and as his head went under the water it hissed briefly, was gone.

The man in the doorway turned, disappeared.

The water reddened. Faintly, the phonograph lisped: "Hi de ho . . ."

Doolin grinned up at the waiter. "An' see the eggs are four minutes, an' don't put any cream in my coffee."

The waiter bobbed his head sullenly and disappeared through swinging doors.

Doolin unfolded his paper and turned to the comic page. He read it carefully, chuckling, from top to bottom. Then he spread pages two and three across the counter and began at the top of page two. Halfway across he read the headline: "Winfield, Motion Picture Executive, Slain by Sweetheart: Story continued from page one."

He turned to the front page and stared at a two-column cut of Winfield, read the accompanying account, turned back to page two and finished it. There was another cut of Winfield, and a woman. The caption under the woman's picture read: "Elma O'Shea Darmond, well-known screen actress and friend of Winfield, who was found unconscious in his apartment with the automatic in her hand."

Doolin yawned and shoved the paper aside to make room for the eggs and toast and coffee that the sour-faced waiter carried. He devoured the eggs and had half finished his coffee before he saw something that interested him on page three. He put his cup down, leaned over the paper, read: "Man Shot in Glendale Mystery. H. J. (Jake) Coleman, alleged gambler, was shot and killed as he came out of the Lyric Billiard Parlors in Glendale yesterday evening. The shots were fired from a mysterious black roadster which the police are attempting to trace."

Doolin read the rest of the story, finished his coffee. He sat several minutes staring expressionlessly at his reflection in the mirror behind the counter, got up, paid his check, and went out into the bright morning.

He walked briskly down Hill Street to First, over First to the *Los Angeles Bulletin* Building. He was whistling as the elevator carried him up.

In the back files of the *Bulletin* he found what he was looking for, a front-page spread in the home edition of December 10:

MASSACRE IN NIGHTCLUB
Screen Stars Duck for Cover as Machine Guns Belch Death

Early this morning The Hotspot, famous cabaret near Culver City, was the scene of the bloodiest battle the local gang war has afforded to date. Two men who police believe to be Frank Riccio and Edward (Whitey) Conroy of the Purple Gang in Detroit were instantly killed when a private room in the club was invaded by four men with submachine guns. A third man, a companion of Riccio and Conroy, was seriously wounded and is not expected to live.

Doolin skimmed down the column, read:

R. E. Winfield, prominent motion-picture executive, who was one of the party in the private room, said that he could not identify any of the killers. He said it all happened too quickly to be sure of any of them, and explained his presence in the company of the notorious gangsters as the result of his desire for firsthand information about the underworld in connection with a picture of that type which he is supervising. The names of others in the party are being withheld. . . .

Under a subhead Doolin read:

H. J. Coleman and his companion, Miss Mazie Decker, were in the corridor leading to the private room when the killers entered. Miss Decker said she could positively identify two of them. Coleman, who is nearsighted, was equally positive that he could not. . . .

An hour and a half later, Doolin left the *Bulletin* Building. He had gone carefully through the December file, and up to the middle of January. He had called into service the city directory, telephone book, Dun & Bradstreet, and the telephone, and he had wheedled all the inside dope he could out of a police reporter whom he knew casually.

He stood on the wide stone steps and looked at the sheet of paper on which he had scrawled notes. It read:

People in private room and corridor who might be able to identify killers of Riccio and Conroy:

Winfield. Dead.

Coleman. Dead.

Martha Grainger. Actress. In show in N.Y.

Betty Crane. Hustler. Died of pneumonia January 4.

Isabel Dolly. Hustler and extra girl. Was paralyzed drunk during shooting; probably not important. Can't locate.

Mazie Decker. Taxi dancer. Works at Dreamland on Sixth and Hill. Failed to identify killers from rogues-gallery photographs.

Nelson Halloran. Man about town. Money. Friend of Winfield's. Lives at Fontenoy, same apartment house as Winfield.

Doolin folded and creased the sheet of paper. He wound it abstractedly around his forefinger and walked down the steps, across the sidewalk to a cab. He got into the cab and sat down and leaned back.

The driver slid the glass, asked: "Where to?"

Doolin stared at him blankly, then laughed. He said: "Wait a minute," spread the sheet of paper across his knee. He took a stub of pencil out of his pocket and slowly, thoughtfully, drew a line through the first five names; that left Mazie Decker and Nelson Halloran.

Doolin leaned forward and spoke to the driver: "Is that Dreamland joint at Sixth an' Hill open in the afternoon?"

The driver thought a moment, shook his head.

Doolin said: "All right, then—Fontenoy Apartment—on Whitley in Hollywood."

Nelson Halloran looked like death. His white face was extremely long, narrow; his sharp chin tapered upward in unbroken lines to high sharp cheekbones, great deep-sunken eyes; continued to a high, almost degenerately narrow, forehead. His mouth was wide, thin, dark against the whiteness of his skin. His hair was the color of water. He was six feet three inches tall, weighed a hundred and eighty.

He half lay in a deeply upholstered chair in the living room of his apartment and watched a round spot of sunlight move across the wall. The shades were drawn and the apartment was in semidarkness. It was a chaos of modern furniture, books, magazines, papers, bottles; there were several good but badly hung reproductions on the pale walls.

Halloran occasionally lifted one long white hand languidly to his mouth, inhaled smoke deeply and blew it upward into the ray of sunlight.

When the phone buzzed he shuddered involuntarily, leaned sidewise and took it up from a low table.

He listened a moment, said: "Send him up." His voice was very low. There was softness in it, and there was coldness and something faraway.

He moved slightly in the chair so that one hand was near his side, in the folds of his dressing gown. There was a Luger there in the darkness of the chair. He was facing the door.

With the whirl of the buzzer he called: "Come in."

The door opened and Doolin came a little way into the room, closed the door behind him.

Halloran did not speak.

Doolin stood blinking in the half-light, and Halloran watched him and was silent.

Doolin was around thirty, of medium height, inclined to thickness through all the upper part of his body. His face was round and on the florid side and his eyes were wide-set, blue. His clothes didn't fit him very well.

He stood with his hat in his hand, his face expressionless, until Halloran said coldly: "I didn't get the name."

"Doolin. D—double o-l-i-n."

His voice was pleasant, his vowels colored slightly by brogue.

Halloran waited.

Doolin said: "I read a couple of things in the paper this morning that gave me an idea. I went over to the *Bulletin* an' worked on the idea, an' it pans out you're in a very bad spot."

Halloran took a drag of his cigarette, stared blankly at Doolin, waited. Doolin waited, too. They were both silent, looking at one another for more than a minute. Doolin's eyes were bright, pleased.

Halloran finally said: "This is a little embarrassing." He hesitated a moment. "Sit down."

Doolin sat on the edge of a wide steel and canvas chair against the wall. He dropped his hat on the floor and leaned forward, put his elbows on his knees. The little circle of sunlight moved slowly across the wall above him.

Halloran mashed his cigarette out, said: "Go on."

"Have you read the papers?" Doolin took a cellophane-wrapped cigar out of his pocket and ripped off the wrapper, clamped the cigar between his teeth.

Halloran nodded, if moving his head the merest fraction of an inch could be called a nod.

Doolin spoke around the cigar: "Who rubbed Riccio and Conroy?"

Halloran laughed.

Doolin took the cigar out of his mouth. He said very earnestly: "Listen. Last night Winfield was murdered—an' Coleman. You're next. I don't know why the people who did it waited so long—maybe because the trial of a couple of the boys they've been holding comes up next week. . . ."

Halloran's face was a blank white mask.

Doolin leaned back and crossed his legs. "Anyway—they got Winfield an' Coleman. That leaves the Decker broad—the one who was with Coleman—an' you. The rest of them don't count—one's in New York an' one died of pneumonia an' one was cockeyed. . . ."

He paused to chew his cigar. Halloran rubbed his left hand down over one side of his face, slowly.

Doolin went on: "I used to be a stunt man in pictures. For the last year all the breaks have been bad out at Pathé— They gave me a job as special dick, but that wasn't so hot. I haven't worked for five months." He leaned forward, emphasized his words with the cigar held like a pencil: "I want to work for you."

There was thin amusement in Halloran's voice: "What are your qualifications?"

"I can shoot straight, an' fast, an' I ain't afraid to take a chance—any kind of a chance! I'd make a hell of a swell bodyguard."

Doolin stood up in the excitement of his sales talk, took two steps toward Halloran.

Halloran said: "Sit down." His voice was icy. The Luger glistened in his hand.

Doolin looked at the gun and smiled a little, stuck the cigar in his mouth and backed up and sat down.

Halloran said: "How am I supposed to know you're on the level?"

Doolin scratched his nose with the nail of his thumb and shook his head slowly, grinning.

"Anyway—it sounds like a pipe dream to me," Halloran went on. "The paper says Miss Darmond killed Winfield." He smiled. "And Coleman was a gambler —any one of a half-dozen suckers is liable to have shot him."

Doolin shrugged elaborately. He leaned forward and picked up his hat and put it on, stood up.

Halloran laughed again. His laugh was not a particularly pleasing one.

"Don't be in a hurry," he said.

They were silent awhile and then Halloran lighted a cigarette and stood up. He was so tall and spare that Doolin stared involuntarily as he crossed, holding the Luger loosely at his side, patted Doolin's pockets, felt under his arms with his free hand. Then Halloran went to a table across a corner of the room and dropped the Luger into a drawer.

He turned and smiled warmly at Doolin, said: "What will you drink?"

"Gin."

"No gin."

Doolin grinned.

Halloran went on: "Scotch, rye, bourbon, brandy, rum, Kirsch, champagne. No gin."

Doolin said: "Rye."

Halloran took bottles from a tall cabinet, poured two drinks. "Why don't you go to the Decker girl? She's the one who said she could identify the men who killed Riccio and Conroy. She's the one who needs a bodyguard."

Doolin went over to the table and picked up his drink. "I ain't had a chance," he said. "She works at Dreamland downtown, an' it ain't open in the afternoon."

They drank.

Halloran's mouth was curved to a small smile. He picked up a folded newspaper, pointed to a headline, handed it to Doolin.

Doolin took the paper, a late edition of the *Morning Bulletin,* read:

MURDERED GIRL IDENTIFIED AS TAXI DANCER

The body of the girl who was found stabbed to death on the road near Lankershim early this morning has been identified as Mazie Decker of 308 S. Lake Street, an employee of the Dreamland Dancing Studio.

The identification was made by Peggy Galbraith, the murdered girl's roommate. Miss Decker did not return home last night, and upon reading an account of the tragedy in the early editions, Miss Galbraith went to the morgue and positively identified Miss Decker. The police are . . .

Doolin put the paper down, said: "Well, well. . . . Like I said . . ." There was a knock at the door, rather a curious rhythmic tapping of fingernails.

Halloran called: "Come in."

The door opened and a woman came in slowly, closed the door. She went to Halloran and put her arms around him and tilted her head back.

Halloran kissed her lightly. He smiled at Doolin, said: "This is Mrs. Sare." He turned his smile to the woman. "Lola—meet Mr. Doolin—my bodyguard."

Her hair was red, so dark that it was black in certain lights. Her eyes slanted, were so dark a green they were usually black. Her nose was straight, but the nostrils flared the least bit too much; her mouth red and full, too wide and curved. Her skin was smooth, very dark. Her figure was good, on the slender side. She was ageless; perhaps twenty-six, perhaps thirty-six.

She wore a dark green robe of heavy silk, black mules; her hair was gathered in a large roll at the nape of her neck.

She inclined her head sharply toward Doolin, without expression.

Doolin said: "Very happy to know you, Mrs. Sare."

She went to one of the wide windows and jerked the drape aside. A broad flat beam of sunshine yellowed the darkness.

She said: "Sorry to desecrate the tomb." Her voice was deep, husky.

Halloran poured three drinks and went back to his chair and sat down. Mrs. Sare leaned against the table, and Doolin, after a hesitant glance at her, sat down again on the chair against the wall.

Halloran sipped his drink. "The strange part of it all," he said, "is that I couldn't identify any of the four men who came in that night if my life depended upon it—and I'm almost sure Winfield couldn't. We'd been on a bender together for three days—and my memory for faces is bad, at best. . . ."

He put his glass on the floor beside the chair, lighted a cigarette. "Who else did you mention, besides the Decker girl and Coleman and Winfield and myself, who might . . . ?"

Doolin took the folded sheet of paper out of his pocket, got up and handed it to Halloran.

Halloran studied it awhile, said: "You missed one."

Mrs. Sare picked up the two bottles and went to Doolin, refilled his glass.

Doolin stared questioningly at Halloran, his eyebrows raised to a wide inverted V.

"The man who was with Riccio and Conroy," Halloran went on. "The third man, who was shot . . ."

Doolin said: "I didn't see any more about him in the files—the paper said he wasn't expected to live. . . ."

Halloran clicked the nail of his forefinger against his teeth, said: "I wonder."

Mrs. Sare had paused to listen. She went to Halloran and refilled his glass and put the bottles on the floor, sat down on the arm of Halloran's chair.

"Winfield and I went to The Hotspot alone," Halloran went on. "We had some business to talk over with a couple girls in the show." He grinned faintly, crookedly at Mrs. Sare. "Riccio and Conroy and this third man—I think his name was Martini or something dry like that—and the three girls on your list passed our table on their way to the private room. . . ."

Doolin was leaning forward, chewing his cigar, his eyes bright with interest.

Halloran blew smoke up into the wedge of sun. "Winfield knew Conroy casually

—had met him in the East. Conroy invited us to join their party. Winfield went for that—he was doing a gangster picture, and Conroy was a big shot in the East —Winfield figured he could get a lot of angles. . . ."

Doolin said: "That was on the level, then?"

"Yes," Halloran nodded emphatically. "Winfield even talked of making Conroy technical expert on the picture—before the fireworks started."

"What did this third man—this Martini, look like?"

Halloran looked a little annoyed. He said: "I'll get to that. There were eight of us in the private room—the three men and the three girls and Winfield and I. Riccio was pretty drunk, and one of the girls was practically under the table. We were all pretty high."

Halloran picked up his glass, leaned forward. "Riccio and Martini were all tangled up in some kind of drunken argument and I got the idea it had something to do with drugs—morphine. Riccio was pretty loud. Winfield and I were talking to Conroy, and the girls were amusing themselves gargling champagne, when the four men—I guess there were four—crashed in and opened up on Riccio and Conroy. . . ."

"What about Martini?" Doolin's unlighted cigar was growing rapidly shorter.

Halloran looked annoyed again. "That's the point," he said. "They didn't pay any attention to Martini—they wanted Riccio and Conroy. And it wasn't machine guns—that was newspaper color. It was automatics. . . ."

Doolin said: "What about Martini?"

"For Christ's sake—shut up!" Halloran grinned cheerlessly, finished his drink. "Riccio shot Martini."

Doolin stood up slowly, said: "Can I use the phone?"

Halloran smiled at Mrs. Sare, nodded.

Doolin called several numbers, asked questions, said "Yes" and "No" monotonously.

Halloran and Mrs. Sare talked quietly. Between two calls, Halloran spoke to Doolin: "You've connections—haven't you." It was an observation, not a question.

Doolin said: "If I had as much money as I have connections, I'd retire."

He finished after a while, hung up and put the phone back on the low round table.

"Martinelli," he said, "not Martini. Supposed to have been Riccio and Conroy's partner in the East. They had the drug business pretty well cornered. He showed up out here around the last of November, and Riccio and Conroy came in December tenth, were killed the night they got in. . . ."

Halloran said: "I remember that—they were talking about the trip."

Doolin took the cigar out of his mouth long enough to take a drink. "Martinelli was discharged from St. Vincent's Hospital January sixteenth—day before yesterday. He's plenty bad—beat four or five murder raps in the East and was figured for a half-dozen others. They called him The Executioner. Angelo Martinelli—The Executioner."

Mrs. Sare said: "Come and get it."

Doolin and Halloran got up and went into the little dining room. They sat down at the table, and Mrs. Sare brought in a steaming platter of bacon and scrambled eggs, a huge double globe of bubbling coffee.

Doolin said: "Here's the way it looks to me: If Martinelli figured you an' Winfield an' whoever else was in the private room had seen Riccio shoot him, he'd want to shut you up; it was a cinch he'd double-crossed Riccio, and if it came out at the trial, the Detroit boys would be on his tail."

Halloran nodded, poured a large rosette of chili sauce on the plate beside his scrambled eggs.

"But what did he want to rub Coleman an' Decker for?"

Halloran started to speak with his mouth full, but Doolin interrupted him: "The answer to that is that Martinelli had hooked up with the outfit out here, the outfit that Riccio and Conroy figured on moving in on. . . ."

Halloran said: "Martinelli probably came out to organize things for a narcotic combination between here and Detroit, in opposition to our local talent. He liked the combination here the way it was and threw in with them—and when Riccio and Conroy arrived, Martinelli put the finger on them, for the local boys. . . ."

Doolin swallowed a huge mouthful of bacon and eggs, said: "Swell," out of the corner of his mouth to Mrs. Sare.

He picked up his cigar and pointed it at Halloran. "That's the reason he wanted all of you—you an' Winfield because you'd get the Detroit outfit on his neck if you testified; Decker an' Coleman because they could spot the L.A. boys. He didn't try to proposition any of you—he's the kind of guy who would figure killing was simpler."

Halloran said: "He's got to protect himself against the two men who are in jail too. They're liable to spill their guts. If everybody who was in on it was bumped, there wouldn't be a chance of those two guys being identified—everything would be rosy."

They finished their bacon and eggs in silence.

With the coffee, Doolin said: "Funny he didn't make a pass at you last night —before or after he got Winfield. The same building an' all . . ."

"Maybe he did." Halloran put his arm around Mrs. Sare who was standing beside his chair. "I didn't get home till around three—he was probably here, missed me."

Doolin said: "We better go downtown an' talk to the D.A. That poor gal of Winfield's is probably on the grill. We can clear that up an' have Martinelli picked up. . . ."

Halloran said: "No." He said it very emphatically.

Doolin opened his eyes wide, slowly. He finished his coffee, waited.

Halloran smiled faintly, said: "In the first place, I hate coppers." He tightened his arm around Mrs. Sare. "In the second place, I don't particularly care for Miss Darmond—she can goddamned well fry on the griddle from now on, so far as I'm concerned. In the third place—I like it. . . ."

Doolin glanced at Mrs. Sare, turned his head slowly back toward Halloran.

"I've got three months to live," Halloran went on—"at the outside." His voice was cold, entirely unemotional. "I was shell-shocked and gassed and kicked around pretty generally in France in 'eighteen. They stuck me together and sent me back, and I've lasted rather well. But my heart is shot, and my lungs are bad, and so on —the doctors are getting pretty sore because I'm still on my feet. . . ."

He grinned widely. "I'm going to have all the fun I can in whatever time is left. We're not going to call copper, and we're going to play this for everything we can get out of it. You're my bodyguard and your salary is five hundred a week, but your job isn't to guard me—it's to see that there's plenty of excitement. And instead of waiting for Martinelli to come to us, we're going to Martinelli."

Doolin looked blankly at Mrs. Sare. She was smiling in a very curious way.

Halloran said: "Are you working?"

Doolin smiled slowly with all his face. He said: "Sure."

Doolin dried his hands and smoothed his hair, whistling tunelessly, went through the small cheaply furnished living room of his apartment to the door of the kitchenette. He picked up a newspaper from a table near the door, unfolded it and glanced at the headlines, said: "They're calling the Winfield kill 'Murder in Blue' because it happened in a blue bathtub. Is that a laugh!"

A rather pretty fresh-faced girl was stirring something in a white saucepan on the little gas stove. She looked up and smiled and said: "Dinner'll be ready in a minute," wiped her hands on her apron and began setting the table.

Doolin leaned against the wall and skimmed through the rest of the paper. The Coleman case was limited to a quarter-column—the police had been unable to trace the car. There was even less about Mazie Decker. The police were "working on a theory. . . ."

The police were working on a theory, too, on the Winfield killing. Miss Darmond had been found near the door of Winfield's apartment with a great bruise on her head, the night of the murder; she said the last she remembered was opening the door and struggling with someone. The "best minds" of the force believed her story up to that point; they were working on the angle that she had an accomplice.

Doolin rolled up the paper and threw it on a chair. He said: "Five hundred a week—an' expenses! Is that swell!" He was grinning broadly.

The girl said: "I'm awfully glad about the money, darling—if you're *sure* you'll be safe. God knows it's about time we had a break." She hesitated a moment. "I hope it's all right. . . ."

She was twenty-three or four, a honey-blond pink-cheeked girl with wide gray eyes, a slender well-curved figure.

Doolin went to her and kissed the back of her neck.

"Sure, it's all right, Mollie," he said. "Anything is all right when you get paid enough for it. The point is to make it last—five hundred is a lot of money, but a thousand will buy twice as many lamb chops."

She became very interested in a tiny speck on one of the cheap white plates, rubbed it industriously with a towel. She spoke without looking up: "I keep thinking about that Darmond girl—in jail. What do you suppose Halloran has against her?"

"I don't know." Doolin sat down at the table. "Anyway—she's okay. We can spring her anytime, only we can't do it now because we'd have to let the law in on the Martinelli angle an' they'd pick him up—an' Halloran couldn't have his fun."

"It's a funny kind of fun."

Doolin said: "He's a funny guy. Used to be a police reporter in Chi—maybe that has something to do with it. Anyway, the poor bastard's only got a little while to go—let him have any kind of fun he wants. He can afford it. . . ."

They were silent while the girl cut bread and got the butter out of the Frigidaire and finished setting the table.

Doolin was leaning forward with his elbows on the table, his chin in his hands. "As far as the Darmond gal is concerned, a little of that beef stew they dish up at the county will be good for her. These broads need a little of that—to give them perspective."

The girl was heaping mashed potatoes into a big bowl. She did not speak.

"The way I figure it," Doolin went on, "Halloran hasn't got the guts to bump himself off. He's all washed up, an' he knows it—an' the idea has made him a little batty. Then along comes Martinelli—a chance for him to go out dramatically— the way he's lived—an' he goes for it. Jesus! So would I if I was as near the edge as he is. He doesn't give a goddamn about anything—he doesn't have to. . . ."

The girl finished putting food on the table, sat down. Doolin heaped their plates with chops and potatoes and cauliflower while she served salad. They began to eat.

"As far as Halloran is concerned," he went on—"I'm just another actor in his show. Instead of sitting and waiting for Martinelli to come to get him—we go after Martinelli. That's Halloran's idea of fun—that's the kind of sense of humor he's got. What the hell! He's got nothing to lose. . . ."

The girl said: "Eat your dinner before it gets cold."

They were silent awhile.

Finally she said: "What if Martinelli shoots first?"

Doolin laughed. "Martinelli isn't going to shoot at all. Neither am I—an' neither is Mr. Halloran."

The girl lighted a cigarette, sipped her coffee. She stared expressionlessly at Doolin, waited.

"Halloran is having dinner with Mrs. Sare," Doolin went on. "Then they're going to a show an' I'm picking them up afterward—at the theatre. Then Halloran an' I are going to have a look around for Martinelli."

He finished his coffee, refilled both their cups. "In the meantime I'm supposed to be finding out where we're most likely to find him—Halloran is a great believer in my 'connections.' "

Doolin grinned, went on with a softly satisfied expression, as if he were taking a rabbit out of a hat: "I've already found Martinelli—not only where he hangs out, but where he lives. It was a cinch. He hasn't any reason to think he's pegged for anything—he's not hiding out."

The girl said: "So what?"

He stood up, stretched luxuriously. "So I'm going to Martinelli right now." He paused dramatically. "An' I'm going to tell him what kind of a spot he's in—with half a dozen murder raps hanging over his head, an' all. I'm going to tell him that plenty people besides myself know about it an' that the stuff's on the way to the D.A.'s office an' that he'd better scram toot sweet. . . ."

The girl said: "You're crazy."

Doolin laughed extravagantly. "Like a fox," he said. "Like a fox. I'm doing Martinelli a big favor—so I'm set with him. I'm keeping Halloran from running a chance of being killed—an' he'll think he's still running the chance, an' get his throb out of it. I'm keeping five hundred smackers coming into the cash register every week as long as Halloran lives, or as long as I can give him a good show. An' everybody's happy. What more do you want?"

"Sense." The girl mashed her cigarette out, stood up. "I never heard such a crazy idea in all my life! . . ."

Doolin looked disgusted. He walked into the living room, came back to the doorway. "Sure, it's crazy," he said. "Sure, it's crazy. So is Halloran—an' you—an' me. So is Martinelli—probably. It's the crazy ideas that work—an' this one is going to work like a charm."

The girl said: "What about Darmond? If Martinelli gets away, she'll be holding the bag for Winfield's murder."

"Oh, no, she won't! As soon as the Halloran angle washes up, I'll turn my evidence over to the D.A. an' tell him it took a few weeks to get it together—an' be sure about it. It's as plain as the nose on your face that Martinelli killed all three of them. Those chumps downtown are too sappy to see it now, but they won't be when I point it out to them. It's a setup case against Martinelli!"

The girl smiled coldly. She said: "You're the most conceited, bullheaded mick that ever lived. You've been in one jam after another ever since we were married. This is one time I'm not going to let you make a fool of yourself—an' probably get killed. . . ."

Doolin's expression was stubborn, annoyed. He turned and strode across the living room, squirmed into his coat, put on his hat and jerked it down over his eyes.

She stood in the doorway. Her face was very white and her eyes were wide, round.

She said: "Please. Johnny . . ."

He didn't look at her. He went to the desk against one wall and opened a drawer, took a nickel-plated revolver out of the drawer and dropped it into his coat pocket.

She said: "If you do this insane thing—I'm leaving." Her voice was cold, brittle.

Doolin went to the outer door, went out, slammed the door.

She stood there a little while looking at the door.

Angelo Martinelli stuck two fingers of his left hand into the little jar, took them out pale, green, sticky with Smoothcomb Hair Dressing. He dabbed it on his head, held his hands stiff with the fingers bent backward, and rubbed it vigorously into his hair. Then he wiped his hands and picked up a comb, bent toward the mirror.

Martinelli was very young—perhaps twenty-four or -five. His face was pale, unlined, pallor shading to blue toward his long angular jaw; his eyes red-brown, his nose straight and delicately cut. He was of medium height, but the high padded shoulders of his coat made him appear taller.

The room was small, garishly furnished. A low bed and two chairs in the worst modern manner were made a little more objectionable by orange and pink batik throws; there was an elaborately wrought-iron floor lamp, its shade made of whiskey labels pasted on imitation parchment.

Martinelli finished combing his hair, spoke over his shoulder to a woman who lounged across the foot of the bed: "Tonight does it. . . ."

Lola Sare said: "Tonight does it—if you're careful. . . ."

Martinelli glanced at his wristwatch. "I better get going—it's nearly eight. He said he'd be there at eight."

Lola Sare leaned forward and dropped her cigarette into a half-full glass on the floor.

"I'll be home from about eight-thirty on," she said. "Call as soon as you can."

Martinelli nodded. He put on a lightweight black felt hat, tilted it to the required angle in front of the mirror. He helped her into her coat, and then he put his arms around her, kissed her mouth lingeringly.

She clung to him, whispered: "Make it as fast as you can, darling."

They went to the door, and Martinelli snapped off the light and they went out.

Martinelli said: "Turn right at the next corner."

The cab driver nodded; they turned off North Broadway into a dimly lighted street, went several blocks over bad pavement.

Martinelli pounded on the glass, said: "Oke."

The cab slid to an abrupt stop, and Martinelli got out and paid the driver, stood at the curb until the cab had turned around in the narrow street, disappeared.

He went to a door above which one pale electric globe glittered, felt in the darkness for the button, pressed it. The door clicked open; Martinelli went in and slammed it shut behind him.

There were a half-dozen or so men strung out along the bar in the long dim room. A few more sat at tables against the wall.

Martinelli walked to the far end of the bar, leaned across it to speak quietly to a chunky bald-headed man who sat on a high stool near the cash register: "Chief here?"

The bald man bobbed his head, jerked it toward a door behind Martinelli.

Martinelli looked surprised, said mildly: "He's on time for once in his life!"

The man bobbed his head. His face was blank.

Martinelli went through the door, up two short flights of stairs to a narrow hallway. At the end of the hallway he knocked at a heavy steel-sheathed fire door.

After a little while the door opened and a voice said: "Come in."

Doolin stood on his toes and tried to make out the number above the door, but the figures were too faded by weather, time; the electric light was too dim.

He walked down the dark street a half-block and then walked back and pressed the button beside the door; the door clicked open and he went through the short passageway into the long barroom.

A bartender wiped off the stained wood in front of him, questioned with his eyes. Doolin said: "Rye."

He glanced idly at the men at the bar, at the tables, at the heavily built bald man who sat on a stool at the far end of the bar. The little bald man was stooped over a widespread newspaper.

The bartender put a glass on the bar in front of Doolin, put a flat brightly labeled flask beside it.

Doolin said: "Seen Martinelli tonight?"

The bartender watched Doolin pour his drink, picked up the bottle and put it under the bar, said: "Yeah. He came in a little while ago. He's upstairs."

Doolin nodded, tasted the rye. It wasn't too bad. He finished it and put a quarter on the bar, sauntered toward the door at the back of the room.

The little bald man looked up from his paper.

Doolin said: "Martinelli's expecting me. He's upstairs—ain't he?"

The little man looked at Doolin. He began at his face and went down to his feet and then back up, slowly. "He didn't say anything about you." He spat with the admirable precision of age and confidence into a cuspidor in the corner.

Doolin said: "He forgot." He put his hand on the doorknob.

The little man looked at him, through him, blankly.

Doolin turned the knob and opened the door, went through, closed the door behind him.

The stairs were dimly lighted by a sputtering gas jet. He went up slowly. There was one door at the top of the first flight; it was dark; there was no light under it, no sound beyond it. Doolin went up another flight very quietly. He put his ear against the steel-sheathed door; he could hear no sound, but a little light filtered through under the door. He doubled up his fist, knocked with the heel of his hand.

Martinelli opened the door. He stood a moment staring questioningly at Doolin and then he glanced over his shoulder, smiled, said: "Come in."

Doolin put his hands in his overcoat pockets, his right hand holding the revolver tightly, went forward into the room.

Martinelli closed the door behind him, slid the heavy bolt.

The room was large, bare; somewhere around thirty-five by forty. It was lighted by a single green-shaded droplight over a very large round table in the center; there were other tables and chairs stacked in the dusk of the corner. There were no windows, no other doors.

Halloran sat in one of the four chairs at the table. He was leaning slightly forward with his elbows on the table, his long waxen hands framing his face. His face was entirely cold, white, expressionless.

Martinelli stood with his back against the door, his hands behind him.

Doolin glanced over his shoulder at Martinelli, looked back at Halloran. His eyebrows were lifted to the wide V; his mouth hung a little open.

Halloran said: "Well, well—this is a surprise."

He moved his eyes to Martinelli, said: "Angelo. Meet Mr. Doolin—my body-guard. . . ." For an instant his wide thin mouth flickered a fraction of an inch upward; then his face became a blank, white mask again. "Mr. Doolin—Mr. Martinelli. . . ."

Martinelli had silently come up behind Doolin, suddenly thrust his hands into Doolin's pockets, hard, grabbed Doolin's hands. Doolin bent sharply forward. They struggled for possibly half a minute, silently except for the tearing sound of their breath; then Martinelli brought his knee up suddenly, savagely; Doolin groaned, sank to his knees; the nickel-plated revolver clattered to the floor, slid halfway across the room.

Martinelli darted after it.

Halloran had not appeared to move. He said: "Wait a minute, baby. . . ." The blunt Luger that Doolin had experienced in the afternoon glittered on the table between his two hands.

Martinelli made an impatient gesture, stooped to pick up Doolin's gun.

"I *said*, wait a minute!" Halloran's voice was like a cold swift scythe.

Martinelli stood up very straight.

Doolin got to his feet slowly. He bent over and held the middle of his body, rolled his head toward Martinelli, his eyes narrow, malevolent. He said very quietly, as if to himself: "Dirty son of a bitch—dirty, *dirty* son of a bitch!"

Martinelli grinned, stood very straight. His hands, cupped close to his thighs, trembled rigidly.

Halloran said slowly: "Don't do it, baby. I'll shoot both your eyes out before you get that shiv of yours into the air."

Martinelli looked like a clothing-store dummy. He was balanced on the balls of his feet, his hands trembling at his sides, his grin artificial, empty.

Doolin laughed suddenly. He stood up straight and looked at Martinelli and laughed.

Halloran moved his eyes to Doolin, smiled faintly.

He said: "Gentlemen—sit down."

Martinelli tottered forward, sank into one of the chairs.

Halloran said: "Put your hands on the table, please."

Martinelli obediently put his hands on the table. The empty grin seemed to have congealed on his face.

Halloran turned his eyes toward Doolin. Doolin smiled, walked gingerly to the other chair and sat down.

Halloran said: "Now. . . ." He put one hand up to his face; the other held the Luger loosely on the table.

Doolin cleared his throat, said: "What's it all about, Mr. Halloran?"

Martinelli laughed suddenly. The empty grin exploded into loud high-pitched mirth. "What's it all about! Dear God—what's it all about! . . ."

Halloran was watching Doolin, his shadowed sunken eyes half closed.

Martinelli leaned forward, lifted his hands and pointed two fingers at Doolin. "Listen—wise guy . . . you've got minutes to live—if you're lucky. That's what it's all about!"

Doolin regarded Martinelli with faint amusement.

Martinelli laughed again. He moved his hand slowly until the two fingers pointed at Halloran. "He killed Coleman," he said. "He shot Coleman an' I drove the car. An' he killed Winfield himself. An' his outfit killed Riccio an' Conroy. . . ."

Doolin glanced at Halloran, turned back to smile dimly, dumbly at Martinelli.

"He propositioned me into killing the dance-hall dame," Martinelli went on— "an' now he's going to kill you an' me. . . ."

Doolin looked at Halloran. Halloran's face was white and immovable as plaster.

"Listen—wise guy!" Martinelli leaned forward, moved his hand back to point at Doolin. He was suddenly very intense; his dark eyes burned into Doolin's. "I came out here for Riccio to make connections to peddle M—a lot of it—an' I met Mr. Halloran." Martinelli moved his head an eighth of an inch toward Halloran. "Mr. Halloran runs the drug racket out here—did you know that?"

Doolin glanced swiftly at Halloran, looked back at Martinelli's tense face.

"Mr. Halloran aced me into double-crossing Frankie Riccio an' Conroy," Martinelli went on. "Mr. Halloran's men rubbed Riccio an' Conroy an' would've taken care of me if Riccio hadn't almost beat 'em to it. . . ."

Halloran said coldly, amusedly: "Oh—come, come, Angelo. . . ."

Martinelli did not look at Halloran. He said: "I met Riccio an' Conroy at the train that night an' took them to that joint in Culver City to talk business to Mr. Halloran—only I didn't know the kind of business Mr. Halloran was going to talk. . . ."

"Is it quite necessary to go into all this?" Halloran spoke sidewise to Martinelli, smiled at Doolin. It was his first definite change of expression since Doolin had come into the room.

Martinelli said: "Yes," emphatically. He scowled at Halloran, his eyes thin black slits. "Bright boy here"—he indicated Doolin with his hand—"wants to know what it's all about. I'd like to have somebody know—besides me. One of us might leave here alive—if I get this all out of my system it's a cinch it won't be bright boy."

Halloran's smile was very cheerful. He said: "Go on."

"One of the men the law picked up for the Hotspot shooting was a good guess —he's on Mr. Halloran's payroll," Martinelli went on. He was accenting the "Mr." a little unnecessarily, a little too much. "When I got out of the hospital Mr. Halloran suggested we clean things up—move Coleman an' Decker an' Winfield —anybody who might identify his man or testify that Riccio shot me—out of the way. He hated Winfield anyway, for beating his time with the Darmond gal—an' he hated her. . . ."

Halloran was beaming at Doolin, his hand tight and steady on the Luger. Doolin thought about the distance across the big table to Halloran, the distance to the light.

Martinelli was leaning forward, talking swiftly, eagerly: "I brought eighty-five grand worth of morphine out with me, an' I turned it over to his nibs here when we threw in together. I ain't had a nickel out of it. That's the reason I went for all this finagling—I wanted my dough. I was supposed to get it tonight, but I found out about ten minutes ago I ain't going to get it at all. . . ."

Martinelli smiled at Halloran, finished: "Mr. Halloran says it was hijacked." He stood up slowly.

Halloran asked: "All through, baby?"

Martinelli was standing very stiff and straight, his hands cupped at his sides.

Doolin ducked suddenly, exerted all his strength to upset the table. For a moment he was protected by the edge, could see neither Martinelli nor Halloran; then the big round tabletop slid off its metal base, crashed to the floor.

Halloran was holding Martinelli very much in the way a great ape would hold a smaller animal. One long arm was out stiff, the long white hand at Martinelli's throat, almost encircling it. Halloran's other hand held Martinelli's wrist, waved it back and forth slowly. The blade of a short curved knife glistened in Martinelli's hand. Except for the slow waving of their two hands they were as if frozen, entirely still. There was nothing human in their position, nothing human in their faces.

Doolin felt in that instant that Halloran was not human. He was mad, insane, but it was not the madness of a man; it was the cold murderous lust of an animal.

The Luger and Doolin's revolver were on the floor near their feet. Doolin circled until he was behind Halloran, moved slowly toward them.

As he dived for one of the guns Halloran swung Martinelli around swiftly, kicked viciously at Doolin's head. He missed once, but the second caught Doolin's hand as it closed over the Luger, sent the Luger spinning to a corner.

As Doolin half rose, Halloran's long leg lashed out again; his heavy shoe struck the side of Doolin's head. Doolin grunted, fell sidewise to the floor.

Doolin lay on his back and the room went around him. Later, in remembering what followed, it was like short strips of motion-picture film, separated by strips of darkness.

Halloran backed Martinelli slowly to the wall. It was as if they were performing some strange ritualistic dance; their steps were measured; Halloran's face was composed, his expression almost tender. Martinelli's face was darkening from the pressure on his throat; Halloran waved the hand holding the knife slowly back and forth.

The next time the darkness in Doolin's head cleared, they were against the wall, his head high, at a curious twisted angle above Halloran's white relentless hand, his face purpling. Halloran's other hand had slipped down over Martinelli's chest.

Martinelli's eyes bulged. His face was the face of a man who saw death coming, and was afraid. Doolin could no longer see Halloran's face. He watched the knife near Martinelli's chest, slowly.

Martinelli, some way, made a high piercing sound in his throat as the knife went into him. And again as Halloran withdrew the knife, pressed it in again slowly. Halloran did not stab mercifully on the left side, but on the right, puncturing the lung again and again, slowly.

Doolin rolled over on his side. The revolver lay on the floor midway between him and Halloran. He shook his head sharply, crawled toward it.

Halloran suddenly released Martinelli, stepped back a pace. Martinelli's knees buckled; he sank slowly down, sat on the floor with his back against the wall, his legs out straight. He sucked in air in great rattling gasps, held both hands tightly against his chest, tightly against the shaft of the knife.

He lifted his head and there was blood on his mouth. He laughed; and Doolin forgot the gun, stopped, stared fascinated at Martinelli. Martinelli laughed, and the sound was as if everything inside him was breaking. His head rolled back and he grinned upward with glazing eyes at Halloran, held his hands tightly against his chest, spoke:

"Tell Lola we can't go away now. . . ." He paused, sucked in air. "She's waiting for me. . . . Tell her Angelo sends his regrets. . . ." His voice was thick, high-pitched, but his words were telling, took deadly effect.

Halloran seemed to grow taller, his great shoulders seemed to widen as Doolin watched.

Martinelli laughed again. He said: "So long—sucker. . . ."

Halloran kicked him savagely in the chest. He drew his long leg back and as Martinelli slumped sidewise he kicked his face, hard, repeatedly.

Doolin scrambled swiftly forward, picked up the revolver, raised it.

Halloran turned slowly.

Doolin held the revolver unsteadily in his right hand, aimed at Halloran's chest, pulled the trigger twice.

Halloran came toward him. Doolin made a harsh sound in his throat, scuttled backward a few feet, held the revolver out limply and fired again.

Halloran's face was cold, impassive; his eyes were great black holes in his skull. He came toward Doolin slowly.

Doolin tried to say something, but the words stuck in his throat, and then

Halloran was above him and there was a terribly crushing weight against Doolin's forehead and it was suddenly dark.

Slowly, Doolin came to, lay a little while with his eyes closed. There were sharp twisting wires of pain in his head; he put his hand up, took it away wet, sticky.

He opened his eyes. It was entirely dark, a cold penetrating darkness; entirely still.

Suddenly he laughed, a curious hysterical sound in the quiet room, and as suddenly, panic seized him. He struggled to his knees, almost fell down again as the pain in his head throbbed to the swift movement. He got to his feet slowly, fumbled in his pockets and found a match, lighted it.

Martinelli's body was slumped in the angle of floor and wall at one side of the room. There was no one else. Doolin's revolver shone dimly on the floor in the flare of the match. The door was ajar.

Doolin lighted another match and picked up his revolver, his hat. He took out a handkerchief and wiped his face, and the handkerchief was wet, dark. He walked unsteadily to the door, down the dark stairs.

One faint globe burned above the deserted bar. Doolin felt his way along the wall, lifted the heavy bar across the outside door and went out, closed the door behind him. It was raining lightly, a thin cold drizzle.

He took air into his lungs in great gulps, soaked the handkerchief in a little puddle of rainwater and tried to clean his face. Then he went down the dark street swiftly toward North Broadway.

The druggist looked at him through thick spectacles, gestured toward the back of the store.

Doolin said: "Fix me up some peroxide an' bandages an' stuff—I had an accident." He went back to the telephone booth, found the number of the Fontenoy, called it, asked for Mrs. Sare.

The operator said Mrs. Sare didn't answer.

Doolin hung up and went out and cleaned the blood from his face in front of a mirror. A little girl stared at him wide-eyed from the soda fountain; the druggist said: "Automobile. . . ?"

Doolin nodded.

The druggist asked: "How much bandage do you want?"

Doolin said: "Let it go—it's not as bad as I thought it was."

He put his hat on the back of his head and went out and got into a cab, said: "Fontenoy Apartments—Hollywood. An' make it snappy."

Doolin opened the door, went in.

She was sitting in a long low chair beneath a crimson-shaded bridge lamp. It was the only light in the room. Her arms were bare, straight on the arms of the chair, her hands hanging limply downward. Her dark head was against the back of the chair and her face was taut, her eyes wide, vacant.

Doolin took off his hat, said: "Why the hell don't you answer your phone?"

She did not speak, nor move.

"You'd better get out of here—quick." Doolin went toward her. "Halloran killed Martinelli—an' Martinelli opened up about you before he died. Halloran will be coming to see you. . . ."

Her blank eyes moved slowly from his face to some place in the dusk behind him. He followed her gaze, turned slowly.

Halloran was standing against the wall near the door. The door had covered him when Doolin entered; he put out one hand and pushed it gently; it swung closed with a sharp click.

As Doolin's eyes became used to the dimness of the room he saw Halloran clearly. He was leaning against the wall, and the right shoulder and breast of his light gray suit was dark, sodden. He held the short blunt Luger in his left hand.

He said: "You're a little late. . . ."

The Luger roared.

Lola Sare put her hands up to the middle of her breast, low; her head came forward slowly. She started to get up and the Luger leaped in Halloran's hand, roared again.

At the same instant Doolin shot, holding the revolver low. The two explosions were simultaneous, thundered in the dark, narrow room.

Halloran fell as a tree falls; slowly, his arm stiff at his sides; crashed to the floor.

Doolin dropped the revolver, walked unsteadily toward Lola Sare. His knees buckled suddenly and he sank forward, down.

There was someone pounding at the door.

Doolin finished dabbing iodine on his head, washed his hands and went into the little living room of his apartment. A first dull streak of morning grayed the windows. He pulled down the shades and went into the kitchenette, lighted the gas under the percolator.

When the coffee was hot he poured a cup, dropped four lumps of sugar into it absently, carried it into the living room. He sat down on the davenport and put the coffee on an end table, picked up the phone and dialed a number.

He said: "Hello, Grace? Is Mollie there? . . ." He listened a moment, went on: "Oh—I thought she might be there. Sorry I woke you. . . ." He hung up, sipped his steaming coffee.

After a few minutes he picked up the phone, dialed again, said: "Listen, Grace —please put Mollie on. . . . I know she's there—please make her talk to me. . . ."

Then he smiled, waited a moment, said: "Hello, darling. . . . Listen—please come on home—will you? . . . Aw listen, honey—I did what you said—everything's all right. . . . Uh-huh. . . . Halloran's dead—an' Martinelli. . . . Uh-huh. . . . The Sare dame is shot up pretty bad, but not too much to give evidence an' clean it all up. . . . Uh-huh. . . ."

He reached over and picked up the cup and took a long drink of coffee, smiled into the phone, said: "Sure—I'm all right—I got a little scratch on my head, but I'm all right. . . . Sure. . . . Sure—we were right. . . . All right, honey—I'll be waiting for you. Hurry up. . . . G'bye. . . ."

He hung up, curved his mouth to a wide grin, finished his coffee, lit a cigarette and waited.

Cain in *Black Mask*

1932–1936

Series characters: Gerry Kells   (GK)
                     Black   (B)

*—indicates use as basis for published novel
•—included in *The* Black Mask *Boys*

*"Fast One" (GK)   March 1932
*"Lead Party" (GK)   April 1932
"Black" (B)   May 1932
*"Velvet" (GK)   June 1932
"Parlor Trick"   July 1932
*"The Heat" (GK)   August 1932
*"The Dark" (GK)   September 1932
"Red 71"   December 1932
"One, Two, Three"   May 1933
•"Murder Done in Blue" (in *BMB* as "Gundown") June 1933
"Pigeon Blood"   November 1933
"Hunch"   March 1934
"Trouble-Chaser" (B)   April 1934
"Chinaman's Chance"   September 1935
"Death Song"   January 1936
"Pineapple"   March 1936
"Dutch Treat"   December 1936

Published Cain Novel Derived from *Black Mask*

Fast One—New York: Doubleday, 1933
   (Derived from "Fast One," "Lead Party," "Velvet," "The Heat," "The Dark")

Behind the Mask: Raymond Chandler

•

When Raymond Chandler wrote his first story for *Black Mask*, in 1933, the hard-boiled genre had been established for a full decade. Hammett's spare, coolly objective writing had set the style and dominated the field.

Chandler arrived relatively late on the *Black Mask* scene and wrote only eleven stories for the magazine, into 1937. Yet his impact was stunning. The shock waves from his work are still being felt in crime fiction.

Classically educated, employing the gifts of an essayist and lyric poet, Raymond Chandler achieved another dimension beyond the lean objectivity of Hammett.

His extraordinary talent for in-depth descriptive prose within a hard-boiled framework brought a unique "poetic realism" to the genre. Added to this, an element of cynical humor that elevated the wisecrack to the level of art.

There is an irony behind Chandler's impressive historical position as an all-time master of the hard-boiled school. Had he been financially successful in his many business ventures, it is unlikely that he would ever have turned to detective fiction.

Raymond Thornton Chandler was born in Chicago on July 23, 1888, to an Irish mother, Florence Dart Thornton Chandler, and a father of Pennsylvania Quaker stock, Maurice Benjamin Chandler. Maurice worked as a railway engineer and was an irresponsible, self-indulgent man whose heavy drinking precipitated bitter family quarrels. Raymond later described his alcoholic father as a "swine."

Chandler's parents were divorced when the boy was seven—and Florence took her young son to England, where they lived with her sister and Chandler's proud, arrogant grandmother.

Natasha Spender, who became a close friend to Chandler in his late years, described the household near London as a place where young Chandler and his

224

mother were made to feel like poor relations, sharing "the humiliation suffered from the moralizing condescension of his aunt and grandmother . . ."

In the autumn of 1900, Chandler became a student at London's Dulwich College (a secondary school). He later rated it as "not quite on a level with Eton." The classical education he received there, into 1905, forged Chandler's early love for the English language.

From a very young age he had determined to be a writer. After further study in France and Germany, he returned to London in 1907 where, at twenty, he had his first poem printed in *Chambers Journal.*

Chandler obtained a job as a clerk with the Admiralty, then shocked his family by quitting after six months to become a free-lance journalist in London. Although he was able to place book reviews and essays with several publications, the financial rewards were meager.

Seeing no future for himself in London, he borrowed 500 pounds from an uncle and booked passage for the United States. On shipboard, Chandler met the Warren Lloyds, who were deeply involved in their family's oil business, and well placed socially on the West Coast. They invited the youth to visit them at their home in Los Angeles.

When Raymond Chandler arrived there in 1912, Los Angeles was still "The New Wild West," and the cultured young man was impressed by the area's raw vitality. It was an "anything can happen here" kind of town, totally removed from the classically rooted European capitals he had known.

Through Warren and Alma Lloyd, his new friends, Chandler obtained a job as a bookkeeper-accountant at the Los Angeles Creamery on South Olive Street.

He began frequenting the weekly social gatherings held at the Lloyd home. Alma was a sculptor and these evenings were devoted to art and music, which Chandler greatly enjoyed.

In his mid-twenties and handsome, he was the natural focus of attention for several unmarried young ladies, but he bypassed all of them to concentrate on Pearl "Cissy" Pascal, eighteen years his senior, the charming and attractive wife of pianist-composer Julian Pascal. A strong mutual attraction developed between them.

"Cissy was still happily married at the time," said a friend who knew them both during this period, "so Ray was very frustrated. He just took off for the war."

Chandler enlisted in the Canadian army at Victoria, British Columbia, in August of 1917, declaring "it was still natural for me to prefer a British uniform." He later claimed that he had been rejected by the United States services because of defective eyesight. At twenty-nine, he became a kilt-wearing member of the 50th Regiment, then known as the Gordon Highlanders of Canada.

Chandler wanted "to see some action," and by the spring of 1918 he was on the front lines in France. As a platoon commander, he was forced to lead his men into direct machine-gun fire. It was a harrowing experience, leaving deep emotional scars. In June of that same year, Chandler became the only member of his unit to survive a devastating attack as eleven-inch German artillery shells killed everyone else in his bunker.

Chandler recuperated from shell-shock in Sussex, England, and was discharged from the service in February of 1919.

"I headed for the States," he later recalled. "Arrived back in California in 1919 with a thick British accent and a thin wallet. I worked for twenty cents an hour on an apricot ranch, then switched to a fifty-four-hour-a-week job stringing tennis rackets. They gave me twelve-fifty a week."

In Los Angeles, he got a job as a writer for the *Daily Express.* He admitted that he was (in his words) "a lousy reporter," and the position lasted just six weeks.

Once again, Chandler was attending social evenings at the Lloyds'. His relationship with Cissy Pascal soon developed into a full romance. She loved her husband, but declared she loved Chandler more. In July of 1919 she filed for divorce.

In 1918, Joseph Dabney, in association with Ralph Lloyd (Warren Lloyd's brother), had formed the Dabney Oil Syndicate. The Lloyds convinced Chandler that there was a "bright future" for him in the oil business. Through Warren, Chandler became a bookkeeper for the company.

Raymond and Cissy were married on February 6, 1924, in Los Angeles. She listed her age as forty-three. Actually, she was a full decade older. (She was fifty-three; Chandler was thirty-five.) The age gap was never a concern. Chandler always spoke of her as a young lover speaks of his college sweetheart. It was a good marriage which was destined to last.

From his starting position as a bookkeeper, Chandler moved rapidly up the business ladder. Eventually he was placed in charge of several smaller branch companies for the Dabney Syndicate.

Ernest Dolley, a friend of this period, recalls that Chandler was not happy as an oil executive. "In those days we'd drive to football games at the Coliseum in his big Hupmobile—Ray loved big cars—and he'd be drinking a lot, complaining about his job. He'd take off for a week's binge. Once he got drunk at the Mayfair Hotel and threatened to jump off the roof, and, another time, tried to sell the entire oil company over the phone!"

These drunken antics cost Chandler his job in 1932, just as the Great Depression was settling over the nation. It was a harsh era. Jobs were impossible to find; Chandler was desperate. Most of all, he wanted to write. The days of his youth were behind him and, at forty-four, he felt he could wait no longer to achieve this goal.

"I took to the road, wandering aimlessly up and down the Pacific Coast," he recalled. During these wanderings Chandler picked up a copy of *Black Mask* and discovered a whole new world of fiction. Here, he felt, was honesty and clean-cut, honed prose. He determined to write for the magazine.

It took him five months to finish "Blackmailers Don't Shoot." Shaw was amazed at its professionalism and happily bought it. The story's locale was Los Angeles, the town that would become "Chandler country."

In the 1930s, when he began writing about Los Angeles, the city was controlled by a powerful crime syndicate that included members of the local police department as well as the town's leading lawyers and politicians. Late 1930s statistics were impressive: 600 brothels, 300 gambling houses, and 1,800 bookie joints were openly doing business.

In his *Mask* stories, Chandler dealt with this corruption. Although writing fictional mysteries, he considered himself, in his words, "a realist—and the realist in murder writes of a world in which gangsters rule cities, in which hotels and apartments and celebrated restaurants are owned by men who make their money out of brothels, in which a screen star can be the finger man for a mob, and the nice man down the hall is boss of the numbers racket; a world where a judge with a cellar full of bootleg liquor can send a man to jail for having a pint in his pocket . . . where no man can walk down a dark street in safety because law and order are things we talk about but refrain from practicing."

Chandler credited Joe Shaw with bringing out the best in him, commenting on Shaw's "great insight into writing." He felt fortunate in having such an editor.

At the close of 1936, when Shaw left the *Mask*, Chandler switched to a better-paying pulp, *Dime Detective*. But even at a higher word rate, he was unable to turn out work fast enough to earn a decent living. (In all, during his seven years with the pulps, Chandler wrote just twenty stories.) Pulp writing had proven to be a financial dead end. He and Cissy were existing on the edge of poverty, their standard of living in sharp decline from the salaried oil company days. Therefore, by the close of the 1930s, Chandler turned to novels as a more substantial source of income. In 1939 Alfred A. Knopf published *The Big Sleep*, the book that introduced Philip Marlowe to the reading public.

Chandler's first novel luridly echoed its pulp origins in its unrestrained violence (six bloody deaths). The overly complex, tangled plot tended to annoy rather than intrigue the casual reader, but the Chandler magic was there, lighting every page. By the climax, when Marlowe's bitter thoughts on death are revealed ("What did it matter where you lay once you were dead . . . You just slept the big sleep, not caring about the nastiness of how you died or where you fell."), the cumulative power of the narrative exerted its effect.

A second novel, *Farewell, My Lovely*, appeared in 1940, and this jet-paced, keenly characterized Marlowe adventure was proof positive of Chandler's ability to fashion permanent literature, however specialized, from the field of perishable pulp fiction. *Farewell* presented the seedy milieu of low-life crime with cunning exactitude. Images and descriptions were diamond-sharp: "He was a windblown blossom of some two hundred pounds with freckled teeth and the mellow voice of a circus barker . . . the kind of cop who spits on his blackjack every night instead of saying his prayers."

Here, in the dank subworld of corruption that Chandler illuminated, the grimy guns-and-gangsters atmosphere was so real you could feel the grit between your fingers. "You gotta play the game dirty or you don't eat," snarls a crooked cop (and Chandler reveled in exposing crooked cops). Marlowe suffered at the hands of gangster and cop alike, but, as he muses after one such encounter: "You can take it. You've been sapped down twice, had your throat choked and been beaten half-silly with a gun barrel. You've been shot full of hop and kept under it until you're as crazy as two waltzing mice. And what does all that amount to? Routine."

By now, Chandler was a self-taught expert in many fields relating to his profession: He knew police procedure; he knew poisons and how they killed; he had studied classic crimes—and he knew slang, the honest kind that hard men used.

By 1943, when two more Marlowe books (*The High Window* and *Lady in the Lake*) had been printed, Chandler was lured to Hollywood (joining what he called "the Roman Circus") to tackle the job of scripting *Double Indemnity* for Billy Wilder. The film proved a great success and he continued to work in the entertainment industry, sporadically, for eight years, turning out some half-dozen screenplays.

One of his most bizarre film experiences began in 1945 when producer John Houseman hired him to write a screenplay for Alan Ladd. The Paramount star was due to enter the service, and the studio was desperate to get one more starring film out of him before he left.

Chandler delivered the first half of the screenplay in just three weeks. Production began as he continued to write, but at the end of a month's shooting the flow of pages suddenly stopped. Chandler was totally blocked on the story. Paramount executives were in a panic; Ladd was due to leave for the army in another ten days!

Chandler told Houseman that the only way he could finish the script was under the stimulating influence of alcohol. He could write it drunk, or not at all. He would require two chauffeured limousines outside his home around the clock, available to bring the doctor to him for daily glucose injections (since he would be eating no food) and to take finished script pages to Paramount. Also, he would require six secretaries, in shifts of two, for dictation and typing, and he also needed a direct, twenty-four-hour phone line to Houseman.

The shaken producer agreed. For eight days Chandler stayed drunk on bourbon, ate no food, survived on glucose injections—and finished the script. *The Blue Dahlia* was completed in time for Ladd's exit into the service. The screenplay's final line is ironic: "Did somebody say something about a drink of bourbon?"

Although Chandler hated working in Hollywood, the money was staggering to a writer who had averaged just $2,000 a year in the pulps. Chandler paid an income tax of $50,000 in 1945, the year *Farewell, My Lovely* was filmed (as *Murder, My Sweet*) with Dick Powell.

In 1946, with Bogart as Marlowe, Warner Bros. released *The Big Sleep*. In 1947, Chandler's *The High Window* was filmed as *The Brasher Doubloon,* a season that also saw the film version of *Lady in the Lake*. None of these motion pictures really did Chandler justice, since the special tart flavor of the Marlowe adventures could not be wholly captured with a camera. The prose brilliance was a vital ingredient, and this extra dimension was missing on the screen. Nonetheless, Chandler was riding the crest of a wave of Hollywood popularity.

By 1946, his wife was past her seventy-fifth year, weak and ill, no longer able to withstand the strain of their continual moves. Chandler felt a need to "settle down" and purchased their first home at a cost of $40,000. The house was located on a quiet bluff overlooking the Pacific Ocean in the Southern California town of La Jolla, and Chandler found it restful and mentally relaxing, a good place to write. He completed his fifth Marlowe novel there, *The Little Sister,* published in 1949.

The Chandler reputation was building with each new book. As critic Robert Kirsch commented:

> He was fascinated with Southern California. He appreciated its physical setting, its paradox of beauty and tawdriness, of rootedness and rootlessness. For him, it was the perfect setting for what he wrote, the modern chivalric tale. For Southern California, with its variation of places, its heterogeneous population, provided the enchanted princesses, the ogres, the castles and the hovels, the wrongs to be righted, the characters and the quests.

After an abortive screen job working for Alfred Hitchcock on a script for *Strangers on a Train* ("He threw out nearly everything I wrote and called in another writer"), Chandler gave up Hollywood to concentrate on a major novel. His 92,000-word rough draft was completed in May of 1952, but the book was still two years (and 33,000 words) away from publication.

As Cissy's health continued to decline, Chandler found it difficult to summon up the breezy, wisecracking world of Philip Marlowe. His style in this sixth novel was far more muted; he was probing emotional pain, deepening his characterizations, extending his range. *The Long Goodbye* was more than another mystery novel. It was Chandler's most ambitious attempt to fashion a work of genuine literature from the restrictive materials of detective fiction.

Cissy's frail condition precluded a social life for the Chandlers, but on occasion a friend would stop by for drinks or dinner. In the last days of Cissy's illness, columnist Neil Morgan, a San Diego newspaper pal of Chandler's, paid them a visit. He had never met Chandler's wife before, and described her as "fragile and wan, dying slowly and hard from fibrosis of the lungs. She had studied to be a concert pianist and on the night I met her she sat at the Steinway and played Chopin waltzes. In my memory, the scene is heavy with lavender and magnolia. Chandler hovered over her, and later took her away and helped her to bed."

Cissy Chandler died on December 12, 1954. Her death had a devastating effect on Chandler. He felt rootless, unloved. A sense of desperate loneliness overwhelmed him.

On February 22, 1955, after drinking heavily, Chandler took a loaded .38-caliber revolver from a drawer and walked into his bathroom. Two bullets were fired, one of which went through the bathroom ceiling. When the police arrived they found Chandler sitting on the floor of the shower, drunkenly trying to place the barrel of the gun in his mouth. . . .

He was taken to a psychiatric ward, then to a private sanitarium for a brief "drying out" period. Feeling that he might regain stability by "returning to my boyhood roots," Chandler booked a flight for England.

Recuperating in London, he was befriended by Natasha Spender, wife of poet Stephen Spender. She tried to help him regain his self-respect, but he remained moody, often suicidal. He drank, pursued younger women, and wrote endless letters bemoaning the loss of Cissy.

During this London trip Chandler met Ian Fleming, the creator of James Bond. They shared a mutual admiration for one another's books, and Fleming was able to draw him out of his shell, get him to talk about his fiction.

"He admitted to working endlessly over his dialogue," reported Fleming. "He produced his pages in longhand, very slowly, and there was much revision. He believed that 'toughness' in writing had to come naturally, and pointed out that 'the best hard-boiled writers never try to be tough, they allow toughness to happen when it seems inevitable for its time, place and conditions.' After more than twenty years of writing he felt that he was going stale. In the end, he told me, as one got older, one grew out of gangsters and blondes and guns—and since they were the chief ingredients of thrillers, that was that."

Chandler became close to his London agent, Helga Greene, who gradually persuaded him to go to work on another Marlowe novel. By the end of 1958 he had completed *Playback,* loosely based on an unproduced screenplay of the same title he had written for Universal in his studio days.

In early 1959, Chandler returned to New York to accept the presidency of the Mystery Writers of America, an honor he deeply appreciated. "I feel very humble about this," he told MWA members. "I take this honor as the token of a long career . . . most of which has been spent in trying to make something out of the mystery story—perhaps a little more than it was intended to be—but I am not at all sure that I have succeeded."

Helga Greene accompanied him on the New York trip, and they now planned to be married. Their union would provide Chandler with the stability he desperately needed.

Unhappily, the marriage never took place. Raymond Chandler died of bronchial pneumonia on March 26, 1959, in La Jolla, four months short of his seventy-first birthday.

"Any man who can write a page of living prose adds something to our life," he once declared.

He had added much. In fashioning that unique landscape known as "Chandler country" he had made the sprawling terrain of Southern California his own.

From seedy, paint-blistered beach bungalows to plush Bel Air apartments, from fog-draped piers to smoke-filled bars, from wide, sun-splashed boulevards to dank, narrow tenement hallways, from the broken-scrolled, decaying mansions on Bunker Hill to the foam-wet sands of Malibu, Raymond Chandler brought this vast, multifaceted area and its people to life in a very special way.

Among the *Black Mask* boys, he had evolved into an all-time master.

Blackmailers Don't Shoot

Late in the 1930s, when Chandler was writing his first novel, *The Big Sleep*, he told his wife that he planned on using Mallory as the hero's name. (Chandler's knight-detective owed much, in moral courage and spirit, to Sir Thomas Malory's *Le Morte d'Arthur.*) She said that Mallory was fine—but she liked Marlowe better. Thus, Philip Mallory became Philip Marlowe.

Here, in Raymond Chandler's first hard-boiled story, the detective is Mallory —and he was brought back to the *Mask* under that name in Chandler's second story for Joe Shaw, "Smart-Aleck Kill."

Mallory . . . Carmady . . . Dalmas . . . Gage . . . Evans . . . The names didn't matter. Chandler freely admitted that all of his detectives were the same man of honor, walking the mean streets as Philip Marlowe. Surely, the roots of Marlowe are plainly evident here, in the character and actions of Mallory.

"Blackmailers Don't Shoot" will not be found among the Chandler stories currently available in paperback. Therefore, it is a pleasure to bring it back into print once again. After more than half a century, this story remains as fresh and powerful as the day it was written—a remarkable *Black Mask* debut by a remarkable writer.

BLACKMAILERS DON'T SHOOT

Series character: Mallory

The man in the powder-blue suit—which wasn't powder-blue under the lights of the Club Bolivar—was tall, with wide-set gray eyes, a thin nose, a jaw of stone. He had a rather sensitive mouth. His hair was crisp and black, ever so faintly touched with gray, as by an almost diffident hand. His clothes fitted him as though they had a soul of their own, not just a doubtful past. His name happened to be Mallory.

He held a cigarette between the strong, precise fingers of one hand. He put the other hand flat on the white tablecloth and said:

"The letters will cost you ten grand, Miss Farr. That's not too much."

He looked at the girl opposite him very briefly; then he looked across empty tables toward the heart-shaped space of floor where the dancers prowled under shifting colored lights.

They crowded the customers around the dance floor so closely that the perspiring waiters had to balance themselves like tightrope walkers to get between the tables. But near where Mallory sat were only four people.

A slim, dark woman was drinking a highball across the table from a man whose fat red neck glistened with damp bristles. The woman stared into her glass morosely and fiddled with a big silver flask in her lap. Farther along two bored, frowning men smoked long thin cigars, without speaking to each other.

Mallory said thoughtfully: "Ten grand does it nicely, Miss Farr."

Rhonda Farr was very beautiful. She was wearing, for this occasion, all black, except a collar of white fur, light as thistledown, on her evening wrap. Except also a white wig which, meant to disguise her, made her look very girlish. Her eyes were cornflower blue, and she had the sort of skin an old rake dreams of.

She said nastily, without raising her head: "That's ridiculous."

"Why is it ridiculous?" Mallory asked, looking mildly surprised and rather annoyed.

Rhonda Farr lifted her face and gave him a look as hard as marble. Then she picked a cigarette out of a silver case that lay open on the table and fitted it into a long slim holder, also black. She went on:

"The love letters of a screen star? Not so much anymore. The public has stopped being a sweet old lady in long lace panties."

A light danced contemptuously in her purplish-blue eyes. Mallory gave her a hard look.

"But you came here to talk about them quick enough," he said, "with a man you never heard of."

She waved the cigarette holder and said: "I must have been nuts."

Mallory smiled with his eyes, without moving his lips. "No, Miss Farr. You had a damn good reason. Want me to tell you what it is?"

Rhonda Farr looked at him angrily. Then she looked away, almost appeared to forget him. She held up her hand, the one with the cigarette holder, looked at it, posing. It was a beautiful hand, without a ring. Beautiful hands are as rare as jacaranda trees in bloom, in a city where pretty faces are as common as runs in dollar stockings.

She turned her head and glanced at the stiff-eyed woman, beyond her toward the mob around the dance floor. The orchestra went on being saccharine and monotonous.

"I loathe these dives," she said thinly. "They look as if they only existed after dark, like ghouls. The people are dissipated without grace, sinful without irony." She lowered her hand to the white cloth. "Oh yes, the letters, what makes them so dangerous, blackmailer?"

Mallory laughed. He had a ringing laugh with a hard quality in it, a grating sound. "You're good," he said. "The letters are not so much perhaps. Just sexy tripe. The memoirs of a schoolgirl who's been seduced and can't stop talking about it."

"That's lousy," Rhonda Farr said in a voice like iced velvet.

"It's the man they're written to that makes them important," Mallory said coldly. "A racketeer, a gambler, a fast-money boy. And all that goes with it. A guy you couldn't be seen talking to—and stay in the cream."

"I don't talk to him, blackmailer. I haven't talked to him in years. Landrey was a pretty nice boy when I knew him. Most of us have something behind us we'd rather not go into. In my case it *is* behind."

"Oh yes? Make mine strawberry," Mallory said with a sudden sneer. "You just got through asking him to help you get your letters back."

Her head jerked. Her face seemed to come apart, to become merely a set of features without control. Her eyes looked like the prelude to a scream—but only for a second.

Almost instantly she got her self-control back. Her eyes were drained of color, almost as gray as his own. She put the black cigarette holder down with exaggerated care, laced her fingers together. The knuckles looked white.

"You know Landrey that well?" she said bitterly.

"Maybe I just get around, find things out. . . . Do we deal, or do we just go on snarling at each other?"

"Where did you get the letters?" Her voice was still rough and bitter.

Mallory shrugged. "We don't tell things like that in our business."

"I had a reason for asking. Some other people have been trying to sell me these same damned letters. That's why I'm here. It made me curious. But I guess you're just one of them trying to scare me into action by stepping the price."

Mallory said: "No, I'm on my own."

She nodded. Her voice was scarcely more than a whisper. "That makes it nice. Perhaps some bright mind thought of having a private edition of my letters made. Photostats . . . Well, I'm not paying. It wouldn't get me anywhere. I don't deal, blackmailer. So far as I'm concerned, you can go out some dark night and jump off the dock with your lousy letters!"

Mallory wrinkled his nose, squinted down it with an air of deep concentration. "Nicely put, Miss Farr. But it doesn't get us anywhere."

She said deliberately: "It wasn't meant to. I could put it better. And if I'd thought to bring my little pearl-handled gun, I could say it with slugs and get away with it! But I'm not looking for that kind of publicity."

Mallory held up two lean fingers and examined them critically. He looked amused, almost pleased. Rhonda Farr put her slim hand up to her white wig, held it there a moment, and dropped it.

A man sitting at a table some way off got up at once and came toward them.

He came quickly, walking with a light, lithe step and swinging a soft black hat against his thigh. He was sleek in dinner clothes.

While he was coming Rhonda Farr said: "You didn't expect me to walk in here alone, did you? Me, I don't go to nightclubs alone."

Mallory grinned. "You shouldn't ought to have to, baby," he said dryly.

The man came up to the table. He was small, neatly put together, dark. He had a little black mustache, shiny like satin, and the clear pallor that Latins prize above rubies.

With a smooth gesture, a hint of drama, he leaned across the table and took one of Mallory's cigarettes out of the silver case. He lit it with a flourish.

Rhonda Farr put her hand to her lips and yawned. She said, "This is Erno, my bodyguard. He takes care of me. Nice, isn't it?"

She stood up slowly. Erno helped her with her wrap. Then he spread his lips in a mirthless smile, looked at Mallory, said:

"Hello, baby."

He had dark, almost opaque eyes with hot lights in them.

Rhonda Farr gathered her wrap about her, nodded slightly, sketched a brief sarcastic smile with her delicate lips, and turned off along the aisle between the tables. She went with her head up and proud, her face a little tense and wary, like a queen in jeopardy. Not fearless, but disdaining to show fear. It was nicely done.

The two bored men gave her an interested eye. The dark woman brooded glumly over the task of mixing herself a highball that would have floored a horse. The man with the fat sweaty neck seemed to have gone to sleep.

Rhonda Farr went up the five crimson-carpeted steps to the lobby, past a bowing headwaiter. She went through looped-back gold curtains, and disappeared.

Mallory watched her out of sight, then he looked at Erno. He said: "Well, punk, what's on your mind?"

He said it insultingly, with a cold smile. Erno stiffened. His gloved left hand jerked the cigarette that was in it so that some ash fell off.

"Kiddin' yourself, baby?" he inquired swiftly.

"About what, punk?"

Red spots came into Erno's pale cheeks. His eyes narrowed to black slits. He moved his ungloved right hand a little, curled the fingers so that the small pink nails glittered. He said thinly:

"About some letters, baby. Forget it! It's out, baby, out!"

Mallory looked at him with elaborate, cynical interest, ran his fingers through his crisp black hair. He said slowly: "Perhaps I don't know what you mean, little one."

Erno laughed. A metallic sound, a strained deadly sound. Mallory knew that kind of laugh; the prelude to gun music in some places. He watched Erno's quick little right hand. He spoke raspingly.

"On your way, red hot. I might take a notion to slap that fuzz off your lip."

Erno's face twisted. The red patches showed startlingly in his cheeks. He lifted the hand that held his cigarette, lifted it slowly, and snapped the burning cigarette straight at Mallory's face. Mallory moved his head a little, and the white tube arced over his shoulder.

There was no expression on his lean, cold face. Distantly, dimly, as though another voice spoke, he said:

"Careful, punk. People get hurt for things like that."

Erno laughed the same metallic, strained laugh. "Blackmailers don't shoot, baby," he snarled. "Do they?"

"Beat it, you dirty little wop!"

The words, the cold sneering tone, stung Erno to fury. His right hand shot up like a striking snake. A gun whisked into it from a shoulder holster. Then he stood motionless, glaring. Mallory bent forward a little, his hands on the edge of the table, his fingers curled below the edge. The corners of his mouth sketched a dim smile.

There was a dull screech, not loud, from the dark woman. The color drained from Erno's cheeks, leaving them pallid, sunk in. In a voice that whistled with fury he said:

"Okay, baby. We'll go outside. March, you—!"

One of the bored men three tables away made a sudden movement of no significance. Slight as it was it caught Erno's eye. His glance flickered. Then the table rose into his stomach, knocked him sprawling.

It was a light table, and Mallory was not a lightweight. There was a complicated thudding sound. A few dishes clattered, some silver. Erno was spread on the floor with the table across his thighs. His gun settled a foot from his clawing hand. His face was convulsed.

For a poised instant of time it was as though the scene were imprisoned in glass and would never change. Then the dark woman screeched again, louder. Everything became a swirl of movement. People on all sides came to their feet. Two waiters put their arms straight up in the air and began to spout violent Neapolitan. A moist, overdriven bus-boy charged up, more afraid of the headwaiter than of sudden death. A plump, reddish man with corn-colored hair hurried down steps, waving a bunch of menus.

Erno jerked his legs clear, weaved to his knees, snatched up his gun. He swiveled, spitting curses. Mallory, alone, indifferent in the center of the babble, leaned down and cracked a hard fist against Erno's flimsy jaw.

Consciousness evaporated from Erno's eyes. He collapsed like a half-filled sack of sand.

Mallory observed him carefully for a couple of seconds. Then he picked his cigarette case up off the floor. There were still two cigarettes in it. He put one of them between his lips, put the case away. He took some bills out of his trouser pocket, folded one lengthwise, and poked it at a waiter.

He walked away without haste, toward the five crimson-carpeted steps and the entrance.

The man with the fat neck opened a cautious and fishy eye. The drunken woman staggered to her feet with a cackle of inspiration, picked up a bowl of ice cubes in her thin jeweled hands, and dumped it on Erno's stomach, with fair accuracy.

Mallory came out from under the canopy with his soft hat under his arm. The doorman looked at him inquiringly. He shook his head and walked a little way down the curving sidewalk that bordered the semicircular private driveway. He stood at the edge of the curbing, in the darkness, thinking hard. After a little while an Isotta-Fraschini went by him slowly.

It was an open phaeton, huge even for the calculated swank of Hollywood. It glittered like a Ziegfeld chorus as it passed the entrance lights, then it was all dull gray and silver. A liveried chauffeur sat behind the wheel as stiff as a poker, with a peaked cap cocked rakishly over one eye. Rhonda Farr sat in the backseat, under the half-deck, with the rigid stillness of a wax figure.

The car slid soundlessly down the driveway, passed between a couple of squat stone pillars, and was lost among the lights of the boulevard. Mallory put on his hat absently.

Something stirred in the darkness behind him, between tall Italian cypresses. He swung around, looked at faint light on a gun barrel.

The man who held the gun was very big and broad. He had a shapeless felt hat on the back of his head, and an indistinct overcoat hung away from his stomach. Dim light from a high-up, narrow window outlined bushy eyebrows, a hooked nose. There was another man behind him.

He said: "This is a gun, buddy. It goes boom-boom, and guys fall down. Want to try it?"

Mallory looked at him emptily and said: "Grow up, flattie! What's the act?"

The big man laughed. His laughter had a dull sound, like the sea breaking on rocks in a fog. He said with heavy sarcasm:

"Bright boy has us spotted, Jim. One of us must look like a cop." He eyed Mallory, and added: "Saw you pull a rod on a little guy inside. Was that nice?"

Mallory tossed his cigarette away, watched it arc through the darkness. He said carefully:

"Would twenty bucks make you see it some other way?"

"Not tonight, mister. Most any other night, but not tonight."

"A C note?"

"Not even that, mister."

"That," Mallory said gravely, "must be damn tough."

The big man laughed again, came a little closer. The man behind him lurched out of the shadows and planted a soft fattish hand on Mallory's shoulder. Mallory slid sidewise, without moving his feet. The hand fell off. He said:

"Keep your paws off me, gumshoe!"

The other man made a snarling sound. Something swished through the air. Something hit Mallory very hard behind his left ear. He went to his knees. He kneeled swaying for a moment, shaking his head violently. His eyes cleared. He could see the lozenge design in the sidewalk. He got to his feet again rather slowly.

He looked at the man who had blackjacked him and cursed him in a thick dull voice, with a concentration of ferocity that set the man back on his heels with his slack mouth working like melting rubber.

The big man said: "Damn your soul, Jim! What in hell'd you do that for?"

The man called Jim put his soft fat hand to his mouth and gnawed at it. He shuffled the blackjack into the side pocket of his coat.

"Forget it!" he said. "Let's take the——and get on with it. I need a drink."

He plunged down the walk. Mallory turned slowly, followed him with his eyes, rubbing the side of his head. The big man moved his gun in a businesslike way and said:

"Walk, buddy. We're takin' a little ride in the moonlight."

Mallory walked. The big man fell in beside him. The man called Jim fell in on the other side. He hit himself hard in the pit of the stomach, said:

"I need a drink, Mac. I've got the jumps."

The big man said peacefully: "Who don't, you poor egg?"

They came to a touring car that was double-parked near the squat pillars at the edge of the boulevard. The man who had hit Mallory got in behind the wheel. The big man prodded Mallory into the backseat and got in beside him. He held his gun across his big thigh, tilted his hat a little further back, and got out a crumpled pack of cigarettes. He lit one carefully, with his left hand.

The car went out into the sea of lights, rolled east a short way, then turned south down the long slope. The lights of the city were an endless glittering sheet. Neon signs glowed and flashed. The languid ray of a searchlight prodded about among high faint clouds.

"It's like this," the big man said, blowing smoke from his wide nostrils. "We got you spotted. You were tryin' to peddle some phony letters to the Farr twist."

Mallory laughed shortly, mirthlessly. He said: "You flatties give me an ache."

The big man appeared to think it over, staring in front of him. Passing electro-liers threw quick waves of light across his broad face. After a while he said:

"You're the guy, all right. We got to know these things in our business."

Mallory's eyes narrowed in the darkness. His lips smiled. He said: "What business, copper?"

The big man opened his mouth wide, shut it with a click. He said:

"Maybe you better talk, bright boy. Now would be a hell of a good time. Jim and me ain't tough to get on with, but we got friends who ain't so dainty."

Mallory said: "What would I talk about, Lieutenant?"

The big man shook with silent laughter, made no answer. The car went past the oil well that stands in the middle of La Cienega Boulevard, then turned off on to a quiet street fringed with palm trees. It stopped halfway down the block, in front of an empty lot. Jim cut the motor and the lights. Then he got a flat bottle out of the door pocket and held it to his mouth, sighed deeply, passed the bottle over his shoulder.

The big man took a drink, waved the bottle, said:

"We got to wait here for a friend. Let's talk. My name's Macdonald—detective bureau. You was tryin' to shake the Farr girl down. Then her protection stepped in front of her. You bopped him. That was a nice routine and we liked it. But we didn't like the other part."

Jim reached back for the whiskey bottle, took another drink, sniffed at the neck, said: "This liquor is lousy."

Macdonald went on: "We was stashed out for you. But we don't figure your play out in the open like that. It don't listen."

Mallory leaned an arm on the side of the car and looked out and up at the calm, blue, star-spattered sky. He said:

"You know too much, copper. And you didn't get your dope from Miss Farr. No screen star would go to the police on a matter of blackmail."

Macdonald jerked his big head around. His eyes gleamed faintly in the dark interior of the car.

"We didn't say how we got our dope, bright boy. So you *was* tryin' to shake her down, huh?"

Mallory said gravely: "Miss Farr is an old friend of mine. Somebody is trying to blackmail her, but not me. I just have a hunch."

Macdonald said swiftly: "What the wop pull a gun on you for?"

"He didn't like me," Mallory said in a bored voice. "I was mean to him."

Macdonald said: "Horsefeathers!" He rumbled angrily. The man in the front seat said: "Smack him in the kisser, Mac. Make the——like it!"

Mallory stretched his arms downward, twisting his shoulders like a man cramped from sitting. He felt the bulge of his Luger under his left arm. He said slowly, wearily:

"You said I was trying to peddle some phony letters. What makes you think the letters would be phony?"

Macdonald said softly: "Maybe we know where the right ones are."

Mallory drawled: "That's what I thought, copper," and laughed.

Macdonald moved suddenly, jerked his balled fist up, hit him in the face, but not very hard. Mallory laughed again, then he touched the bruised place behind his ear with careful fingers.

"That went home, didn't it?" he said.

Macdonald swore dully. "Maybe you're just a bit too damn smart, bright boy. I guess we'll find out after a while."

He fell silent. The man in the front seat took off his hat and scratched at a mat of gray hair. Staccato horn blasts came from the boulevard a half-block away. Headlights streamed past the end of the street. After a time a pair of them swung around in a wide curve, speared white beams along below the palm trees. A dark bulk drifted down the half-block, slid to the curb in front of the touring car. The lights went off.

A man got out and walked back. Macdonald said: "Hi, Slippy. How'd it go?"

The man was a tall thin figure with a shadowy face under a pulled-down cap. He lisped a little when he spoke. He said:

"Nothin' to it. Nobody got mad."

"Okay," Macdonald grunted. "Ditch the hot one and drive this heap."

Jim got into the back of the touring car and sat on Mallory's left, digging a hard elbow into him. The lanky man slid under the wheel, started the motor, and drove back to La Cienega, then south to Wilshire, then west again. He drove fast and roughly.

They went casually through a red light, passed a big movie palace with most of its lights out and its glass cashier's cage empty; then through Beverly Hills, over interurban tracks. The exhaust got louder on a long hill with high banks paralleling the road. Macdonald spoke suddenly:

"Hell, Jim, I forgot to frisk this baby. Hold the gun a minute."

He leaned in front of Mallory, close to him, blowing whiskey breath in his face. A big hand went over his pockets, down inside his coat around the hips, up under his left arm. It stopped there a moment, against the Luger in the shoulder holster. It went on to the other side, went away altogether.

"Okay, Jim. No gun on bright boy."

A sharp light of wonder winked into being deep in Mallory's brain. His eyebrows drew together. His mouth felt dry.

"Mind if I light up a cigarette?" he asked, after a pause.

Macdonald said with mock politeness: "Now why would we mind a little thing like that, sweetheart?"

The apartment house stood on a hill above Westward Village, and was new and rather cheap-looking. Macdonald and Mallory and Jim got out in front of it, and the touring car went on around the corner, disappeared.

The three men went through a quiet lobby past a switchboard where no one sat at the moment, up to the seventh floor in the automatic elevator. They went along a corridor, stopped before a door. Macdonald took a loose key out of his pocket, unlocked the door. They went in.

It was a very new room, very bright, very foul with cigarette smoke. The furniture was upholstered in loud colors, the carpet was a mess of fat green and yellow lozenges. There was a mantel with bottles on it.

Two men sat at an octagonal table with tall glasses at their elbows. One had red hair, very dark eyebrows, and a dead white face with deep-set dark eyes. The other one had a ludicrous big bulbous nose, no eyebrows at all, hair the color of the inside of a sardine can. This one put some cards down slowly and came across the room with a wide smile. He had a loose, good-natured mouth, an amiable expression.

"Have any trouble, Mac?" he said.

Macdonald rubbed his chin, shook his head sourly. He looked at the man with the nose as if he hated him. The man with the nose went on smiling. He said:

"Frisk him?"

Macdonald twisted his mouth to a thick sneer and stalked across the room to the mantel and the bottles. He said in a nasty tone:

"Bright boy don't pack a gun. He works with his head. He's smart."

He recrossed the room suddenly and smacked the back of his rough hand across Mallory's mouth. Mallory smiled thinly, did not stir. He stood in front of a big bile-colored davenport spotted with angry-looking red squares. His hands hung down at his sides, and cigarette smoke drifted up from between his fingers to join the haze that already blanketed the rough, arched ceiling.

"Keep your pants on, Mac," the man with the nose said. "You've done your act. You and Jim check out now. Oil the wheels and check out."

Macdonald snarled: "Who you givin' orders to, big shot? I'm stickin' around till this chiseler gets what's coming to him, Costello."

The man called Costello shrugged his shoulders briefly. The red-haired man at the table turned a little in his chair and looked at Mallory with the impersonal air of a collector studying an impaled beetle. Then he took a cigarette out of a neat black case and lit it carefully with a gold lighter.

Macdonald went back to the mantel, poured some whiskey out of a square bottle into a glass, and drank it raw. He leaned, scowling, with his back to the mantel.

Costello stood in front of Mallory, cracking the joints of long, bony fingers.

He said: "Where do you come from?"

Mallory looked at him dreamily and put his cigarette in his mouth. "McNeil's Island," he said with vague amusement.

"How long since?"

"Ten days."

"What were you in for?"

"Forgery." Mallory gave the information in a soft, pleased voice.

"Been here before?"

Mallory said: "I was born here. Didn't you know?"

Costello's voice was gentle, almost soothing. "No-o, I didn't know that," he said. "What did you come for—ten days ago?"

Macdonald heaved across the room again, swinging his thick arms. He slapped Mallory across the mouth a second time, leaning past Costello's shoulder to do it. A red mark showed on Mallory's face. He shook his head back and forth. Dull fire was in his eyes.

"Jeeze, Costello, this crumb ain't from McNeil. He's ribbin' you." His voice blared. "Bright boy's just a cheap chiseler from Brooklyn or K. C.—one of those hot towns where the cops are all cripples."

Costello put a hand up and pushed gently at Macdonald's shoulder. He said: "You're not needed in this, Mac," in a flat, toneless voice.

Macdonald balled his fist angrily. Then he laughed, lunged forward, and ground his heel on Mallory's foot. Mallory said: "——damn!" and sat down hard on the davenport.

The air in the room was drained of oxygen. Windows were in one wall only, and heavy net curtains hung straight and still across them. Mallory got out a handkerchief and wiped his forehead, patted his lips.

Costello said: "You and Jim check out, Mac," in the same flat voice.

Macdonald lowered his head, stared at him steadily through a fringe of eyebrow. His face was shiny with sweat. He had not taken his shabby, rumpled overcoat off. Costello didn't even turn his head. After a moment Macdonald barged back to the mantel, elbowed the gray-haired cop out of the way, and grabbed at the square bottle of Scotch.

"Call the boss, Costello," he blared over his shoulder. "You ain't got the brains for this deal. For——sake do something besides talk!" He turned a little toward Jim, thumped him on the back, said sneeringly: "Did you want just one more drink, copper?"

"What did you come here for?" Costello asked Mallory again..

"Looking for a connection." Mallory stared up at him lazily. The fire had died out of his eyes.

"Funny way you went about it, boy."

Mallory shrugged. "I thought if I made a play, I might get in touch with the right people."

"Maybe you made the wrong kind of play," Costello said quietly. He closed his eyes and rubbed his nose with a thumbnail. "These things are hard to figure sometimes."

Macdonald's harsh voice boomed across the close room. "Bright boy don't make mistakes, mister. Not with his brains."

Costello opened his eyes and glanced back over his shoulder at the red-haired man. The red-haired man swiveled loosely in his chair. His right hand lay along his leg, slack, half closed. Costello turned the other way, looked straight at Macdonald.

"Move out!" he snapped coldly. "Move out now. You're drunk, and I'm not arguing with you."

Macdonald ground his shoulders against the mantel and put his hands in the side pockets of his suit coat. His hat hung formless and crumpled on the back of his big, square head. Jim, the gray-haired cop, moved a little away from him, stared at him strainedly, his mouth working.

"Call the boss, Costello!" Macdonald shouted. "You ain't givin' me orders. I don't like you well enough to take 'em."

Costello hesitated, then moved across to the telephone. His eyes stared at a spot high up on the wall. He lifted the instrument off the prongs and dialed with his back to Macdonald. Then he leaned against the wall, smiling thinly at Mallory over the cup. Waiting.

"Hello . . . yes . . . Costello. Everything's oke except Mac's loaded. He's pretty hostile . . . won't move out. Don't know yet . . . some out-of-town boy. Okay."

Macdonald made a motion, said: "Hold it . . ."

Costello smiled and put the phone aside without haste. Macdonald's eyes gleamed at him with a greenish fire. He spit on the carpet, in the corner between a chair and the wall. He said:

"That's lousy. Lousy. You can't dial Montrose from here." Costello moved his hands vaguely. The red-haired man got to his feet. He moved away from the table and stood laxly, tilting his head back so that the smoke from his cigarette rose clear of his eyes.

Macdonald rocked angrily on his heels. His jawbone was a hard white line against his flushed face. His eyes had a deep, hard glitter.

"I guess we'll play it this way," he stated. He took his hands out of his pockets in a casual manner, and his blued service revolver moved in a tight, business-like arc.

Costello looked at the red-haired man and said: "Take him, Andy."

The red-haired man stiffened, spit his cigarette straight out from between his pale lips, flashed a hand up like lightning.

Mallory said: "Not fast enough. Look at this one."

He had moved so quickly and so little that he had not seemed to move at all. He leaned forward a little on the davenport. The long black Luger lined itself evenly on the red-haired man's belly.

The red-haired man's hand came down slowly from his lapel, empty. The room was very quiet. Costello looked once at Macdonald with infinite disgust, then he put his hands out in front of him, palms up, and looked down at them with a blank smile.

Macdonald spoke slowly, bitterly. "The kidnapping is one too many for me, Costello. I don't want any part of it. I'm takin' a powder from this toy mob. I took a chance that bright boy might side me."

Mallory stood up and moved sidewise toward the red-haired man. When he had gone about half the distance, the gray-haired cop, Jim, let out a strangled sort of yell and jumped for Macdonald, clawing at his pocket. Macdonald looked at him with quick surprise. He put his big left hand out and grabbed both lapels of Jim's overcoat tight together, high up. Jim flailed at him with both fists, hit him in the face twice. Macdonald drew his lips back over his teeth. Calling to Mallory, "Watch those birds," he very calmly laid his gun down on the mantel, reached down into the pocket of Jim's coat, and took out the woven leather blackjack. He said:

"You're a louse, Jim. You always were a louse."

He said it rather thoughtfully, without rancor. Then he swung the blackjack and hit the gray-haired man on the side of the head. The gray-haired man sagged slowly to his knees. He clawed freely at the skirts of Macdonald's coat. Macdonald stooped over and hit him again with the blackjack, in the same place, very hard.

Jim crumpled down sidewise and lay on the floor with his hat off and his mouth open. Macdonald swung the blackjack slowly from side to side. A drop of sweat ran down the side of his nose.

Costello said: "Rough boy, ain't you, Mac?" He said it dully, absently, as though he had very little interest in what went on.

Mallory went on toward the red-haired man. When he was behind him he said: "Put the hands way up, wiper."

When the red-haired man had done this, Mallory put his free hand over his shoulder, down inside his coat. He jerked a gun loose from a shoulder holster and dropped it on the floor behind him. He felt the other side, patted pockets. He stepped back and circled to Costello. Costello had no gun.

Mallory went to the other side of Macdonald, stood where everyone in the room was in front of him. He said:

"Who's kidnapped?"

Macdonald picked up his gun and glass of whiskey. "The Farr girl," he said. "They got her on her way home, I guess. It was planned when they knew from the wop bodyguard about the date at the Bolivar. I don't know where they took her."

Mallory planted his feet wide apart and wrinkled his nose. He held his Luger easily, with a slack wrist. He said:

"What does your little act mean?"

Macdonald said grimly: "Tell me about yours. I gave you a break."

Mallory nodded, said: "Sure—for your own reasons. . . . I was hired to look for some letters that belong to Rhonda Farr." He looked at Costello. Costello showed no emotion.

Macdonald said: "Okay by me. I thought it was some kind of a plant. That's why I took the chance. Me, I want an out from this connection, that's all." He waved his hand around to take in the room and everything in it.

Mallory picked up a glass, looked into it to see if it was clean, then poured a little Scotch into it and drank it in sips, rolling his tongue around in his mouth.

"Let's talk about the kidnapping," he said. "Who was Costello phoning to?"

"Atkinson. Big Hollywood lawyer. Front for the boys. He's the Farr girl's lawyer, too. Nice guy, Atkinson. A louse."

"He in on the kidnapping?"

Macdonald laughed and said: "Sure."

Mallory shrugged, said: "It seems like a dumb trick—for him."

He went past Macdonald, along the wall to where Costello stood. He stuck the muzzle of the Luger against Costello's chin, pushed his head back against the rough plaster.

"Costello's a nice old boy," he said thoughtfully. "He wouldn't kidnap a girl. Would you, Costello? A little quiet extortion maybe, but nothing rough. That right, Costello?"

Costello's eyes went blank. He swallowed. He said between his teeth: "Can it. You're not funny."

Mallory said: "It gets funnier as it goes on. But perhaps you don't know it all."

He lifted the Luger and drew the muzzle down the side of Costello's big nose, hard. It left a white mark that turned to a red weal. Costello looked a little worried.

Macdonald finished pushing a nearly full bottle of Scotch into his overcoat pocket and said:

"Let me work on the——!"

Mallory shook his head gravely from side to side, looking at Costello.

"Too noisy. You know how these places are built. Atkinson is the boy to see. Always see the head man—if you can get to him."

Jim opened his eyes. Flapped his hands on the floor, tried to get up. Macdonald lifted a large foot and planted it carelessly in the gray-haired man's face. Jim lay down again. His face was a muddy gray color.

Mallory glanced at the red-haired man and went over to the telephone stand. He lifted the instrument down and dialed a number awkwardly, with his left hand.

He said: "I'm calling the man who hired me. . . . He has a big fast car. . . . We'll put these boys in soak for a while."

Landrey's big black Cadillac rolled soundlessly up the long grade to Montrose. Lights shone low on the left, in the lap of the valley. The air was cool and clear, and the stars were very bright. Landrey looked back from the front seat, draped an arm over the back of the seat, a long black arm that ended in a white glove.

He said, for the third or fourth time: "So it's her own mouthpiece shaking her down. Well, well, well."

He smiled smoothly, deliberately. All his movements were smooth and deliberate. Landrey was a tall, pale man with white teeth and jet-black eyes that sparkled under the dome light.

Mallory and Macdonald sat in the backseat. Mallory said nothing; he stared out of the car window. Macdonald took a pull at his square bottle of Scotch, lost the cork on the floor of the car, and swore as he bent over to grope for it. When he found it he leaned back and looked morosely at Landrey's clear, pale face above the white silk scarf.

He said: "You still got that place on Highland Drive?"

Landrey said: "Yes, copper, I have. And it's not doin' so well."

Macdonald growled. He said: "That's a damn shame, Mr. Landrey." Then he put his head back against the upholstery and closed his eyes.

The Cadillac turned off the highway. The driver seemed to know just where he was going. He circled around into a landscaped subdivision of rambling elaborate homes. Tree frogs sounded in the darkness, and there was a smell of orange blossoms.

Macdonald opened his eyes and leaned forward. "The house on the corner," he told the driver.

The house stood well back from a wide curve. It had a lot of tiled roof, an entrance like a Norman arch, and wrought-iron lanterns lit on either side of the door. By the sidewalk there was a pergola covered with climbing roses. The driver cut his lights and drifted expertly up to the pergola.

Mallory yawned and opened the car door. Cars were parked along the street around the corner. The cigarette tips of a couple of lounging chauffeurs spotted the soft bluish dark.

"Party," he said. "That makes it nice."

He got out, stood a moment looking across the lawn. Then he walked over soft grass to a pathway of dull bricks spaced so that the grass grew between them. He stood between the wrought-iron lanterns and rang the bell.

A maid in cap and apron opened the door. Mallory said:

"Sorry to disturb Mr. Atkinson, but it's important. Macdonald is the name."

The maid hesitated, then went back into the house, leaving the front door open a crack. Mallory pushed it open carelessly, looked into a roomy hallway with Indian rugs on the floor and walls. He went in.

A few yards down the hallway a doorway gave on a dim room lined with books, smelling of good cigars. Hats and coats were spread around on the chairs. From the back of the house a radio droned dance music.

Mallory took his Luger out and leaned against the jamb of the door, inside.

A man in evening dress came along the hall. He was a plump man with thick white hair above a shrewd, pink, irritable face. Beautifully tailored shoulders failed to divert attention from rather too much stomach. His heavy eyebrows were drawn together in a frown. He walked fast and looked mad.

Mallory stepped out of the doorway and put his gun in Atkinson's stomach.

"You're looking for me," he said.

Atkinson stopped, heaved a little, made a choked sound in his throat. His eyes were wide and startled. Mallory moved the Luger up, put the cold muzzle into the flesh of Atkinson's throat, just above the V of his wing collar. The lawyer partly lifted one arm, as though to make a sweep of the gun. Then he stood quite still, holding the arm up in the air.

Mallory said: "Don't talk. Just think. You're sold out. Macdonald has ratted on you. Costello and two other boys are taped up at Westwood. We want Rhonda Farr."

Atkinson's eyes were dull blue, opaque, without interior light. The mention of Rhonda Farr's name did not seem to make much impression on him. He squirmed against the gun and said:

"Why do you come to me?"

"We think you know where she is," Mallory said tonelessly. "But we won't talk about it here. Let's go outside."

Atkinson jerked, sputtered. "No . . . no, I have guests."

Mallory said coldly: "The guest we want isn't here." He pressed on the gun.

A sudden wave of emotion went over Atkinson's face. He took a short step back and snatched at the gun. Mallory's lips tightened. He twisted his wrist in a tight circle, and the gun sight flicked across Atkinson's mouth. Blood came out on his lips. His mouth began to puff. He got very pale.

Mallory said: "Keep your head, fat boy, and you may live through the night."

Atkinson turned and walked straight out of the open door, swiftly, blindly.

Mallory took his arm and jerked him to the left, on to the grass. "Make it slow, mister," he said gratingly.

They rounded the pergola. Atkinson put his hands out in front of him and floundered at the car. A long arm came out of the open door and grabbed him. He went in, fell against the seat. Macdonald clapped a hand over his face and forced him back against the upholstery. Mallory got in and slammed the car door.

Tires squealed as the car circled rapidly and shot away. The driver drove a block before he switched the lights on again. Then he turned his head a little, said: "Where to, boss?"

Mallory said: "Anywhere. Back to town. Take it easy."

The Cadillac turned on to the highway again and began to drop down the long grade. Lights showed in the valley once more, little white lights that moved ever so slowly along the floor of the valley. Headlights.

Atkinson heaved up in the seat, got a handkerchief out and dabbed at his mouth. He peered at Macdonald and said in a composed voice:

"What's the frame, Mac? Shakedown?"

Macdonald laughed gruffly. Then he hiccuped. He was a little drunk. He said thickly:

"Hell, no. The boys hung a snatch on the Farr girl tonight. Her friends here don't like it. But you wouldn't know anything about it, would you, big shot?" He laughed again, jeeringly.

Atkinson said slowly: "It's funny . . . but I wouldn't." He lifted his white head higher, went on: "Who are these men?"

Macdonald didn't answer him. Mallory lit a cigarette, guarding the match flame with cupped hands. He said slowly:

"That's not important, is it? Either you know where Rhonda Farr was taken, or you can give us a lead. Think it out. There's lots of time."

Landrey turned his head and looked back. His face was a pale blur in the dark.

"It's not much to ask, Mr. Atkinson," he said gravely. His voice was cool, suave, pleasant. He tapped on the seatback with his gloved fingers.

Atkinson stared toward him for a while, then put his head back against the upholstery. "Suppose I don't know anything about it," he said wearily.

Macdonald lifted his hand and hit him in the face. The lawyer's head jerked against the cushions. Mallory said in a cold, unpleasant voice:

"A little less of your crap, copper."

Macdonald swore at him, turned his head away. The car went on.

They were down in the valley now. A three-colored airport beacon swung through the sky not far away. There began to be wooded slopes and little beginnings of valley between dark hills. A train roared down from the Newhall tunnel, gathered speed and went by with a long shattering crash.

Landrey said something to his driver. The Cadillac turned off on to a dirt road. The driver switched the lights off and picked his way by moonlight. The dirt road ended in a spot of dead brown grass with low bushes around it. There were old cans and torn discolored newspapers faintly visible on the ground.

Macdonald got his bottle out, hefted it, and gurgled a drink. Atkinson said thickly:

"I'm a bit faint. Give me one."

Macdonald turned, held the bottle out, then growled: "Aw, go to hell!" and put it away in his coat. Mallory took a flash out of the door pocket, clicked it on, and put the beam on Atkinson's face. He said:

"Talk, kidnapper."

Atkinson put his hands on his knees and stared straight at the beacon of the flashlight. His eyes were glassy and there was blood on his chin. He spoke:

"This is a frame by Costello. I don't know what it's all about. But if it's Costello, a man named Slippy Morgan will be in on it. He has a shack on the mesa by Baldwin Hills. They might have taken Rhonda Farr there."

He closed his eyes, and a tear showed in the glare of the flash. Mallory said slowly:

"Macdonald should know that."

Atkinson kept his eyes shut, said: "I guess so." His voice was dull and without any feeling.

Macdonald balled his fist, lurched sidewise, and hit him in the face again. The lawyer groaned, sagged to one side. Mallory's hand jerked; jerked the flash. His voice shook with fury. He said:

"Do that again and I'll put a slug in your guts, copper. So help me I will."

Macdonald rolled away, with a foolish laugh. Mallory snapped off the light. He said, more quietly:

"I think you're telling the truth, Atkinson. We'll case this shack of Slippy Morgan's."

The driver swung and backed the car, picked his way back to the highway again.

A white picket fence showed up for a moment before the headlights went off. Behind it on a rise the gaunt shapes of a couple of derricks groped toward the sky. The darkened car went forward slowly, stopped across the street from a small frame house. There were no houses on that side of the street, nothing between the car and the oil field. The house showed no light.

Mallory got to the ground and went across. A gravel driveway led along to a shed without a door. There was a touring car parked under the shed. There was thin worn grass along the driveway and a dull patch of something that had once been a lawn at the back. There was a wire clothesline and a small stoop with a rusted screen door. The moon showed all this.

Beyond the stoop there was a single window with the blind drawn; two thin cracks of light showed along the edges of the blind. Mallory went back to the car, walking on the dry grass and the dirt road surface without sound.

He said: "Let's go, Atkinson."

Atkinson got out heavily, stumbled across the street like a man half asleep. Mallory grabbed his arm sharply. The two men went up the wooden steps, crossed the porch quietly. Atkinson fumbled and found the bell. He pressed it. There was a dull buzz inside the house. Mallory flattened himself against the wall, on the side where he would not be blocked by the opening screen door.

Then the house door came open without sound, and a figure loomed behind the screen. There was no light behind the figure. The lawyer said mumblingly:

"It's Atkinson."

The screen hook was undone. The screen door came outward.

"What's the big idea?" said a lisping voice that Mallory had heard before.

Mallory moved, holding his Luger waist high. The man in the doorway whirled at him. Mallory stepped in on him swiftly, making a clucking sound with tongue and teeth, shaking his head reprovingly.

"You wouldn't have a gun, would you, Slippy?" he said, nudging the Luger forward. "Turn slow and easy, Slippy. When you feel something against your spine go on in, Slippy. We'll be right with you."

The lanky man put his hands up and turned. He walked back into the darkness, Mallory's gun in his back. A small living room smelled of dust and casual cooking. A door had light under it. The lanky man put one hand down slowly and opened the door.

An unshaded light bulb hung from the middle of the ceiling. A thin woman in a dirty white smock stood under it, limp arms at her sides. Dull colorless eyes brooded under a mop of rusty hair. Her fingers fluttered and twitched in involuntary contractions of the muscles. She made a thin plaintive sound, like a starved cat.

The lanky man went and stood against the wall on the opposite side of the room, pressing the palms of his hands against wallpaper. There was a fixed, meaningless smile on his face.

Landrey's voice said from behind: "I'll take care of Atkinson's pals."

He came into the room with a big automatic in his gloved hand. "Nice little home," he added pleasantly.

There was a metal bed in a corner of the room. Rhonda Farr was lying on it, wrapped to the chin in a brown army blanket. Her white wig was partly off her head and damp golden curls showed. Her face was bluish white, a mask in which the rouge and lip paint glared. She was snoring.

Mallory put his hand under the blanket, felt for her pulse. Then he lifted an eyelid and looked closely at the upturned pupil.

He said: "Doped."

The thin woman in the smock wet her lips. "A shot of M," she said in a slack voice. "No harm done, mister."

Atkinson sat down on a hard chair that had a dirty towel on the back of it. His dress shirt was dazzling under the unshaded light. The lower part of his face was smeared with dry blood. The lanky man looked at him contemptuously and patted the stained wallpaper with the flat of his hands. Then Macdonald came into the room.

His face was flushed and sweaty. He staggered a little and put a hand up along the door frame. "Hi ho, boys," he said vacantly. "I ought to rate a promotion for this."

The lanky man stopped smiling. He ducked sidewise very fast, and a gun jumped into his hand. Roar filled the room, a great crashing roar. And again a roar.

The lanky man's duck became a slide and the slide degenerated into a fall. He spread himself out on the bare carpet in a leisurely sort of way. He lay quite still, one half-open eye apparently looking at Macdonald. The thin woman opened her mouth wide, but no sound came out of it.

Macdonald put his other hand up to the door frame, leaned forward, and began to cough. Bright red blood came out on his chin. His hands came down the door frame slowly. Then his shoulder twitched forward; he rolled like a swimmer in a breaking wave and crashed. He crashed on his face, his hat still on his head, the mouse-colored hair at the nape of his neck showing below it in an untidy curl.

Mallory said: "Two down," and looked at Landrey with a disgusted expression. Landrey looked down at his big automatic and put it away out of sight, in the side pocket of his thin dark overcoat.

Mallory stooped over Macdonald, put a finger to his temple. There was no heartbeat. He tried the jugular vein with the same result. Macdonald was dead, and he still smelled violently of whiskey.

There was a faint trace of smoke under the light bulb, an acrid fume of powder. The thin woman bent forward at the waist and scrambled toward the door. Mallory jerked a hard hand against her chest and threw her back.

"You're fine where you are, sister," he snapped.

Atkinson took his hands off his knees and rubbed them together as if all the feeling had gone out of them. Landrey went over to the bed, put his gloved hand down, and touched Rhonda Farr's hair.

"Hello, baby," he said lightly. "Long time no see." He went out of the room, saying: "I'll get the car over on this side of the street."

Mallory looked at Atkinson. He said casually: "Who has the letters, Atkinson? The letters belonging to Rhonda Farr?"

Atkinson lifted his blank face slowly, squinted as though the light hurt his eyes He spoke in a vague, far-off sort of voice.

"I—I don't know. Costello, maybe. I never saw them."

Mallory let out a short harsh laugh which made no change in the hard cold lines of his face. "Wouldn't it be funny as hell if that's true!" he said jerkily

He stooped over the bed in the corner and wrapped the brown blanket closely around Rhonda Farr. When he lifted her she stopped snoring, but she did not wake.

A window or two in the front of the apartment house showed light. Mallory held his wrist up and looked at the curved watch on the inside of it. The faintly glowing hands were at half-past three. He spoke back into the car:

"Give me ten minutes or so. Then come on up. I'll fix the doors."

The street entrance to the apartment house was locked. Mallory unlocked it with a loose key, put it on the latch. There was a little light in the lobby, from one bulb in a floor lamp and from a hooded light above the switchboard. A wizened, white-haired little man was asleep in a chair by the switchboard, with his mouth open and his breath coming in long, wailing snores, like the sounds of an animal in pain.

Mallory walked up one flight of carpeted steps. On the second floor he pushed the button for the automatic elevator. When it came rumbling down from above, he got in and pushed the button marked "7." He yawned. His eyes were dulled with fatigue.

The elevator lurched to a stop, and Mallory went down the bright, silent corridor. He stopped at a gray olive wood door and put his ear to the panel. Then he fitted the loose key slowly into the lock, turned it slowly, moved the door back an inch or two. He listened again, went in.

There was light from a lamp with a red shade that stood beside an easy chair. A man was sprawled in the chair, and the light splashed on his face. He was bound at the wrists and ankles with strips of wide adhesive tape. There was a strip of adhesive across his mouth.

Mallory fixed the door latch and shut the door. He went across the room with quick silent steps. The man in the chair was Costello. His face was a purplish color above the white adhesive that plastered his lips together. His chest moved in jerks and his breath made a snorting noise in his big nose.

Mallory yanked the tape off Costello's mouth, put the heel of one hand on the man's chin, forced his mouth wide open. The cadence of the breathing changed a bit. Costello's chest stopped jerking, and the purplish color of his face faded to pallor. He stirred, made a groaning sound.

Mallory took an unopened pint bottle of rye off the mantel and tore the metal strip from the cap with his teeth. He pushed Costello's head far back, poured some whiskey into his open mouth, slapped his face hard. Costello choked, swallowed convulsively. Some of the whiskey ran out of his nostrils. He opened his eyes, focused them slowly. He mumbled something confused.

Mallory went through velour curtains that hung across a doorway at the inner end of the room, into a short hall. The first door led into a bedroom with twin beds. A light burned, and a man was lying bound on each of the beds.

Jim, the gray-haired cop, was asleep or still unconscious. The side of his head was stiff with congealed blood. The skin of his face was a dirty gray.

The eyes of the red-haired man were wide open, diamond bright, angry. His mouth worked under the tape, trying to chew it. He had rolled over on his side and almost off the bed. Mallory pushed him back toward the middle, said:

"Sorry, punk. It's all in the game."

He went back to the living room and switched on more light. Costello had struggled up in the easy chair. Mallory took out a pocket knife and reached behind him, sawed the tape that bound his wrists. Costello jerked his hands apart, grunted, and rubbed the backs of his wrists together where the tape had pulled hairs out. Then he bent over and tore tape off his ankles. He said:

"That didn't do me any good. I'm a mouth breather." His voice was loose, flat, and without cadence.

He got to his feet and poured two inches of rye into a glass, drank it at a gulp, sat down again and leaned his head against the high back of the chair. Life came into his face; glitter came into his washed-out eyes.

He said: "What's new?"

Mallory spooned at a bowl of water that had been ice, frowned, and drank some whiskey straight. He rubbed the left side of his head gently with his fingertips and winced. Then he sat down and lit a cigarette.

He said: "Several things. Rhonda Farr is home. Macdonald and Slippy Morgan got gunned. But that's not important. I'm after some letters you were trying to peddle to Rhonda Farr. Dig 'em up."

Costello lifted his head and grunted. He said: "I don't have the letters."

Mallory said: "Get the letters, Costello. Now." He sprinkled cigarette ash carefully in the middle of a green and yellow diamond in the carpet design.

Costello made an impatient movement. "I don't have them," he insisted. "Straight goods. I never saw them."

Mallory's eyes were slate-gray, very cold, and his voice was brittle. He said: "What you heels don't know about your racket is just pitiful. . . . I'm tired, Costello. I don't feel like an argument. You'd look lousy with that big beezer smashed over on one side of your face with a gun barrel."

Costello put his bony hand up and rubbed the reddened skin around his mouth where the tape had chafed it. He glanced down the room. There was a slight movement of the velour curtains across the end door, as though a breeze had stirred them. But there was no breeze. Mallory was staring down at the carpet.

Costello stood up from the chair, slowly. He said: "I've got a wall safe. I'll open it up."

He went across the room to the wall in which the outside door was, lifted down a picture, and worked the dial of a small inset circular safe. He swung the little round door open and thrust his arm into the safe.

Mallory said: "Stay just like that, Costello."

He stepped lazily across the room and passed his left hand down Costello's arm, into the safe. It came out again holding a small pearl-handled automatic. He made a sibilant sound with his lips and put the little gun into his pocket.

"Just can't learn, can you, Costello?" he said in a tired voice.

Costello shrugged, went back across the room. Mallory plunged his hands into the safe and tumbled the contents out on to the floor. He dropped on one knee. There were some long white envelopes, a bunch of clippings fastened with a paper clip, a narrow, thick checkbook, a small photograph album, an address book, some loose papers, some yellow bank statements with checks inside. Mallory spread one of the long envelopes carelessly, without much interest.

The curtains over the end door moved again. Costello stood rigid in front of the mantel. A gun came through the curtains in a small hand that was very steady. A slim body followed the hand, a white face with blazing eyes—Erno.

Mallory came to his feet, his hands breast high, empty.

"Higher, baby," Erno croaked. "Much higher, baby!"

Mallory raised his hands a little more. His forehead was wrinkled in a hard frown. Erno came forward into the room. His face glistened. A lock of oily black hair drooped over one eyebrow. His teeth showed in a stiff grin.

He said: "I think we'll give it to you right here, two-timer."

His voice had a questioning inflection, as if he waited for Costello's confirmation.

Costello didn't say anything.

Mallory moved his head a little. His mouth felt very dry. He watched Erno's eyes, saw them tense. He said rather quickly:

"You've been crossed, mugg, but not by me."

Erno's grin widened to a snarl, and his head went back. His trigger finger whitened at the first joint. Then there was a noise outside the door, and it came open.

Landrey came in. He shut the door with a jerk of his shoulder and leaned against it, dramatically. Both his hands were in the side pockets of his thin dark overcoat. His eyes under the soft black hat were bright and devilish. He looked pleased. He moved his chin in the white silk evening scarf that was tucked carelessly about his neck. His handsome pale face was like something carved out of old ivory.

Erno moved his gun slightly and waited. Landrey said cheerfully:

"Bet you a grand you hit the floor first!"

Erno's lips twitched under his shiny little mustache. Two guns went off at the same time. Landrey swayed like a tree hit by a gust of wind; the heavy roar of his .45 sounded again, muffled a little by cloth and the nearness to his body.

Mallory went down behind the davenport, rolled, and came up with the Luger straight out in front of him. But Erno's face had already gone blank.

He went down slowly; his light body seemed to be drawn down by the weight of the gun in his right hand. He bent at the knees as he fell and slid forward on the floor. His back arched once and then went loose.

Landrey took his left hand out of his coat pocket and spread the fingers away from him as though pushing at something. Slowly and with difficulty he got the big automatic out of the other pocket and raised it inch by inch, turning on the balls of his feet. He swiveled his body toward Costello's rigid figure and squeezed the trigger again. Plaster jumped from the wall at Costello's shoulder.

Landrey smiled vaguely, said: "Damn!" in a soft voice. Then his eyes went up in his head and the gun plunged down from his nerveless fingers, bounded on the carpet. Landrey went down joint by joint, smoothly and gracefully, kneeled, swaying a moment before he melted over sidewise, spread himself on the floor almost without sound.

Mallory looked at Costello and said in a strained, angry voice: "Boy, are you lucky!"

* * *

The buzzer droned insistently. Three little lights glowed red on the panel of the switchboard. The wizened, white-haired little man shut his mouth with a snap and struggled sleepily upright.

Mallory jerked past him with his head turned the other way, shot across the lobby, out of the front door of the apartment house, down the three marble-faced steps, across the sidewalk and the street. The driver of Landrey's car had already stepped on the starter. Mallory swung in beside him, breathing hard, and slammed the car door.

"Get goin' fast!" he rasped. "Stay off the boulevard. Cops here in five minutes!"

The driver looked at him and said: "Where's Landrey? . . . I heard shootin'."

Mallory held the Luger up, said swiftly and coldly: "Move, baby!"

The gears went in; the Cadillac jumped forward; the driver took a corner recklessly, the tail of his eye on the gun.

Mallory said: "Landrey stopped lead. He's cold." He held the Luger up, put the muzzle under the driver's nose. "But not from my gun. Smell that, punk! It hasn't been fired!"

The driver said: "Jeeze!" in a shattered voice, swung the big car wildly, missing the curb by inches.

It was getting to be daylight.

Rhonda Farr said: "Publicity, darling. Just publicity. Any kind is better than none at all. I'm not so sure my contract is going to be renewed, and I'll probably need it."

She was sitting in a deep chair, in a large, long room. She looked at Mallory with lazy, indifferent purplish-blue eyes and moved her hand to a tall, misted glass. She took a drink.

The room was enormous. Mandarin rugs in soft colors swathed the floor. There was a lot of teakwood and red lacquer. Gold frames glinted high up on the walls, and the ceiling was remote and vague, like the dusk of a hot day. A huge carved radio gave forth muted and unreal strains.

Mallory wrinkled his nose and looked amused in a grim sort of way. He said: "You're a nasty little rat. I don't like you."

Rhonda Farr said: "Oh, yes, you do, darling. You're crazy about me."

She smiled and fitted a cigarette into a jade-green holder that matched her jade-green lounging pajamas. Then she reached out her beautifully shaped hand and pushed the button of a bell that was set into the top of a low nacre and teakwood table at her side. A silent, white-coated Japanese butler drifted into the room and mixed more highballs.

"You're a pretty wise lad, aren't you, darling?" Rhonda Farr said, when he had gone out again. "And you have some letters in your pocket you think are body and soul to me. Nothing like it, mister, nothing like it." She took a sip of the fresh highball. "The letters you have are phony. They were written about a month ago. Landrey never had them. He gave *his* letters back a long time ago. . . . What you have are just props." She put a hand to her beautifully waved hair. The experience of the previous night seemed to have left no trace on her.

Mallory looked at her carefully. He said: "How do you prove that, baby?"

"The notepaper—if I have to prove it. There's a little man down at Fourth and Spring who makes a study of that kind of thing."

Mallory said: "The writing?"

Rhonda Farr smiled dimly. "Writing's easy to fake, if you have plenty of time. Or so I'm told. That's my story anyhow."

Mallory nodded, sipped at his own highball. He put his hand into his inside breast pocket and took out a flat manila envelope, legal size. He laid it on his knee.

"Four men got gunned out last night on account of these phony letters," he said carelessly.

Rhonda Farr looked at him mildly. "Two crooks, a double-crossing policeman make three of them. I should lose my sleep over that trash! Of course, I'm sorry about Landrey."

Mallory said politely: "It's nice of you to be sorry about Landrey. Swell."

She said peacefully: "Landrey, as I told you once, was a pretty nice boy a few years ago, when he was trying to get into pictures. But he chose another business, and in that business he was bound to stop a bullet sometime."

Mallory rubbed his chin. He said: "It's funny he didn't remember he'd given you back your letters. Very funny."

"He wouldn't care, darling. He was that kind of actor, and he'd like the show. It gave him a chance for a swell pose. He'd like that terribly."

Mallory let his face get hard and disgusted. He said: "The job looked on the level to me. I didn't know much about Landrey, but he knew a good friend of mine in Chicago. He figured a way to the boys who were working on you, and I played his hunch. Things happened that made it easier—but a lot noisier."

Rhonda Farr tapped little bright nails against her little bright teeth. She said: "What are you back where you live, darling? One of those hoods they call private dicks?"

Mallory laughed harshly, made a vague movement, and ran his fingers through his crisp dark hair. "Let it go, baby," he said softly. "Let it go."

Rhonda Farr looked at him with a surprised glance, then laughed rather shrilly. "It gets mad, doesn't it?" she cooed. She went on, in a dry voice: "Atkinson has been bleeding me for years, one way and another. I fixed the letters up and put them where he could get hold of them. They disappeared. A few days afterward a man with one of those tough voices called up and began to apply the pressure. I let it ride. I figured I'd hang a pinch on Atkinson somehow, and our two reputations put together would be good for a write-up that wouldn't hurt me too much. But the thing seemed to be spreading out, and I got scared. I thought of asking Landrey to help me out. I was sure he would like it."

Mallory said roughly: "Simple, straightforward kid, ain't you? Like hell!"

"You don't know much about this Hollywood racket, do you, darling?" Rhonda

Farr said. She put her head on one side and hummed softly. The strains of a dance band floated idly through the quiet air. "That's a gorgeous melody. . . . It's swiped from a Weber sonata. . . . Publicity has to hurt a bit out here. Otherwise nobody believes it."

Mallory stood up, lifting the manila envelope off his knee. He dropped it in her lap.

"Five grand these are costing you," he said.

Rhonda Farr leaned back and crossed her jade-green legs. One little green slipper fell off her bare foot to the rug, and the manila envelope fell down beside it. She didn't stir toward either one.

She said: "Why?"

"I'm a businessman, baby. I get paid for my work. Landrey didn't pay me. Five grand was the price. The price to him, and now the price to you."

She looked at him almost casually, out of placid, cornflower-blue eyes, and said: "No deal . . . blackmailer. Just like I told you at the Bolivar. You have all my thanks, but I'm spending my money myself."

Mallory said curtly: "This might be a damn good way to spend some of it."

He leaned over and picked up her highball, drank a little of it. When he put the glass down, he tapped the nails of two fingers against the side for a moment. A small tight smile wrinkled the corners of his mouth. He lit a cigarette and tossed the match into a bowl of hyacinths.

He said slowly: "Landrey's driver talked, of course. Landrey's friends want to see me. They want to know how come Landrey got rubbed out in Westwood. The cops will get around to me after a while. Someone is sure to tip them off. I was right beside four killings last night, and naturally I'm not going to run out on them. I'll probably have to spill the whole story. The cops will give you plenty of publicity, baby. Landrey's friends—I don't know what they'll do. Something that will hurt a lot, I should say."

Rhonda Farr jerked to her feet, fumbling with her toe for the green slipper. Her eyes had gone wide and startled.

"You'd . . . sell me out?" she breathed.

Mallory laughed. His eyes were bright and hard. He stared along the floor at a splash of light from one of the standing lamps. He said in a bored voice:

"Why the hell should I protect you? I don't owe you anything. And you're too damn tight with your dough to hire me. I haven't a record, but you know how the law boys love my sort. And Landrey's friends will just see a dirty plant that got a good lad killed. ——sake, why should I front for a chiseler like you, baby?"

He snorted angrily and flung his cigarette at the bowl of hyacinths. Red spots showed in his tanned cheeks.

Rhonda Farr stood quite still and shook her head slowly from side to side. She said: "No deal, blackmailer . . . no deal." Her voice was small and f   ', but her chin stuck out hard and brave.

Mallory reached out and picked up his hat. "You're a hell of a guy, baby," he said, grinning. "——! but you Hollywood frails must be hard to get on with!"

He leaned forward suddenly, put his left hand behind her head, and kissed her on the mouth hard. Then he flipped the tips of his fingers across her cheek.

"You're a nice kid—in some ways," he said. "And a fair liar. Just fair. You didn't fake any letters, baby. Atkinson wouldn't fall for a trick like that." Rhonda Farr stooped over, snatched the manila envelope off the rug, and tumbled out what was in it—a number of closely written gray pages, deckle-edged, with thin gold monograms. She stared down at them with quivering nostrils.

She said slowly: "I'll send you the money."

Mallory put his hand against her chin and pushed her head back.

He said rather gently:

"I was kidding you, baby. I have that bad habit. But there are two funny things about these letters. They haven't any envelopes, and there's nothing to show who they were written to—nothing at all. The second thing is, Landrey had them in his pocket when he was killed."

He nodded once, turned away. Rhonda Farr said sharply: "Wait!" Her voice was suddenly terrified. She flopped down into the chair, sat limp.

Mallory said: "It gets you when it's over, baby. Take a drink."

He went a little way down the room, turned his head. He said: "I have to go. Got a date with a big black spot. . . . Send me some flowers, baby. Wild, blue flowers, like your eyes."

He went out under an arch. A door opened and shut heavily. Rhonda Farr sat without moving for a long time.

Cigarette smoke laced the air. A group of people in evening clothes stood sipping cocktails at one side of a curtained opening that led to the gambling rooms. Beyond the curtains, light blazed down on one end of a roulette table.

Mallory put his elbows on the bar, and the bartender left two young girls in party gowns and slid a white towel along the polished wood toward him. He said:

"What'll it be, chief?"

Mallory said: "A small beer."

The bartender gave it to him, smiled, went back to the two girls. Mallory sipped the beer, made a face, and looked into the long mirror that ran all the way behind the bar and slanted forward a little, so that it showed the floor all the way over to the far wall. A door opened in the wall and a man in dinner clothes came through. He had a wrinkled brown face and hair the color of steel wool. He met Mallory's glance in the mirror and came across the room nodding.

He said, "I'm Mardonne. Nice of you to come." He had a soft, husky voice, the voice of a fat man, but he was not fat.

Mallory said: "It's not a social call."

Mardonne said: "Let's go up to my office."

Mallory drank a little more of the beer, made another face, and pushed the glass away from him across the bar top. They went through the door, up a carpeted staircase that met another staircase halfway up. An open door shone light on the landing. They went in where the light was.

The room had been a bedroom, and no particular trouble had been taken to make it over into an office. It had gray walls, two or three prints in narrow frames. There was a big filing cabinet, a good safe, chairs. A parchment-shaded lamp stood on a walnut desk. A very blond young man sat on a corner of the desk swinging one leg over the other. He was wearing a soft hat with a gay band.

Mardonne said: "All right, Henry. I'll be busy."

The blond young man got off the desk, yawned, put his hand to his mouth with an affected flirt of the wrist. There was a large diamond on one of his fingers. He looked at Mallory, smiled, went slowly out of the room, closing the door.

Mardonne sat down in a blue leather swivel chair. He lit a thin cigar and pushed a humidor across the grained top of the desk. Mallory took a chair at the end of the desk, between the door and a pair of open windows. There was another door, but the safe stood in front of it. He lit a cigarette, said:

"Landrey owed me some money. Five grand. Anybody here interested in paying it?"

Mardonne put his brown hands on the arms of his chair and rocked back and forth. "We haven't come to that," he said.

Mallory said: "Right. What have we come to?"

Mardonne narrowed his dull eyes. His voice was flat and without tone. "To how Landrey got killed."

Mallory put his cigarette in his mouth and clasped his hands together behind his head. He puffed smoke and talked through it at the wall above Mardonne's head.

"He crossed everybody up and then he crossed himself. He played too many parts and got his lines mixed. He was gun-drunk. When he got a rod in his hand he had to shoot somebody. Somebody shot back."

Mardonne went on rocking, said: "Maybe you could make it a little more definite."

"Sure . . . I could tell you a story . . . about a girl who wrote some letters once. She thought she was in love. They were reckless letters, the sort a girl would write who had more guts than was good for her. Time passed, and somehow the letters got on the blackmail market. Some workers started to shake the girl down. Not a high stake, nothing that would have bothered her, but it seems she liked to do things the hard way. Landrey thought he would help her out. He had a plan, and the plan needed a man who could wear a tux, keep a spoon out of a coffee cup, and wasn't known in this town. He got me. I run a small agency in Chicago."

Mardonne swiveled toward the open windows and stared out at the tops of some trees. "Private dick, huh?" he grunted impassively. "From Chicago."

Mallory nodded, looked at him briefly, looked back at the same spot on the wall. "And supposed to be on the level, Mardonne. You wouldn't think it from some of the company I've been keeping lately."

Mardonne made a quick impatient gesture, said nothing.

Mallory went on: "Well, I gave the job a tumble, which was my first and worst mistake. I was making a little headway when the shakedown turned into a kidnapping. Not so good. I got in touch with Landrey, and he decided to show with me. We found the girl without a lot of trouble. We took her home. We still had to get the letters. While I was trying to pry them loose from the guy I thought had them, one of the bad boys got in the back way and wanted to play with his gun. Landrey made a swell entrance, struck a pose, and shot it out with the hood, toe to toe. He stopped some lead. It was pretty, if you like that sort of thing, but it left me in a spot. So perhaps I'm prejudiced. I had to lam out and collect my ideas."

Mardonne's dull brown eyes showed a passing flicker of emotion. "The girl's story might be interesting, too," he said coolly.

Mallory blew a pale cloud of smoke. "She was doped and doesn't know anything. She wouldn't talk, if she did. And I don't know her name."

"I do," Mardonne said. "Landrey's driver also talked to me. So I won't have to bother you about that."

Mallory talked on, placidly. "That's the tale from the outside, without notes. The notes make it funnier—and a hell of a lot dirtier. The girl didn't ask Landrey for help, but he knew about the shakedown. He'd once had the letters, because they were written to him. His scheme to get on their trail was for me to make a wrong pass at the girl myself, make her think *I* had the letters, talk her into a meeting at a nightclub where we could be watched by the people who were working on her. She'd come, because she had that kind of guts. She'd be watched, because there would be an inside—maid, chauffeur, or something. The boys would want to know about me. They'd pick me up, and if I didn't get conked out of hand, I might learn who was who in the racket. Sweet setup, don't you think so?"

Mardonne said coldly: "A bit loose in places. . . . Go on talking."

"When the decoy worked, I knew it was fixed. I stayed with it, because for the time being I had to. After a while there was another sour play, unrehearsed this time. A big flattie who was taking graft money from the gang got cold feet and threw the boys for a loss. He didn't mind a little extortion, but a snatch was going off the deep end on a dark night. The break made things easier for me, and it didn't hurt Landrey any, because the flattie wasn't in on the clever stuff. The hood who got Landrey wasn't either, I guess. That one was just sore, thought he was being chiseled out of his cut."

Mardonne flipped his brown hands up and down on the chair arms, like a purchasing agent getting restless under a sales talk. "Were you supposed to figure things out this way?" he asked with a sneer.

"I used my head, Mardonne. Not soon enough, but I used it. Maybe I wasn't hired to think, but that wasn't explained to me, either. If I got wise, it was Landrey's hard luck. He'd have to figure an out to that one. If I didn't I was the nearest thing to an honest stranger he could afford to have around."

Mardonne said smoothly: "Landrey had plenty of dough. He had some brains. Not a lot, but some. He wouldn't go for a cheap shake like that."

Mallory laughed harshly: "It wasn't so cheap to him, Mardonne. He wanted the girl. She'd got away from him, out of his class. He couldn't pull himself up, but he could pull her down. The letters were not enough to bring her into line. Add a kidnapping and a fake rescue by an old flame turned racketeer, and you have a story no rag could be made to soft-pedal. If it was spilled, it would blast her right out of her job. *You* guess the price for not spilling it, Mardonne."

Mardonne said: "Uh-huh," and kept on looking out of the window.

Mallory said: "But all that's on the cuff, now. I was hired to get some letters, and I got them—out of Landrey's pocket when he was bumped. I'd like to get paid for my time."

Mardonne turned in his chair and put his hands flat on the top of the desk. "Pass them over," he said. "I'll see what they're worth to me."

Mallory let out another harsh laugh. His eyes got sharp and bitter. He said: "The trouble with you heels is that you can't figure anybody to be on the up and up. . . . The letters are withdrawn from circulation, Mardonne. They passed around too much and they wore out."

"It's a sweet thought," Mardonne sneered. "For somebody else. Landrey was my partner, and I thought a lot of him. . . . So you give the letters away, and I pay you dough for letting Landrey get gunned. I ought to write that one in my diary. My hunch is you've been paid plenty already—by Miss Rhonda Farr."

Mallory said, sarcastically: "I figured it would look like that to you. Maybe *you'd* like the story better this way. . . . The girl got tired of having Landrey trail her around. She faked some letters and put them where her smart lawyer could lift them, pass them along to a man who was running a strong-arm squad the lawyer used in his business sometimes. The girl wrote to Landrey for help and he got me. The girl got to me with a better bid. She hired me to put Landrey on the spot. I played along with him until I got him under the gun of a wiper that was pretending to make a pass at me. The wiper let him have it, and I shot the wiper with Landrey's gun, to make it look good. Then I had a drink and went home to get some sleep."

Mardonne leaned over and pressed a buzzer on the side of his desk. He said: "I like that one a lot better. I'm wondering if I could make it stick."

"You could try," Mallory said lazily. "I don't guess it would be the first lead quarter you've tried to pass."

The room door came open and the blond boy strolled in. His lips were spread in a pleased grin and his tongue came out between them. He had an automatic in his hand.

Mardonne said: "I'm not busy anymore, Henry."

The blond boy shut the door. Mallory stood up and backed slowly toward the wall. He said grimly:

"Now for the funny stuff, eh?"

Mardonne put brown fingers up and pinched the fat part of his chin. He said curtly:

"There won't be any shooting here. Nice people come to this house. Maybe you didn't spot Landrey, but I don't want you around. You're in my way."

Mallory kept on backing until he had his shoulders against the wall. The blond boy frowned, took a step toward him. Mallory said:

"Stay right where you are, Henry. I need room to think. You might get a slug into me, but you wouldn't stop my gun from talking a little. The noise wouldn't bother me at all."

Mardonne bent over his desk, looking sidewise. The blond boy slowed up. His tongue still peeped out between his lips. Mardonne said:

"I've got some C notes in the desk here. I'm giving Henry ten of them. He'll go to your hotel with you. He'll even help you pack. When you get on the train east he'll pass you the dough. If you come back after that, it will be a new deal —from a cold deck." He put his hand down slowly and opened the desk drawer.

Mallory kept his eyes on the blond boy. "Henry might make a change in the continuity," he said unpleasantly. "Henry looks kind of unstable to me."

Mardonne stood up, brought his hand from the drawer. He dropped a packet of notes on top of the desk. He said:

"I don't think so. Henry usually does what he is told."

Mallory grinned tightly. "Perhaps *that's* what I'm afraid of," he said. His grin got tighter still, and crookeder. His teeth glittered between his pale lips. "You said you thought a lot of Landrey, Mardonne. That's hooey. You don't care a thin dime about Landrey, now he's dead. You probably stepped right into his half of the joint, and nobody around to ask questions. It's like that in the rackets. You want me out because you think you can still peddle your dirt—in the right place—for more than this small-time joint would net in a year. But you can't peddle it, Mardonne. The market's closed. Nobody's going to pay you a plugged nickel either to spill it or not to spill it."

Mardonne cleared his throat softly. He was standing in the same position, leaning forward a little over the desk, both hands on top of it, and the packet of notes between his hands. He licked his lips, said:

"All right, mastermind. Why not?"

Mallory made a quick but expressive gesture with his right thumb.

"I'm the sucker in this deal. *You're* the smart guy. I told you a straight story the first time, and my hunch says Landrey wasn't in that sweet frame alone. *You* were in it up to your fat neck! . . . But you aced yourself backward when you let Landrey pack those letters around with him. The girl can talk now. Not a whole lot, but enough to get backing from an outfit that isn't going to scrap a million-dollar reputation because some cheap gambler wants to get smart. . . . If your money says different, you're going to get a jolt that'll have you picking your eyeteeth out of your socks. You're going to see the sweetest cover-up even Hollywood ever fixed."

He paused, flashed a quick glance at the blond boy. "Something else, Mardonne.

When you figure on gunplay, get yourself a loogan that knows what it's all about. The gay caballero here forgot to thumb back his safety."

Mardonne stood frozen. The blond boy's eyes flinched down to his gun for a split second of time. Mallory jumped fast along the wall, and his Luger snapped into his hand. The blond boy's face tensed; his gun crashed. Then the Luger cracked, and a slug went into the wall beside the blond boy's gay felt hat. Henry faded down gracefully, squeezed lead again. The shot knocked Mallory back against the wall. His left arm went dead.

His lips writhed angrily. He steadied himself; the Luger talked twice, very rapidly.

The blond boy's gun arm jerked up and the gun sailed against the wall high up. His eyes widened; his mouth came open in a yell of pain. Then he whirled, wrenched the door open, and pitched straight out on the landing with a crash.

Light from the room streamed after him. Somebody shouted somewhere. A door banged. Mallory looked at Mardonne, saying evenly:

"Got me in the arm——! I could have killed the——four times!"

Mardonne's hand came up from the desk with a blued revolver in it. A bullet splashed into the floor at Mallory's feet. Mardonne lurched drunkenly, threw the gun away like something red hot. His hands groped high in the air. He looked scared stiff.

Mallory said: "Get in front of me, big shot! I'm moving out of here."

Mardonne came out from behind the desk. He moved jerkily, like a marionette. His eyes were as dead as stale oysters. Saliva drooled down his chin.

Something loomed in the doorway. Mallory heaved sidewise, firing blindly at the door. But the sound of the Luger was overborne by the terrific flat booming of a shotgun. Searing flame stabbed down Mallory's right side. Mardonne got the rest of the load.

He plunged to the floor on his face, dead before he landed.

A sawed-off shotgun dumped itself in through the open door. A thick-bellied man in shirt-sleeves eased himself down in the door frame, clutching and rolling as he fell. A strangled sob came out of his mouth, and blood spread on the pleated front of a dress shirt.

Sudden noise flared out down below. Shouting, running feet, a shrilling off-key laugh, a high sound that might have been a shriek. Cars started outside; tires screeched on the driveway. The customers were getting away. A pane of glass went out somewhere. There was a loose clatter of running feet on a sidewalk.

Across the lighted patch of landing nothing moved. The blond boy groaned softly, out there on the floor, behind the dead man in the doorway.

Mallory plowed across the room, sank into the chair at the end of the desk. He wiped sweat from his eyes with the heel of his gun hand. He leaned his ribs against the desk, panting, watching the door.

His left arm was throbbing now, and his right leg felt like the plagues of Egypt. Blood ran down his sleeve inside, down on his hand, off the tips of two fingers.

After a while he looked away from the door, at the packet of notes lying on the desk under the lamp. Reaching across, he pushed them into the open drawer with the muzzle of the Luger. Grinning with pain, he leaned far enough over to pull the drawer shut. Then he opened and closed his eyes quickly, several times, squeezing them tight together, then snapping them open wide. That cleared his head a little. He drew the telephone toward him.

There was silence below stairs now. Mallory put the Luger down, lifted the phone off the prongs and put it down beside the Luger.

He said out loud: "Too bad, baby. . . . Maybe I played it wrong after all. . . . Maybe the louse hadn't the guts to hurt you at that . . . well . . . there's got to be talking done now."

As he began to dial, the wail of a siren got louder coming up the long hill from Sherman. . . .

The uniformed officer behind the typewriter desk talked into a Dictaphone, then looked at Mallory and jerked his thumb toward a glass-paneled door that said: "Captain of Detectives. Private."

Mallory got up stiffly from a hard chair and went across the room, leaned against the wall to open the glass-paneled door, went on in.

The room he went into was paved with dirty brown linoleum, furnished with the peculiar sordid hideousness only municipalities can achieve. Cathcart, the captain of detectives, sat in the middle of it alone, between a littered rolltop desk that was not less than twenty years old and a flat oak table large enough to play Ping-Pong on.

Cathcart was a big shabby Irishman with a sweaty face and a loose-lipped grin. His white mustache was stained in the middle by nicotine. His hands had a lot of warts on them.

Mallory went towards him slowly, leaning on a heavy cane with a rubber tip. His right leg felt large and hot. His left arm was in a sling made from a black silk scarf. He was freshly shaved. His face was pale and his eyes were as dark as slate.

He sat down across the table from the captain of detectives, put his cane on the table, tapped a cigarette and lit it. Then he said casually:

"What's the verdict, chief?"

Cathcart grinned. "How you feel, kid? You look kinda pulled down."

"Not bad. A bit stiff."

Cathcart nodded, cleared his throat, fumbled unnecessarily with some papers that were in front of him. He said:

"You're clear. It's a lulu, but you're clear. Chicago gives you a clean sheet—damn clean. Your Luger got Mike Corliss, a two-time loser. I'm keepin' the Luger for a souvenir. Okay?"

Mallory nodded, said: "Okay. I'm getting me a twenty-five with copper slugs. A sharpshooter's gun. No shock effect, but it goes better with evening clothes."

Cathcart looked at him closely for a minute, then went on: "Mike's prints are on the shotgun. The shotgun got Mardonne. Nobody's cryin' about that much. The blond kid ain't hurt bad. That automatic we found on the floor had his prints, and that will take care of him for a while."

Mallory rubbed his chin slowly, wearily. "How about the others?"

The captain raised tangled eyebrows, and his eyes looked absent. He said: "I don't know of nothin' to connect you there. Do you?"

"Not a thing," Mallory said apologetically. "I was just wondering."

The captain said firmly: "Don't wonder. And don't get to guessin', if anybody should ask you. . . . Take that Baldwin Hills thing. The way we figure it, Macdonald got killed in the line of duty, takin' with him a dope peddler named Slippy Morgan. We have a tag out for Slippy's wife, but I don't guess we'll make her. Mac wasn't on the narcotic detail, but it was his night off and he was a great guy to gumshoe around on his night off. Mac loved his work."

Mallory smiled faintly, said politely: "Is that so?"

"Yeah," the captain said. "In the other one, it seems this Landrey, a known gambler—he was Mardonne's partner too. That's kind of a funny coincidence—went down to Westwood to collect dough from a guy called Costello that ran a book on the eastern tracks. Jim Ralston, one of our boys, went with him. Hadn't ought to, but he knew Landrey pretty well. There was a little trouble about the money. Jim got beaned with a blackjack, and Landrey and some little hood fogged each other. There was another guy there we don't trace. We got Costello, but he won't talk and we don't like to beat up an old guy. He's got a rap comin' on account of the blackjack. He'll plead, I guess."

Mallory slumped down in his chair until the back of his neck rested on top of it. He blew smoke straight up toward the stained ceiling. He said:

"How about night before last? Or was that the time the roulettè wheel backfired and the trick cigar blew a hole in the garage floor?"

The captain of detectives rubbed both his moist cheeks briskly, then hauled out a very large handkerchief and snorted into it.

"Oh, that," he said negligently, "that wasn't nothin'. The blond kid—Henry Anson or something like that—says it was all his fault. He was Mardonne's bodyguard, but that didn't mean he could go shootin' anyone he might want to. That takes care of him, but we let him down easy for tellin' a straight story."

The captain stopped short and stared at Mallory hard-eyed. Mallory was grinning. "Of course if you don't *like* his story . . ." the captain went on coldly.

Mallory said: "I haven't heard it yet. I'm sure I'll like it fine."

"Okay," Cathcart rumbled, mollified. "Well, this Anson says Mardonne buzzed him in where you and the boss were talkin'. You was makin' a kick about something, maybe a crooked wheel downstairs. There was some money on the desk, and Anson got the idea it was a shake. You looked pretty fast to him, and not knowing you was a dick he gets kinda nervous. His gun went off. You didn't shoot right away, but the poor sap lets off another round and plugs you. Then, by——you drilled him in the shoulder, as who wouldn't, only if it had been me, I'd of pumped his guts. Then the shotgun boy comes bargin' in, lets go without asking any questions, fogs Mardonne and stops one from you. We kinda thought at first the guy might of got Mardonne on purpose, but the kid says no, he tripped in the door comin' in. . . . Hell, we don't like for you to do all that shooting, you being a stranger and all that, but a man ought to have a right to protect himself against illegal weapons."

Mallory said gently: "There's the D.A. and the coroner. How about them? I'd kind of like to go back as clean as I came away."

Cathcart frowned down at the dirty linoleum and bit his thumb as if he liked hurting himself.

"The coroner don't give a damn about that trash. If the D.A. wants to get funny, I can tell him about a few cases his office didn't clean up so good."

Mallory lifted his cane off the table, pushed his chair back, put weight on the cane and stood up. "You have a swell police department here," he said. "I shouldn't think you'd have any crime at all."

He moved across toward the outer door. The captain said to his back: "Goin' on to Chicago?"

Mallory shrugged carefully with his right shoulder, the good one. "I might stick around," he said. "One of the studios made me a proposition. Private extortion detail. Blackmail and so on."

The captain grinned heartily. "Swell," he said. "Eclipse Films is a swell outfit. They always been swell to me. . . . Nice easy work, blackmail. Oughtn't to run into any rough stuff."

Mallory nodded solemnly. "Just light work, chief. Almost effeminate, if you know what I mean."

He went on out, down the hall to the elevator, down to the street. He got into a taxi. It was hot in the taxi. He felt faint and dizzy going back to his hotel.

Chandler in *Black Mask*

1933–1937

Series characters: Mallory (M)
                       Ted Carmady (TC)

*—indicates use as basis for published novel
•—included in *The* Black Mask *Boys*

•"Blackmailers Don't Shoot" (M)   December 1933
"Smart-Aleck Kill" (M)   July 1934
"Finger Man"   October 1934
*"Killer in the Rain"   January 1935
"Nevada Gas"   June 1935

'Spanish Blood" November 1935
"Guns at Cyrano's" January 1936
*"The Man Who Liked Dogs" (TC) March 1936
"Goldfish" (TC) June 1936
*"The Curtain" (TC) September 1936
*"Try the Girl" (TC) January 1937

Published Chandler Novels Derived from *Black Mask*

The Big Sleep—New York: Knopf, 1939
   (Derived from "Killer in the Rain," "The Curtain," and other material)
Farewell, My Lovely—New York: Knopf, 1940
   (Derived from "The Man Who Liked Dogs," "Try the Girl," and other material)
Note: Chandler's other five Marlowe novels did not originate in *Black Mask*.

The Rivals of
Black Mask

•

A Checklist of Mystery-Detective-Crime Pulp Magazines

In order to place *Black Mask* in its proper historical perspective, it is necessary to be aware of the vast number of crime-genre pulp magazines that competed with *Mask* for reader attention and newsstand space from the 1920s into the early 1950s. Prior to World War II, 25 million readers devoured 200 million bimonthly and monthly words ground out by more than 1,300 pulp writers. In any given month, some 200 pulps in all genres (war, western, romance, adventure, science fiction, etc.) crowded the stands.

This listing of 178 titles, while extensive, does *not* include digest-sized crime publications (such as *Ellery Queen's Mystery Magazine*). Nor does it include nongenre magazines (such as *Argosy*) that printed crime and detective fiction as part of a mixed editorial contents.

Ace-High Detective
Ace G-Man Stories
Ace Mystery
Action Detective
Alibi
All Detective
All-Fiction Detective Stories
All Star Detective Stories

All Story Detective
Amazing Detective Tales
Angel Detective
The Avenger

Baffling Detective Mysteries
Best Detective
Big Book Detective

Black Aces
Black Bat Detective
Black Book Detective
Black Hood Detective

Candid Detective
Captain Satan, King of Detectives
Clues
Complete Detective Novel
Complete Mystery Novelettes
Complete Underworld Novelettes
Courtroom Stories
Crack Detective Stories
Crack Detective and Mystery Stories
Crime Busters
Crime Detective
Crime Mysteries

Dan Dunn Detective
Dare Devil Detective
Detective Action Stories
Detective and Murder Mysteries
Detective Book
Detective Classics
Detective Dime Novels
Detective-Dragnet
Detective Fiction
Detective Fiction Weekly
Detective Mysteries
Detective Mystery Novel
Detective Novels
Detective Romances
Detective Short Story
Detective Story
Detective Tales
Detective Trails
Detective Yarns
Dime Detective
Dime Mystery
Dime Mystery Book
Doc Savage
Doctor Death
Double-Action Detective

Double Action Gang
Double Detective
Dragnet

Eerie Mysteries
Exciting Detective
Exciting Mystery

Famous Detective
Fast-Action Detective Mystery
F.B.I. Detective Stories
Federal Agent
The Feds
Fifteen Detective Stories
Fifteen Mystery Stories
Fifteen-Story Detective
Five Detective Novels
Four Big Mystery Novels

Gangland Stories
The Gang
Gangster Stories
Gang World
The Ghost Super Detective
Giant Detective
Girl Rackets
Girls' Detective
G-Men Detective
Gold Seal Detective
Great Detective
Greater Gangster Stories
The Green Ghost Detective
The Green Lama
Gun Molls

Hardboiled
Headquarters Detective
Hollywood Detective
Hooded Detective

International Detective
Illustrated Detective

Lone Wolf Detective

Mammoth Detective
Mammoth Mystery
Masked Detective
Mobsters
Mystery
Mystery Adventure
Mystery Book
Mystery League
Mystery Novels
Mystery Novels and Short Stories
Mystery Stories
Mystery Tales

New Detective
New Mystery Adventures
Nick Carter
Nickel Detective

The Octopus
Operator #5

Phantom Detective
Pocket Detective
Popular Detective
Prison Life Stories
Prison Stories
Private Detective Stories
Private Eye Stories
Prize Detective
Public Enemy

Racketeer Stories
Rapid-Fire Detective Stories
Real Police Story
Real Mystery
Red Hood Detective
Red Mask Detective Stories
Red Star Detective
Red Star Mystery
Romantic Detective

Scotland Yard Detective Stories
Scientific Detective
Secret Agent Detective Mysteries
Secret Agent X
Secret Service Detective
The Shadow
Smashing Detective
Snappy Detective Mysteries
Speakeasy Stories
Special Detective
Speed Detective
Speed Mystery
Spicy Detective
Spicy Mystery Stories
The Spider
Star Detective
Startling Detective Adventures
Startling Mystery
Stirring Detective and Western Stories
Strange Detective Mystery
Strange Detective Stories
Street & Smith's Mystery
Super-Detective
Sure-Fire Detective

Ten Detective Aces
Ten Story Detective
Ten Story Gang
Ten Story Mystery
Thrilling Detective
Thrilling Mysteries
Thrilling Mystery
Thrilling Mystery Novels
Thrilling Spy Stories
Top Detective
Top-Notch Detective
Triple Detective
True Gang Life
Two Book Detective
Two Complete Detective Books
Two Detective Mystery Novels

Undercover Detective

The Underworld
Underworld Detective
Underworld Love
Underworld Romances

Variety Detective

The Whisperer
World Manhunters

Acknowledgments

●

My primary debt is to Professor E. R. Hagemann. His superb reference work, *A Comprehensive Index to* Black Mask, *1920–1951* (Bowling Green, Ohio: Bowling Green State University Popular Press, 1982), proved an essential source of data on titles, series characters, pseudonyms, and much else. Professor Hagemann was also extremely generous in providing me with copies of personal file material on *Black Mask,* and on Raoul Whitfield and Paul Cain. Additionally, this book profited from Professor Hagemann's valuable compilation of hard-boiled pieces for the Fall/Winter 1981 issue of *Clues.* (His 116-page section on pulp detective fiction is a small book in itself.)

I am also indebted to a variety of individuals with regard to my eight author profiles.

- On Daly: My thanks to G. A. Finch for his detailed analysis of Daly in *The Armchair Detective,* to Michael S. Barson for his essay on Race Williams in *Clues,* and to Robert Lowndes for his letter on the Spillane-Daly connection.
- On Hammett: My thanks to Richard Layman, whose biography *Shadow Man* (New York: Harcourt Brace Jovanovich, 1981) provided necessary data, and to novelist Joe Gores for critical insight.
- On Gardner: My thanks to Dorothy B. Hughes; her biography *Erle Stanley Gardner: The Case of the Real Perry Mason* (New York: William Morrow, 1978) remains the definitive source. And thanks to Gardner aficionados Francis M. Nevins and Marvin Lachman, and I am also grateful to Jean Bethell Gardner for her generous cooperation.
- On Whitfield: My thanks to Frank D. McSherry, Jr., for additional checklist data; to E. R. Hagemann, whose ground-breaking piece on Whitfield in *The*

Armchair Detective was of great help; and to Carolyn See for criticism.

- On Nebel: My chief debt here is to Dave Lewis, who has done extensive research on Nebel, and whose article in *Clues* aided me considerably. Also, my thanks to crime critic Will Murray for perceptive commentary, to Mrs. Dorothy Nebel and to Robert Randisi for bio data.
- On McCoy: I am particularly grateful to Thomas Sturak, the leading McCoy authority. His unpublished dissertation, "The Life and Writings of Horace McCoy: 1897–1955" (UCLA, 1966), is definitive. Special thanks to Stanley Rem for sending me a microfilm of this work. I am also indebted to John Whitley for critical input.
- On Cain: My thanks to Clifford McCarty, who tracked down biographical data on this obscure author, and, once again, to E. R. Hagemann for his piece on Cain in *The Armchair Detective.* And to Irvin Faust, for commentary.
- On Chandler: My thanks to Ruth and Al Windfeldt for use of material from their presentation "Raymond Chandler's Los Angeles," and to Frank Mac-Shane whose biography *The Life of Raymond Chandler* (New York: E. P. Dutton, 1976) provided primary data.

On my history of *Black Mask,* I owe thanks to John L. Apostolou, J. Randolph Cox, Ron Goulart, Nils Hardin, Stephen Mertz, William Nadel, Herbert Ruhm, and Robert Sampson.

I wish to thank Bill Pronzini for personal advice; William Blackbeard for story-copy services; and my wife, Kam Nolan, for her sharp critical eye and fine typing. Thanks, also, to the American Comic Book Company for crime-pulp data, and to the research library, UCLA Special Collections, in Los Angeles for access to the Joseph Thompson Shaw Papers.

For readers who wish to sample more hard-boiled fiction from the *Mask,* I recommend the following anthologies:

- *The Hard-Boiled Omnibus: Early Stories from* Black Mask, edited by Joseph T. Shaw. New York: Simon and Schuster, 1946.

   A dozen tales from the Shaw decade by Hammett, Chandler, Whitfield, Cain, Torrey, and other boys of the *Mask.*
- *As Tough As They Come,* edited by Will Oursler. Garden City, New York: Permabooks, 1951.

   Genre scholars seem to have overlooked this hard-to-find paperback collection, but it's the genuine goods, with many hard-boiled gems from Hammett, Bruno Fischer, James M. Cain, George Harmon Coxe, and other tough talents.
- *The Hardboiled Dicks,* edited by Ron Goulart. Los Angeles: Sherbourne Press, 1965.

Another solid pioneering effort. Four of the eight bare-knuckle tales are from *Black Mask*—by Nebel, Whitfield, Gruber, and Dent.

- *The Hard-Boiled Detective: Stories from* Black Mask *Magazine (1920–1951)*, edited by Herbert Ruhm. New York: Vintage Books, 1977.

  Of special value: the first book printings of Hammett's "The Road Home" and Daly's "The False Burton Combs." With a dozen others by Nebel, Chandler, Davis, Gardner, Dent, et al.

- *The Great American Detective*, edited by William Kittredge and Steven M. Krauzer. New York: New American Library, 1978.

  This book of assorted private eyes collects Daly's first Race Williams tale, "Knights of the Open Palm."

- *The Arbor House Treasury of Detective and Mystery Stories from the Great Pulps*, edited by Bill Pronzini. New York: Arbor House, 1983.

  Five of the fifteen entries are from *Black Mask*. Here is Dashiell Hammett's first Continental Op tale, "Arson Plus." The roster includes Daly, McCoy, Nebel, and Paul Cain.

In addition to these six genre anthologies, I also recommend two important reference volumes, both of which were utilized extensively in the preparation of this book.

Encyclopedia of Mystery and Detection, edited by Chris Steinbrunner and Otto Penzler. New York: McGraw-Hill, 1976.

Particularly notable for its separate entries on series characters such as the Op, Race Williams, Perry Mason, etc.

Twentieth Century Crime and Mystery Writers, edited by John M. Reilly. New York: St. Martin's Press, 1980.

Of special value: detailed checklists on each of the book's 600 writers. A massive undertaking.

Finally, I wish to acknowledge my debt to the late Philip Durham for his pioneering essay, "The 'Black Mask' School," in *Tough Guy Writers of the Thirties,* edited by David Madden. Carbondale, Illinois: Southern Illinois University Press, 1968.

This critical anthology has much else of value to the hard-boiled enthusiast, including work on Chandler, Hammett, McCoy, and other *Black Mask* boys.

—W.F.N.